ADVANCE PRAISE FOR

THE GOSPEL IN EVERY BOOK OF THE OLD TESTAMENT

"Joseph Farah has set a magnifying glass down on the pages of the Old Testament and shares with readers what many fail to see when reading through the biblical stories of antiquity—Jesus—the great 'I Am' of Scripture. In his latest work, 'The Gospel in Every Book of the Old Testament,' you will be thrilled at the passages that speak of Jesus before He came to earth in human form as the Christmas Child. The foreshadowing of Christ speaks clearly of the salvation He offers to mankind because Jesus, Himself, is the Gospel. Don't miss the true adventure of seeing God's perfect plan of redemption from beginning to end."
—FRANKLIN GRAHAM, President & CEO, Billy Graham Evangelistic Association and Samaritan's Purse

"If you ever wondered why Christians need to understand the Old Testament, you'll get a vivid understanding after reading Joseph Farah's enlightening work, 'The Gospel in Every Book of the Old Testament.' He skillfully reveals the thread of Christ that not only brings unity to the Old Testament, but he masterfully makes clear that the Old Testament is the very foundation upon which the New Testament record of Jesus is built. You'll understand why all 66 books of the Bible have a singular message—the Messiah has come!"
—MIKE HUCKABEE, former Governor of Arkansas, former GOP presidential candidate

"Never before has anyone offered a more complete and comprehensive, book-by-book exploration of the Gospel in the Hebrew Scriptures. Joseph Farah's 'The Gospel in Every Book of the Old Testament' is a triumph and an amazing resource for every pastor and every Bible study leader who understands the importance of the Gospel of the Kingdom Jesus preached. It's even more important for those pastors and Bible study teachers who don't understand it. Revolutionary!"
—DR. JACK VAN IMPE, Jack Van Impe Ministries International

"I was not only educated but also inspired and encouraged by 'The Gospel in Every Book of the Old Testament,' and you will be, too. I wholeheartedly recommend it to every person who either venerates the Bible as the Word of God or is simply curious to expound its original intent and often lost meanings."
—CHUCK NORRIS, world karate champion, actor, film producer and screenwriter

"'In the beginning was the Word. The Word was with God and the Word was God.' Jesus was the Word in the flesh, in bodily form. And Peter reminds us, 'For prophecy never came by the will of man, but holy men of God spoke as they were moved by the Holy Spirit.' Is it any wonder then that the Living Word, as he was inspiring all the Old Testament scriptures, was dropping in hints of his own existence? Joseph Farah has researched and revealed this marvelous truth. And he, like I, has come to the full realization that not only are 'all scriptures inspired by God,' but that the whole Bible from Genesis to Revelation is written by Jews, about Jews and for Jews—focused on little Israel and God's chosen people through whom the whole world might be saved if they receive their own Messiah. Get excited as you read this!"
—PAT BOONE, singer, composer, actor, writer, television personality

"*Just as the Nazis tried to unlink the Old and New Testaments, Dietrich Bonhoeffer wrote his very last book, Prayerbook of the Bible, about how the Old Testament Psalms were the very prayers of Jesus. He was thenceforth banned from publishing in the Third Reich, but Bonhoeffer knew one cannot have a genuine Christian faith unless one understands how the Old Testament books speak of Jesus; and to see that for yourself, I am thrilled to recommend Joseph Farah's superb new book.*"
—ERIC METAXAS, New York Times bestselling author of "Bonhoeffer: Pastor, Martyr, Prophet, Spy" and "Martin Luther: The Man Who Rediscovered God and Changed the World"

"*Joseph Farah has done an amazing job of uncovering a singular message of God's redemptive plan for mankind interwoven through the Bible, from Genesis to Revelation. He has discovered the forgotten key to finding the Gospel in all the books of the Hebrew Scriptures. It's what Jesus called 'the Gospel of the Kingdom'—one of the profound lessons of this unique book. This is a terrific resource for pastors and Bible study leaders and for all those who just want to understand how the Scriptures, from beginning to end, offer one consistent message of redemption.*"
—JONATHAN BERNIS, "Jewish Voice" TV show

"*After Jesus rose from the dead, He appeared to two disciples who had lost hope. They felt He had somehow failed in His mission, when, in fact, everything was going according to schedule, God's schedule. Jesus gave them a personal tour of the Old Testament and what passages pointed to Him. When their journey ended, these two down-hearted disciples who had hope restored spoke of how their hearts burned when Christ opened up the Scriptures to them. In his new book, 'The Gospel in Every Book of the Old Testament,' my friend Joseph Farah helps us to see the vital connection between the Old and New Testaments. I know this book will be a blessing to you.*"
—GREG LAURIE, author, senior pastor of Harvest Christian Fellowship in Riverside, California

"It's amazing that this book hasn't been written before! It's a great way to rediscover the Old Testament, and it proves the Bible—from cover to cover—is a thoroughly integrated book with one consistent message."
—DINESH D'SOUZA, bestselling author and documentary filmmaker

"Joseph Farah has discovered the spiritual key to seeing the Gospel in every book of the Old Testament. The secret is revealed in what Jesus called 'The Gospel of the Kingdom,' a redemption message that transcends 'the Gospel of personal salvation.' This was the great hope of all the prophets from Creation onward, Peter said in Acts 3. By applying this paradigm to his search of all 39 books of the Tanach, the good news of the world's future restoration through the return of Jesus to Earth literally leaps off the pages of the inspired ancient writings."
—DAVID BARTON, founder of WallBuilders, bestselling author

"This book is a goldmine of information, comprehensively tying Old and New Testament Scriptures together regarding the first and second comings of the Lord Jesus Christ; the promised Jewish Messiah and Savior of the world who came first as the Lamb of God to take away the sins of the world, and second, the Lion from the tribe of Judah who is just as literally coming back to rule and reign over His millennial kingdom. If there is another book like this one in print, I have neither seen it nor read it. I have often wondered just what the Lord Jesus Christ said to the two men He walked with on the way to Emmaus after His resurrection from the dead, 'And beginning with Moses and all the prophets, He interpreted to them in all the Scriptures the things concerning Himself.' My friend Joseph Farah has helped answer my question in a very readable and systematic fashion through his newest book, 'The Gospel In Every Book Of The Old Testament.' Once I began reading this manuscript, I could not put it down. The materials written on the book of Isaiah alone are worth the price of the book and the time it takes to read. I wish I could have read this book more than forty years ago as part of my Bible School or Seminary studies. This is that good! Good teachers take complex ideas and share them

in a way that others can understand what is being taught. Joseph Farah is a good teacher and this book is worth buying and reading."
—DR. KARL I. PAYNE, Pastor of Leadership Development and Discipleship Training, Antioch Bible Church, Redmond, Washington, author of "Spiritual Warfare: Christians, Demonization and Deliverance," former Chaplain of the Seattle Seahawks, 1994-2015

"Joseph Farah offers up a rich buffet featuring hundreds of delectable meals— beautiful insights about Jesus the Messiah found in the pages of the Hebrew Scriptures. You might not agree with every insight offered (I found myself passing on a few of the offerings), but you will be enriched and enlightened on page after page of this engagingly written and edifying book. You will see Jesus-Yeshua as you have not seen Him before!"
—DR. MICHAEL L. BROWN, host of the Line of Fire radio and TV broadcast and author of "The Real Kosher Jesus"

"There is no greater goal than to look for Jesus. There is no better place to look than the Holy Scriptures. Joseph Farah brings his incredible skill as an investigative reporter with a keen mind into the task of looking for Jesus in the Old Testament. Although I have been a Christian for over sixty years and have been well taught and am well-read, I was fascinated to discover new insights about Jesus as Farah explores the books of the Old Testament. If you want to see Jesus more clearly—read this book."
—MICHAEL FARRIS, President, Chief Executive Officer and General Counsel, Alliance Defending Freedom

"Joseph Farah is a master communicator, teacher and author. 'The Gospel in Every Book of the Old Testament' challenges traditional Christian thinking and understanding about the Old Testament as well as the New Testament. As a Messianic Jew, I found it fascinating, engaging and enriching reading. I heartily recommend this latest literary offering from Joseph Farah. Congratulations Joseph!"
—JOEL CHERNOFF, General Secretary and Chief Executive Officer, Messianic Jewish Alliance of America

"What an exciting concept! The gospel in every book of the Old Testament. The subject of this publication cannot but cause our hearts to burn within us, as it did when Jesus opened up the Old Testament for His disciples, on the Emmaus road. Joseph Farah's scholarly digging will place into your hands the most valuable of gold nuggets."
—RAY COMFORT, evangelist, author, founder of Living Waters Publications and The Way of the Master in Bellflower, California

"There is nothing new in the New Covenant! It is all 'hidden' in the Old Covenant Jewish Scriptures. Not only is it all in the Jewish Scriptures, but Joseph Farah's teaching will fortify and give you a richer understanding of the New Covenant from this amazing breakthrough revelation!"
—SID ISRAEL ROTH, Host, "It's Supernatural!"

"Wow, another amazing timely book written by Joseph Farah! This book brings out and clarifies the 'gospel' message that Yeshua [Jesus] said must necessarily be preached as a witness to all nations just before He returns. Get a copy to read for yourself and get some extra copies to share with others. For this is our great end of age commission."
—RICHMOND DOUGLAS, ministerial and worldwide missions director, Gospel for All Nations

"This book is a page turner, with the power to transform a Bible reader into a biblical scholar."
—BEN KINCHLOW, TV host, author

"Joseph Farah's marvelous book, 'The Gospel in Every Book of the Old Testament,' is both an eye-opener and a case-closer: Jesus of the New Testament is the Messiah promised in the Old Testament. The first 39 books of the Bible are a read ahead for the coming of Jesus and the salvation that came with Him. Bishop Fulton Sheen once said that in terms of the prophecies of the

Old Testament and the realities of the New Testament, it is a mathematical impossibility that Jesus was not the Messiah. 'The Gospel' lays that truth out book by book in fascinating and refreshing detail. The magic of this book is that those viewing the same passages in the past, on multiple occasions, will find new and inspiring messages in those same passages. The Bible surely plays a key role in our salvation, it educates and inspires, but it has been virtually banned from the public square. I hope this book will help bring it back by uniting both books into one gospel and one message for salvation for all."
—GENERAL PATRICK HENRY BRADY, Medal of Honor recipient, former President of the Medal of Honor Society, most decorated living soldier

"If today's church could get a vision of Jesus in the Old Testament, we could diminish the blight of Replacement Theology raging through the contemporary church. Jesus is a very Jewish concept. Christianity is Jewish. And this theme is in all 66 books of the Bible, not just the New Testament. Joseph Farah's book will help readers understand that."
—JAN MARKELL, Founder/Director, Olive Tree Ministries

"Joseph Farah in his revealing new book 'The Gospel in Every Book of the Old Testament' takes you on a journey where your eyes are opened to see the Scriptures in a whole new light. You realize the importance of walking those ancient paths where the Good Way has always been there but only hidden."
—MARK BILTZ, Founder, El Shaddai Ministries

"Joseph Farah's latest work is a timely remedy to the disease of Old Testament illiteracy that has plagued the Body of Christ for far too long. The Bible declares that it is the 'glory of kings' to uncover a matter. This book does a fantastic job of mining out many precious Gospel gems hidden throughout the Hebrew Scriptures by their divine author. Christians and Messianic Jews alike will benefit much from this thoughtful new study."
—JOEL RICHARDSON, author, documentary filmmaker, human rights activist

"As a Jewish believer I have longed for someone to write a guide to the Gospel in The Old Testament. Once again, Joseph Farah has stepped up to the plate and has written a 'tell all' guide to God's Plan of Redemption revealed from the very beginning of His Word. The research is impeccable and the insights are life-changing to those who have made the claim that Yeshua/Jesus is not in The Old Testament. I believe that new dialogues will open up across all segments of Judaism and Christianity to embrace irrefutable evidence that The Gospel was there at the beginning of Creation. This book reveals God's Plan from an eternity past that will take the reader straight into the promises of a future eternity. This book is a 'must read' for those who are searching for the One Truth that will deepen their understanding of their faith and equip them to bring others into the knowledge of the One Book that clearly shows salvation from the very beginning."

—REV./RABBI ERIC WALKER, host of "Revealing the Truth"

"There are 66 books in the Bible—39 Old Testament Books and 27 New Testament books—the entire Bible is 'His-Story,' that is, it tells the story of Jesus, God's Messiah, from beginning to end. He is the Alpha and the Omega! In Joseph Farah's new book, 'The Gospel in Every Book of the Old Testament,' we clearly see what is hidden to many. No matter which book you read, the Gospel, the 'good news of God in Jesus Christ,' is there—not hidden but revealed. May your heart be touched, may your life be changed, may your faith be rewarded as you read this wonderful book."

—RICHIE FURAY, Founding Pastor, Calvary Chapel Broomfield, Broomfield, Colorado, 1997 inductee into the Rock & Roll Hall of Fame (Buffalo Springfield)

"What's Old is what's New! It's inspiring and wonderful to see a book where the good news about the kingdom of God is explained the same way Jesus and the apostles explained it, from the Old Testament Scriptures. Far too many Christians are missing out on important points about God and His Master Plan when they limit themselves to the New Testament alone. Joseph Farah makes it more than obvious the story of the Messiah and His coming kingdom does not commence in the Gospel of Matthew. It goes all the way back to the first words in Genesis, 'In the beginning.' Well done!"

—JOE KOVACS, author, "Shocked by the Bible" and Shocked by the Bible 2"

"Without doubt the most important study that Christians can make as they read their New Testament is to pursue the quotes from the Old Testament. Following the exhortation of Jesus in Luke 24:25-27, 44-47, we gain great insight in how to interpret correctly the Bible. As Joseph Farah shows, the gospel extensively pervades the message of the former Testament."

—JAMES B. DE YOUNG, senior professor of New Testament Language and Literature, Western Seminary, co-author of "Beyond the Obvious: Discover the Deeper Meaning of Scripture" (1995)

"I have asked my adult Sunday school class on a couple of occasions to write down one prophecy to take place by the beginning of the following year. Not fortune cookie-type statements, but specific things yet to take place. Despite scores of us making predictions, including me, none of us made even the slightest prophecy of the future. Yet in the Old Testament, we have the fore-telling of Jesus Christ in remarkable detail. Now, best-selling author Joseph Farah goes further in showing how Jesus is to be found not only in Isaiah 53, Psalm 22, Micah 5, etc., but in every book of the Hebrew Bible. Only God knows the future. Only God could have written the Bible. Every Christian should read this new book!"

—DR. JERRY NEWCOMBE, senior producer and on-air host, D. James Kennedy Ministries, WND columnist, author/co-author of 29 books, including (with D. James Kennedy), "What If Jesus Had Never Been Born?"

THE GOSPEL
IN EVERY BOOK
OF THE
OLD TESTAMENT

THE GOSPEL IN EVERY BOOK OF THE OLD TESTAMENT

JOSEPH FARAH

 WND Books

THE GOSPEL IN EVERY BOOK OF THE OLD TESTAMENT

Published by WND Books, Washington, D.C. WND Books is a registered trademark of WorldNetDaily.com, Inc. ("WND")

Book designed by Mark Karis

WND Books are available at special discounts for bulk purchases. WND Books also publishes books in electronic formats. For more information call 1-800-496-3266, email orders@wnd.com, or visit www.wndbooks.com.

Hardcover ISBN: 978-1-944229-88-7

eBook ISBN: 978-1-944229-89-4

Library of Congress Cataloging-in-Publication Data

Printed in the United States of America
16 17 18 19 20 21 XXX 9 8 7 6 5 4 3 2 1

CONTENTS

DEDICATION

I commit this work to the providence of God, for whose glory it is written.
May His blessing go with it to awaken, illuminate, strengthen and cheer some
of God's chosen children in their Kingdom journey.
—JOSEPH FARAH

INTRODUCTION

And beginning at Moses and all the prophets, he expounded unto them in all the scriptures the things concerning himself. —LUKE 24:27

"Did not our heart burn within us, while he talked with us by the way, and while he opened to us the scriptures?" —LUKE 24:32

IT MUST HAVE BEEN a very depressing and confusing Passover week for the closest followers of Jesus, who had trekked with Him for years through the Galilee with the expectation that He would shortly assume the kingship of Israel, reigning and ruling from Jerusalem.

Instead, their teacher, their rabbi, their Lord, was arrested, imprisoned, tortured, tried by a corrupt high priest and the equally corrupt Sanhedrin, and finally crucified like a common criminal by the Roman military authorities on a high holy day.

Peter was so discouraged that he denied three times being one of His followers. The other apostles hid in fear for three days and three nights, not comprehending what had become of their Messiah or what would become of them.

Early Sunday morning, a group of women close to Jesus—Mary Magdalene, Joanna, Mary the mother of James and Joses, Salome, and others—who had prepared spices for embalming his body, walked to the garden tomb. Knowing that the entrance to the tomb would be covered by a huge, rolling stone, they wondered aloud, "Who will help us roll away the stone?"

When they arrived, they were shocked and perplexed to find the large stone, sealed under the watch of Roman guards, already rolled away, the Lord's body gone.

"Two men . . . in shining garments," probably angels, spoke to the women, saying: "Why seek ye the living among the dead? He is not here, but is risen: remember how he spake unto you when he was yet in Galilee, saying, The Son of man must be delivered into the hands of sinful men, and be crucified, and the third day rise again" (Luke 24:4–7).

The women, experiencing both fear and joy, hurried back to tell the eleven apostles and other disciples what they had seen and been told. No sooner had they left than they were met by the risen Jesus Himself, who said, "All hail . . . Be not afraid: go tell my brethren that they go into Galilee, and there they shall see me" (Matthew 28:9–10).

Though some of the men did not believe the story, Peter and John ran to the open tomb and found only Jesus' grave clothes.

That same day, two of the apostles decided to journey to the village of Emmaus, a distance of nearly seven miles. Maybe they needed to clear their heads of all the things they had experienced over the last four days. Perhaps they just wanted to talk through all that had happened.

As they walked and talked, they were joined by the risen Jesus, but they did not recognize Him.

Jesus asked them, "What manner of communications are these

that ye have one to another, as ye walk, and are sad?"

The one named Cleopas responded, "Art thou only a stranger in Jerusalem, and hast not known the things which are come to pass there in these days?"

Jesus said, "What things?"

They said, "Concerning Jesus of Nazareth, which was a prophet mighty in deed and word before God and all the people: And how the chief priests and our rulers delivered him to be condemned to death, and have crucified him. But we trusted that it had been he which should have redeemed Israel: and beside all this, to day is the third day since these things were done. Yea, and certain women also of our company made us astonished, which were early at the sepulchre; And when they found not his body, they came, saying, that they had also seen a vision of angels, which said that he was alive. And certain of them which were with us went to the sepulchre, and found it even so as the women had said: but him they saw not."

Jesus responded, "O fools, and slow of heart to believe all that the prophets have spoken: Ought not Christ to have suffered these things, and to enter into his glory?"

Then, the gospel of Luke tells us, that beginning at Moses and all the Hebrew prophets, Jesus "expounded unto them in all the scriptures the things concerning himself" (24:17–27).

Why is this important for today's believers to understand?

This was the same day Jesus rose from the dead. The only scriptures Jesus could use to explain to Cleopas and his friend on that long walk to Emmaus were those that were already written: the Hebrew Scriptures, which we problematically refer to as "the Old Testament."

It would be decades, at least, before the Greek Scriptures, or, the New Testament, would be written and widely circulated to spread the gospel far and wide.

Think about that. The apostles, we're told in Acts 17:6, had turned the world upside down without the benefit of the gospels of Matthew, Mark, Luke, and John or any other books of the New

Testament, which means their main resource, from which came all of their scriptural references, was the Tanakh, or Hebrew Bible.

That's what Jesus used to explain all to his friends on the road to Emmaus, and it was not merely enough. In fact, after that lesson, Cleopas and his companion agreed: "Did not our heart burn within us, while he talked with us by the way, and while he opened to us the scriptures?" (Luke 24:32).

It must have been quite the Bible study. I look forward to a podcast of it during the coming kingdom.

We've all heard the story about the road to Emmaus, but the point is this: that Jesus explained the good news using only the Old Testament suggests that after two thousand years, we should be able to do likewise. We should be able to mine the Hebrew Scriptures to evangelize our Jewish brothers and sisters. That's what Jesus was doing. After all, it would be decades before His apostles and disciples, all Jewish, would even think about bringing the gospel to the Gentiles.

The Old Testament, or Tanakh, is the foundation for our faith as Christians. Without it, we cannot fully appreciate, or explain, or comprehend the work of Jesus (Heb., Yeshua), the very Jewish God-Man, who came to atone for the sins of the world and build His kingdom here on Earth.

Too many churches and Bible study groups don't spend enough time in the Old Testament. It's there we learn about the richness of who Jesus was and what His mission would be—a mission, by the way, in which the best is yet to come.

Though I have studied the Hebrew Scriptures for more than forty years, I came to appreciate them to the point of excitement through the research for my previous book, *The Restitution of All Things: Israel, Christians and the End of the Age*, a work looking toward the fulfillment of the coming kingdom of God. While Jesus talked much about this future kingdom over which He will preside as absolute ruler of the earth, there's so much more most believers have yet to discover through a systematic study of the Hebrew

Scriptures. And that's the *other* part of the gospel, or "good news," about which most Christians are nearly oblivious.

In fact, my title was inspired by what Peter said about this very topic in Acts 3:18–26 on the day of Pentecost:

> But those things, *which God before had shewed by the mouth of all his prophets*, that Christ should suffer, he hath so fulfilled. Repent ye therefore, and be converted, that your sins may be blotted out, when the times of refreshing shall come from the presence of the Lord. And he shall send Jesus Christ, which before was preached unto you: Whom the heaven must receive until the times of restitution of all things, *which God hath spoken by the mouth of all his holy prophets since the world began.* For Moses truly said unto the fathers, A prophet shall the Lord your God raise up unto you of your brethren, like unto me; him shall ye hear in all things whatsoever he shall say unto you. And it shall come to pass, that every soul, which will not hear that prophet, shall be destroyed from among the people. *Yea, and all the prophets from Samuel and those that follow after, as many as have spoken, have likewise foretold of these days.* Ye are the children of the prophets, and of the covenant which God made with our fathers, saying unto Abraham, And in thy seed shall all the kindreds of the earth be blessed. Unto you first God, having raised up his Son Jesus, sent him to bless you, in turning away every one of you from his iniquities. (Emphasis added)

Yes, the Old Testament is full of the gospel, as Peter explained.

In fact, it was during the writing of my previous book that I got the urge to *read* another. Unfortunately, the book I was searching for didn't seem to exist—or at least I couldn't find it in *my* Christian bookstore. The book I was looking for was *this* one: *The Gospel in Every Book of the Old Testament.* But I had hoped to use such a book to help me identify some of the subject matter I needed to cover in *The Restitution of All Things*. I thought it would be useful in helping me prove Peter's claim that every prophecy spoke of the Messiah to come and the kingdom He would establish on Earth. So, I made a mental note to follow up the book I was already writing with another, even broader in scope: *The Gospel in Every Book of the Old Testament*. It was a project that would take a full two years of research and study.

I should say there was one excellent book, similar in nature, written by a friend of mine, David Limbaugh. It proved to be an inspiration to me. It was *The Emmaus Code: Finding Jesus in the Old Testament*, later retitled, *Finding Jesus in the Old Testament*. I can't recommend that book highly enough, and have done so publicly. This effort is different in one major respect: I wanted its readers to understand that the gospel means more than we, as followers of Jesus, usually think it means.

And what is the gospel? Is it simply that Jesus came to earth and died on the cross for our sins so that we can know eternal life? Or is there more to the gospel than that?

I submit to you that there is indeed much more "good news" in the future to comprehend, and the preponderance of it is found in the Hebrew Scriptures. I speak of the complete restoration of human-kind and all of God's creation. That's the good news many Christians seldom consider, let alone study seriously and systematically.

In Mark 1:14–15, the mission of the gospel is defined: "Now after that John was put in prison, Jesus came into Galilee, preaching the gospel of the kingdom of God, and saying, The time is fulfilled, and the kingdom of God is at hand: repent ye, and believe the gospel."

There is a richness and completeness and depth found in those often-overlooked Old Testament Scriptures. Can we really fully believe, embrace, and effectively share the complete gospel without comprehending its entirety, with all its promises about the coming kingdom?

That's the reason for this book, *The Gospel in Every Book of the*

Old Testament. As I said, I was shocked to discover that I couldn't find such a book in my Christian bookstore. I believe it will enrich the spiritual life of any believer who endeavors to read it.

It is written as a kind of layman's study guide and introduction to each of the thirty-nine books of the Hebrew Scriptures and what they foreshadow and prophesy about the gospel—including those parts yet to be fulfilled. It's more than a study of the Tanakh and how it points to the first coming of Messiah Jesus because it is in the Hebrew Scriptures that a rich treasure trove of future prophecy remains still largely unknown, or at least little understood, by most of His followers today.

This book is not intended to be a scholarly or exhaustive treatment of *everything* the Old Testament has to say that foreshadows the gospel message. It's more like an invitation to explore the Hebrew Scriptures for yourself as I demonstrate that the whole Bible is one divinely integrated and inspired work with no contradictions in the nature of the one true God behind it all. God doesn't change His mind. He doesn't make mistakes. There's no need for corrections on His part.

The book frequently quotes scripture—sometimes at length. I ask you not to skip over those lengthy quotations because you've read them before, because I want you to see the context—and, perhaps, with the leading of the Holy Spirit, something you haven't seen before.

I am old-fashioned, and I use exclusively the King James Version of the Bible throughout this book for several reasons. While I have studied other translations and read even more, the King James Version is familiar and poetic, and I've found it to be highly accurate and surprisingly readable, despite the sometimes-archaic English it employs. If you like another translation more, keep it next to you while you go through this book, and read the cited passages in your favorite translation. If you don't see what I see, it's easy enough with the Bible tools we have at our disposal in this digital age to check the original language. In other words, be a Berean (see Acts 17:10–11).

Use this book as a personal study guide to see if these things be true.

I invite you to take a journey with me, book by book, through the Old Testament to see how the whole Bible is much more than a random series of events and stories. I want you to experience the unity of the whole Bible; to see Jesus at work before we meet Him in the books of Matthew, Mark, Luke, and John; and to better appreciate what He has already accomplished for us and what He will do with us in His coming kingdom on Earth.

Now, let's begin.

1

THE GOSPEL IN GENESIS

Forgive, I pray thee now, the trespass of thy brethren, and their sin; for they did unto thee evil: and now, we pray thee, forgive the trespass of the servants of the God of thy father. —GENESIS 50:17

For I say unto you, Ye shall not see me henceforth, till ye shall say, Blessed is he that cometh in the name of the Lord. —MATTHEW 23:39

DO ALL THINGS HAVE A BEGINNING—including time itself?

Until very recently—the nineteenth and twentieth centuries—secular scientists held on to the idea that the universe has perhaps always existed. Today you would be hard-pressed to find any such holdouts. The late Stephen Hawking called this "probably the most remarkable discovery of modern cosmology."[1]

That doesn't mean Hawking or all the other scientists have come to accept the Genesis account of creation—though some have. What's more surprising, perhaps, is that many who call themselves "believers" today dispute the Genesis account. They scoff at the very first words of God, which were recorded under the inspiration of the Holy Spirit by Moses, the humble man who walked and talked with God and believed every word God told Him, with fear and trembling.

The very first words Moses wrote in the very first book of the Bible were these: "In the beginning God created the heaven and the earth" (Genesis 1:1).

One can reject this proclamation—and many do. Yet it is difficult to do so without rejecting the gospel as well, for it is the undeniable foundation.

In the beginning of the gospel of John, we're told: "In the beginning was the Word, and the Word was with God, and the Word was God. The same was in the beginning with God. All things were made by him; and without him was not any thing made that was made" (vv. 1–3)

Why are the very first words in Genesis so important? Because they are essential to the good news—an essential part of the gospel. One cannot trust the gospel without trusting these words. One cannot have the hope of the good news, which is what "gospel" means, without fully embracing God as the Creator. For if He is not the Creator, how can we trust the good news He brings?

Everything starts at the beginning. If you get that point wrong, then everything that follows is wrong. It's the foundation of the Word of God and the underpinning of the entire framework that is to come. If you want to understand the good news that Jesus delivered, you must accept this, believe it, embrace it, just as you must embrace who Jesus is: the Creator of all things, the Messiah, the One who is about the business of fulfilling all of the expectations of the prophets from creation onward. It's not hard, because the choices we have in understanding who we are, how we got here, and where we're going are somewhat limited.

One materialistic alternative to the creation of all things, as written in the Genesis account, is that the universe is eternal: if the universe wasn't created, then perhaps it always was. What's the problem with that? The same problem materialists have with God: if He was not created, then He always was and always will be. It comes down to whether you believe in an eternal God, who made everything, or an eternal universe, which always was and always will be, from which, inexplicably, given enough time, life spontaneously sprang forth. Today, no serious scientist believes the universe is eternal, for such thinking defies the second law of thermodynamics.

You can believe in an eternal universe if you wish. But there's not much good news for those who do. It means we live and we die—and that's it. Without a Creator and His eternal plan for His creation, there's nothing else for us but these few years of life on earth. Then it's over. Ultimately, there is no right or wrong. There is no good or evil. How can there be with no lawmaker, no authority? It's all just opinion. It's up to every person to make the rules—to do what's right in his or her own eyes.

Today, the scientific position is that the universe *began* to exist. Again quoting Stephen Hawkings "Almost everyone believes that the universe, and time itself, had a beginning." To avoid the tough questions an actual creation raises, some suggest that matter and energy sprang forth from nothingness. So, there's a third alternative you can believe in—put your faith in. There's not really any evidence to support it. But you can choose to do so if you wish. If you get enough people believing this, you can even use your clout to teach it as fact. But that doesn't make it fact, does it? It requires every bit as much "faith" and "belief" as does a Creator God. Some would say more.

Either one of these last two alternative theories of where matter and energy came from have much appeal to those who don't like God's rules as laid out in the Bible. In reality, they don't like the idea of "sin," or the idea of judgment. They don't like the idea of eternal rewards and punishments based on a fixed moral code and the necessity of obedience and repentance.

Man thinks he knows better.

At the end of the day, you can put your faith in man's ways or in God's ways. That's the choice we have. Ultimately, it's the only choice we have.

But—like it or not—believing in man's ways means there's no ultimate justice—except the kind that is determined by man and delivered by man. But what is justice? Who's to say? Remember what Pontius Pilate asked Jesus? "What is truth?" (John 18:38). Apart from God, there is no truth. If it's up to each individual to determine truth, then there are only opinions.

Make no mistake about it: if you follow Jesus, if you love Him, then you must do what He commanded and believe what He said . And Jesus affirmed that God created all things (Mark 10:6; 13:19).

We're told in the gospel of John that Jesus is, in fact, God—the Creator of all things. Remember John's famous words at the beginning of his gospel about the Word being with God and being God? He went on to write, "And the Word was made flesh, and dwelt among us, (and we beheld his glory, the glory as of the only begotten of the Father,) full of grace and truth" (1:14).

We're told in Genesis that God not only made the earth and the universe; He made man and woman too. He created all life. And that's good news. Materialists would have you believe that humankind is the result of random chance over millions and millions of years of evolution. Yet science has no clue as to how life could emerge from nonlife, nor does it have evidence of mutations that led from lower life forms to higher. It has never been observed, even after experimentation in the most "favorable" conditions.

Genesis also tells us God created two human beings—Adam and Eve—from whom all others descended. He created humankind to live with Him in fellowship. But when Adam and Eve broke His commandment, the perfect relationship with God was shattered

How was it broken? Through the temptation and deception of Satan, the fallen angel. He used a mixture of truth and lie to deceive Eve. Even the serpent through whom Satan spoke did not deny God's existence and reality. Instead, he told Eve that if she ate the fruit of the

Tree of the Knowledge of Good and Evil, which God had forbidden, she would become *like* God, knowing good and evil. That was true. Man had become *like* God when Eve and later Adam ate of the fruit. In Genesis 3:22, God Himself said that. They didn't become gods, but, in one sense, they became *like* God—knowing both good and evil.

For redemption to take place, God would need to conquer death and become like man—and He did so by dying in our place.

Adam was created as a perfect man who would sin in a perfect world and cause the fall, not just of man, but of all creation. When Jesus became a man and led a perfect, sinless life, he was called the second or last Adam (1 Cor. 15:45).

When sin entered the world, it changed everything in the blink of an eye. Humankind fell. The garden of Eden, a real paradise on the face of the earth, became off-limits to humankind. Life would become hard, a struggle, because of the curse of being cut out of fellowship with God. Human disobedience, brought on by the temptation of the evil one, affected the whole earth, all life, all creation.

But God provided some good news immediately thereafter. In Genesis 3 we get the first hint of the promise of redemption.

We read in verse 8: "And they heard the voice of the LORD God walking in the garden in the cool of the day: and Adam and his wife hid themselves from the presence of the LORD God amongst the trees of the garden."

God walking in the garden? Does God walk? Yes, He does, when He comes as God's only begotten Son, Jesus, who, we are also told in John 1:3, is the One who made heaven and earth—and all things that were made. Yes, it was not unusual, apparently, for God to walk in the garden with Adam and Eve. Picture those strolls with Jesus. He is, after all, the one and only intermediary between humankind and the Father. We know from scripture that man cannot see the Father and live (Exodus 33:20). So, when we see God, we can only see the Son. When we walk with God, we walk with the Son.

This is more than a hint of the gospel in Genesis—a revelation of things to come.

What did God do when He found Adam and Eve hiding from Him in shame for their nakedness, which they had only just discovered? He clothed them in animal skins. In other words, He sacrificed an animal to cover not just their naked bodies, but their sin. This began the sacrificial system, long before Moses reinstituted it when he led the children of Israel out of Egypt, and long before Jesus gave Himself as a sacrifice for the sins of the whole world.

He also summoned all three participants in the fall: Adam, Eve, and the serpent: "And the LORD God said unto the serpent, Because thou hast done this, thou art cursed above all cattle, and above every beast of the field; upon thy belly shalt thou go, and dust shalt thou eat all the days of thy life: And I will put enmity between thee and the woman, and between thy seed and her seed; it shall bruise thy head, and thou shalt bruise his heel" (Genesis 3:14–15).

Did we have to read the New Testament to know about this plan of redemption? No, we learn about it right there in Genesis 3. Jesus, of course, is the seed of the woman who will ultimately bruise the devil's head, after the devil bruised His heel.

Theologians have known these key verses since the time when the Scriptures could only be read in Hebrew, Greek, and Latin as the "protoevangelium," or the first gospel.

Perhaps you ask, how did the devil bruise His heel?

It may have been the natural result of crucifixion. As a crucifixion victim fights for air, he is forced to push up on his feet so that he can take each breath. That means pushing his full weight upward with one heel, as His feet were nailed together. Because a crucifixion victim had one heel pushed into the cross, that one heel—not both heels, interestingly—would bear a tremendous amount of weight and was, thus, badly bruised.

There is more foreshadowing of Jesus' sacrifice in this chapter in Genesis.

"Cursed is the ground for thy sake . . . Thorns also and thistles shall it bring forth to thee; and thou shalt eat the herb of the field," God tells Adam and Eve (3:17–18).

Apparently, before the fall, there were no thorns in the garden of Eden. Wouldn't you love to live in a world without thorns? As someone who walks with my dog in the woods every day, I think about this often. What purpose do they serve, other than to cause pain and slowly rip one's clothes to shreds? If there were no thorns in Eden, it suggests that in the coming kingdom, when all things are restored, we will not have to endure such nuisances for eternity. But there's more in this passage than that. It also hints at the most famous thorns in the history of the world—the crown of thorns thrust upon Jesus' head before His crucifixion.

Maybe you're one of those believers who doesn't accept the Genesis account or the idea that humankind began with two people, Adam and Eve. Or, perhaps, you think the garden of Eden was just a story or allegory.

But what does the gospel of Luke say? Luke 3:38 says Adam was a real person—in fact, it tells us, he was "the son of God."

Romans 5:14 explains, "Nevertheless death reigned from Adam to Moses, even over them that had not sinned after the similitude of Adam's transgression, who is the figure of him that was to come."

First Corinthians 15:22 states: "For as in Adam all die, even so in Christ shall all be made alive." Verse 45 adds, "And so it is written, The first man Adam was made a living soul; the last Adam [Jesus] was made a quickening spirit."

First Timothy 2:13 states: "For Adam was first formed, then Eve."

Things got bad and then worse in the generations that followed Adam and Eve.

There were some righteous people who walked with God, but by Noah's generation, "God saw that the wickedness of man was great in the earth, and that every imagination of the thoughts of his heart was only evil continually. And it repented the LORD that he had made man on the earth, and it grieved him at his heart. And the LORD said, I will destroy man whom I have created from the face of the earth; both man, and beast, and the creeping thing, and the fowls of the air; for it repenteth me that I have made them" (Genesis 6:5–7).

We see this pattern throughout the Bible, Old Testament and New. While humanity has a sin nature, God judges some righteous because they repent of their sins and demonstrate their faith through obedience. In God's eyes, they are seen as "perfect." Enoch was one such man (Genesis 5:24). Noah was another (Genesis 7:1; Hebrews 11:5). And later in Genesis, we meet Abraham (18:19) and Joseph (39:2).

In Genesis 7:1, God says of Noah, "Come thou and all thy house into the ark; for thee have I seen righteous before me in this generation."

Why? A few verses later, we're told, "And Noah did according unto all that the LORD commanded him" (v. 5). Noah gave humankind a second chance in a world much different from Eden and much different from the world before the flood (see Genesis 6–7). But instead of walking in righteousness, like Noah, his descendants once again decided they wanted to be like God.

They united to build a great tower to reach to the heavens. As a result, God confused their communication by creating new languages to divide them, creating the nations and forestalling another global disaster (Genesis 11:1–9).

Perhaps you don't believe Noah was real—maybe just part of an allegorical story like Adam and Eve. Yet, Jesus referred to Noah in the Gospels as a real man (see Matthew 24:38 and Luke 17:26, where he is referred to as Noe).

Following the flood and the incident at the Tower of Babel, God did not leave the world without hope. A few generations later, God called out Abram, a descendant of Noah's son Shem, to leave his country for Canaan (Genesis 12:1–5). He obeyed. God promised to give Abram— later renamed by God Abraham, meaning "father of many nations"—and his seed this land as an everlasting covenant.

God said: "Get thee out of thy country, and from thy kindred, and from thy father's house, unto a land that I will shew thee: And I will make of thee a great nation, and I will bless thee, and make thy name great; and thou shalt be a blessing: And I will bless them that bless thee, and curse him that curseth thee: and in thee shall

all families of the earth be blessed" (Genesis 12:1–3).

It's a remarkable promise repeated several times to Abraham as if to underline its importance. As Paul wrote in Galatians 3:8, the gospel is preached through this promise. By working through the family of Abraham, God did not intend to restrict His blessings to one family. *All* nations would be blessed through Abraham's seed, especially through the special descendant Paul identified in Galatians 3:16 as Jesus. His death, resurrection and return will fulfill that blessing for all humankind as a demonstration of His grace.

It is in Canaan that we briefly meet the mysterious king of Salem, Melchizedek, a Jesus-like figure who is described as "the priest of the most high God" and who brought forth bread and wine to bless Abraham, while Abraham paid tribute to Melchizedek (Genesis 14:18). Here is a foreshadowing of a Jesus—*the* High Priest and *the* King of kings who also brought forth bread and wine (see Matthew 26:26–28; Mark 6:30–44; John 2:1–11; 6:1–14).

In succeeding chapters, God promises the aging Abraham a son, a genealogical heir, and much more. That heir turns out to be Isaac, his one and only son with Sarah. In Hebrew, the name Isaac is Yitzhak, which demonstrates that God has a sense of humor in addition to abundant love for humankind, which He made in His own image. How?

In Genesis 17:17, we're told: "Then Abraham fell upon his face, and laughed, and said in his heart, Shall a child be born unto him that is an hundred years old? and shall Sarah, that is ninety years old, bear?"

In the next chapter, three heavenly visitors approach Abraham and Sarah. One of the three is referred to as "the LORD" (18:1), which suggests this was a "Christophany," one of several Old Testament physical appearances of Jesus in human form.

> And they said unto him, Where is Sarah thy wife? And he said, Behold, in the tent. And he said, I will certainly return unto thee according to the time of life; and, lo, Sarah thy wife shall have a

son. And Sarah heard it in the tent door, which was behind him. Now Abraham and Sarah were old and well stricken in age; and it ceased to be with Sarah after the manner of women. Therefore Sarah laughed within herself, saying, After I am waxed old shall I have pleasure, my lord being old also? And the LORD said unto Abraham, Wherefore did Sarah laugh, saying, Shall I of a surety bear a child, which am old? Is any thing too hard for the LORD? At the time appointed I will return unto thee, according to the time of life, and Sarah shall have a son. Then Sarah denied, saying, I laughed not; for she was afraid. And he said, Nay; but thou didst laugh" (vv. 9–15).

Remember: Abraham had previously been instructed to name his son Isaac, or Yitzhak in Hebrew. The word *Yitzhak* means "laughter," which is precisely what God's messengers heard from Sarah in response to their prophecy that she would bear a son in old age. Yet, it would be through Isaac that God's covenant with Abraham would be fulfilled.

After Isaac's birth, in one of the most remarkable foreshadowings of the coming Messiah, Redeemer, and Savior in the Old Testament, Abraham was instructed to offer his son, his heir, as a sacrifice to God. "And [God] said, Take now thy son, thine only son Isaac, whom thou lovest, and get thee into the land of Moriah; and offer him there for a burnt offering upon one of the mountains which I will tell thee of" (Genesis 22:2).

Abraham, once again, in one of the most amazing passages in the Bible, proved his faith in God, by doing just what God commanded. He laid the wood for the sacrifice on his son's back, just as Jesus would carry His own death cross to Calvary, and headed toward the mountains.

And Isaac spake unto Abraham his father, and said, My father: and he said, Here am I, my son. And he said, Behold the fire and the wood: but where is the lamb for a burnt offering? And

Abraham said, My son, God will provide himself a lamb for a burnt offering: so they went both of them together. And they came to the place which God had told him of; and Abraham built an altar there, and laid the wood in order, and bound Isaac his son, and laid him on the altar upon the wood. And Abraham stretched forth his hand, and took the knife to slay his son. And the angel of the LORD called unto him out of heaven, and said, Abraham, Abraham: and he said, Here am I. And he said, Lay not thine hand upon the lad, neither do thou any thing unto him: for now I know that thou fearest God, seeing thou hast not withheld thy son, thine only son from me. And Abraham lifted up his eyes, and looked, and behold behind him a ram caught in a thicket by his horns: and Abraham went and took the ram, and offered him up for a burnt offering in the stead of his son. And Abraham called the name of that place Jehovahjireh: as it is said to this day, In the mount of the LORD it shall be seen. And the angel of the LORD called unto Abraham out of heaven the second time, and said, By myself have I sworn, saith the LORD, for because thou hast done this thing, and hast not withheld thy son, thine only son: that in blessing I will bless thee, and in multiplying I will multiply thy seed as the stars of the heaven, and as the sand which is upon the sea shore; and thy seed shall possess the gate of his enemies; And in thy seed shall all the nations of the earth be blessed; because thou hast obeyed my voice (Genesis 22:7–18).

Some question how Abraham could have been prepared to sacrifice his own son that day. But Abraham trusted completely in God. He knew God kept His promises. He believed that Isaac would live to fulfill God's promise to Abraham to continue his line. Therefore, Abraham must have known that his son would live again after the sacrifice he was prepared to make—just as Jesus was resurrected three days after His crucifixion (Hebrews 11:17–19).

That's real faith. And it's the gospel, right there in Genesis.

By the way, where did that near sacrifice of Isaac take place?

On Mount Moriah—in Jerusalem, the hill of Calvary—the same city where Jesus would be crucified and three days later resurrected.

"And the scripture, foreseeing that God would justify the heathen through faith, preached before the gospel unto Abraham, saying, In thee shall all nations be blessed," we're told in Galatians 3:8. And what is the gospel? It's the good news of blessing, redemption, healing, justice, and the restitution of all things as they were meant to be from the beginning.

Abraham's heir Isaac went on to bear twin sons, Esau and Jacob. But it was Jacob, later named "Israel" by God, who would carry forward the torch of redemption.

God revealed Himself to Jacob in Genesis 28 while on a journey from his home in Beersheba to Paran:

> And he dreamed, and behold a ladder set up on the earth, and the top of it reached to heaven: and behold the angels of God ascending and descending on it. And, behold, the LORD stood above it, and said, I am the LORD God of Abraham thy father, and the God of Isaac: the land whereon thou liest, to thee will I give it, and to thy seed; And thy seed shall be as the dust of the earth, and thou shalt spread abroad to the west, and to the east, and to the north, and to the south: and in thee and in thy seed shall all the families of the earth be blessed. And, behold, I am with thee, and will keep thee in all places whither thou goest, and will bring thee again into this land; for I will not leave thee, until I have done that which I have spoken to thee of (vv. 12–15).

This is a reaffirmation of God's covenant with Abraham, revealing that it was through Jacob and his descendants that the promise would be fulfilled. The ladder that Jacob saw upon which the angels of heaven ascended and descended is significant to the gospel story for several reasons:

1. It shows the redemption of humankind comes not by man climbing upward to reach God in heaven, as with the unsuccessful efforts to build the Tower of Babel, but by God linking Himself in relationship to man by descending to earth—just as Jesus would do by becoming a man in the form of a descendant of Jacob.

2. In John 1:51, Jesus Himself prophesied to the apostles that they would see something similar to Jacob's ladder: "Verily, verily, I say unto you, Hereafter ye shall see heaven open, and the angels of God ascending and descending upon the Son of man."

3. It hints that believers were made to live in a perfect earth, one connected to heaven and a part of the kingdom of God, which Jesus will rule and reign over forever in the ultimate restoration of all things as they were originally intended.

Now let's look at Jacob's favorite son, Joseph—his eleventh. He not only represents the glue between the books of Genesis and Exodus, but he is also a Jesus archetype. Though his older brothers considered killing him in a type of grave because of their jealousy (Genesis 37), he became the salvation for his father's entire family—and the whole Abrahamic line in the form of the budding nation of Israel.

Joseph was a prophet and became a kind of king in Egypt as well as the father of two of the tribes of Israel—a true patriarch of the faith. The Lord was with Joseph, we're told in Genesis 39:2. While Joseph was a slave in Egypt, God blessed the house of his master, Potiphar, who placed Joseph in charge of all his affairs. Later, he was tempted by Potiphar's wife to commit adultery, but rejected her because of his love for his master. Nevertheless, because of her accusations against Joseph, he was thrown in prison.

Because of the favor Joseph found in the eyes of the Lord, he was shown mercy and was given responsibility by the prison keeper.

There he met two of Pharaoh's servants who had been cast into prison after falling into disfavor with the king, the chief of the butlers and the chief of the bakers. They learned that Joseph could interpret their dreams with great accuracy, when he predicted that the chief butler would be restored to his position and the chief baker would be hanged, and it came to pass.

Once the chief butler was, indeed, restored to his post, Pharaoh had a troubling dream about a coming famine. The butler remembered Joseph's abilities, and Joseph was summoned to interpret the ruler's dream. Pharaoh was so impressed that he placed Joseph in charge of the country, second only in power and authority to himself.

Because of the preparations that Joseph had ordered, when the famine came, Egypt had plenty of food. But not so the family of Israel. So, Jacob, unaware of his favorite son's position in Egypt, sent his sons there, seeking food.

Upon arrival in Egypt, they were ushered into their brother's presence, but they didn't recognize Joseph because he had all the trappings of an Egyptian. When he revealed himself to them, they were afraid. Yet, despite what his brothers had done to him, Joseph showed mercy to them and brought his entire extended family to Egypt, where they remained for the rest of their lives as favored residents of the Pharaoh because of Joseph. It's a gospel-like story with many analogies to the life of Jesus, who was unrecognized as Messiah and rejected by his brethren, imprisoned unjustly, killed, cast into a tomb and resurrected in glory. Both Joseph and Jesus offered forgiveness to their brothers.

One cannot overstate Joseph's faithfulness in God, typified by what he told his brothers in Genesis 45: "Now therefore be not grieved, nor angry with yourselves, that ye sold me hither: for God did send me before you to preserve life. . . . And God sent me before you to preserve you a posterity in the earth, and to save your lives by a great deliverance. So now it was not you that sent me hither, but God: and he hath made me a father to Pharaoh, and lord of all his house, and a ruler throughout all the land of Egypt" (5–8).

Is that not the gospel? Repentance, forgiveness, life.

Later in Genesis, Joseph's father, Jacob gave a prophecy, and not only did that prophecy foretell of the coming lawgiver, Moses; it also predicted the coming of Messiah. Genesis 49:10 says, "The sceptre shall not depart from Judah, nor a lawgiver from between his feet, until Shiloh come; and unto him shall the gathering of the people be." The word "Shiloh" is believed to mean "the peacemaker," or "that which belongs to him." This prophecy clearly refers to Jesus as the coming King of kings.

It's there in Genesis—from the first chapter through the last—just as it is in every book of the Hebrew Scriptures: the gospel. Sometimes, though it's not so obvious. Often, we need to search it out. I believe God wants us to do that—to develop a ravenous hunger for His Word. It sometimes takes the help of others, especially gifted and anointed teachers.

I've had the good fortune in my lifetime to sit at the feet of some great Bible teachers—from Hal Lindsey to Jack Van Impe to Chuck Smith to Charles Rizzo to Jon Courson to Greg Laurie to Jonathan Cahn to Chuck Missler. They are all great not because they have a monopoly on the truth but because they are gifted expositors of the Bible. You need not agree with all that someone teaches to recognize his or her anointing. But what makes teachers of the Bible great is the ability to draw connections, to reveal parallels, to point out the patterns, to go deep into the Word in ways that make it come alive, to demonstrate what the Holy Spirit allowed them to see in the Scriptures. It can be quite inspiring—challenging you to do the same.

Let me share one of the many astounding things that I learned from my dear friend and Bible teacher Chuck Missler. I've checked it out myself with those much more well-versed in Hebrew than I, and done my own research using the modern tools of the computer age to verify it for myself to see if those teachings were true.

Chuck usually starts his teaching by asking a question, as many great teachers do. Here's how I recall hearing Chuck start this message the first time I heard it: "Where is the first place the gospel message appears in the Bible?"

The answer is a most unlikely place—a passage we often skip over as our eyes see a long genealogy from Adam through Noah in Genesis 5 and wonder why it's important or relevant to us.

It turns out there's a coded gospel message in these sometimes hard-to-pronounce names in their original Hebrew roots. I'm sure some might argue with the translations, but after studying the Bible for more than forty years, I have no problem accepting the theory that the God who created the entire universe left this hidden message there purposely for the diligent student—the man or woman who develops a hunger to find deeper meaning in every passage of the Bible.

Determining the meanings of proper names can be a difficult pursuit, since a direct translation is often not readily available. Even a conventional Hebrew lexicon can prove disappointing. But a study of the original root words behind those names can yield some fascinating insights.

Adam means "man." His son Seth's name means "appointed." You might recall Eve saying of Seth, "For God hath appointed me another seed instead of Abel, whom Cain slew" (Genesis 4:25).

Seth's son was called Enosh, which means "mortal, frail, or miserable." Enosh's son was named Kenan, which can mean "sorrow or dirge." Kenan's son was Mahalalel, which means "blessed God."

Mahalalel's son was named Jared, from the verb *yaradh*, meaning "shall come down." Jared's son was named Enoch, which means "teaching, or commencement." And Enoch was the father of Methuselah—both interesting characters.

Enoch walked with God, we're told in Genesis 5:24 "and he was not; for God took him." But, before he was gone, he was a prophet, whom, we're told in the New Testament book of Jude foretold of the Second Coming of the Messiah and "the restitution of all things," as Peter called the time of Jesus' earthly Kingdom. Methuselah, meanwhile was the oldest man in the Bible, living to the ripe old age of 969. Since Enoch was a prophet, he may well have known Methuselah would die before the flood – and told both his son and others. And, indeed, the flood came immediately after his death.

Interestingly, the name Enoch means "teaching." Methuselah means "his death shall bring."

Methuselah's son was named Lamech, which means "despairing" or "lament." Lamech was the father of Noah, which is derived from the Hebrew word *nacham*, meaning "to bring relief or comfort," as Lamech himself explains in Genesis 5:29.

So what's the coded meaning of this genealogy? Put it all together and there is a clear message—a gospel message: "Man appointed mortal sorrow; the Blessed God shall come down teaching His death shall bring the despairing rest [or comfort]."

If this isn't some shocking unintended coincidence! It means God, from the very beginning, had already laid out His plan of redemption. And if we're to take God literally, we must believe that God declares "the end from the beginning, and from ancient times the things that are not yet done, saying, My counsel shall stand, and I will do all my pleasure" (Isaiah 46:10).

2

THE GOSPEL IN EXODUS

*And [Jesus] said unto them, These are the words which I spake unto you, while
I was yet with you, that all things must be fulfilled, which were written in the
law of Moses, and in the prophets, and in the psalms, concerning me.*
—LUKE 24:44

JESUS HIMSELF PROVIDED US with the critical inside information
that *He* is the unifying theme in *every* book of the Bible. And if we
love Jesus, if we worship Him, if He is our Savior, our Lord, our
Master, our Creator, our King, then we should hunger for every bit
of knowledge and understanding of who He is and what He expects
of us and for us. After all, He is the Word made flesh to bring us
light, truth, and grace (John 1:1–14).

In the book of Genesis, we meet several extraordinary Jesus pro-
totypes, or models—Melchizedek, Isaac, and Joseph. In Exodus, we
meet another: Moses, the author of the first five books of the Bible.

While Joseph was sold into slavery in Egypt by his brothers, Moses was born into slavery and condemned to death, like other Hebrew male babies of his generation (see Exodus 1–2). Just as Jesus was faced with a death sentence proclaimed by the king from His birth (Matthew 2:16), so was Moses. But, miraculously, for God's purposes, he was saved by the daughter of Pharaoh and raised as her son as a prince of Egypt, placing him in a position from which he would one day become the deliverer of his people. This part of the Exodus story is familiar not just to Christians and Jews, but to much of the world through popular movies, children's stories, and books.

While Jesus' family fled to Egypt to save a newborn son, Moses was destined to lead His people out of Egypt. But if you want to see the foreshadowing of Jesus and the gospel in Exodus, it is to be found in the grainy details and subplots of the book.

It was after Moses had fled Egypt and was living with his wife, Zipporah, and tending the flocks of his father-in-law, Jethro, that he had his first encounter with God that would lead him to fulfill his destiny as one of the central characters of the Bible—one whose work, interestingly enough, was not finished when He died before entering the promised land.

For hundreds of years, the Hebrew people, the sons and daughters of Abraham, Isaac, and Jacob, had lived in Egypt as slaves. They had come to Egypt to survive a famine and stayed, under the protection of Joseph, the favored son of Jacob, a kind of prime minister for the pharaoh.

But after Joseph died and new pharaohs assumed power, they couldn't help but notice that the Hebrew population had grown into the millions. Seeing this people as a potential existential threat to Egypt, Pharaoh enslaved and oppressed them, even attempting to limit their population growth.

This period of enslavement was not a punishment by God. Rather, it was a period of *incubation* for the people He planned to be his holy, set-apart nation, which He would use to bring the light of His law and His offer of to all people in all nations.

Moses was God's chosen vehicle to bring His people back to the Holy Land He had promised to the heirs of Abraham, Isaac, and Jacob in Genesis.

Moses' encounter with Jesus came when he was leading his flock to Mount Horeb, also known as Sinai, and saw the burning bush (Exodus 3). How do we know that it was the person of Jesus to whom Moses spoke at Horeb? It is always Jesus when God appears to men throughout the Bible. It is always Jesus who interacts with humankind. As we are told in 1 Timothy 2:5, "For there is one God, and one mediator between God and men, the man Christ Jesus;" As illustrated in Genesis, Jesus, according to Scripture, is the Creator of all things. He is God. He and the Father are One. But Jesus is the one Mediator.

In this specific encounter, Moses asked for God's name so he could speak on His behalf to the children of Israel. God told him in Exodus 3:14: "I AM THAT I AM: and he said, Thus shalt thou say unto the children of Israel, I AM hath sent me unto you."

"I AM."

When Jesus was asked by His accusers whether He was the promised One of God, His response shocked them. He said, "I Am." The response is found in three of the four gospel accounts. So it is with all encounters between humankind and God throughout the Bible—past and future. It's Jesus who is the Word, the Creator of all things (John 1:3)—and it is Jesus who is the intermediary between humankind and the Father.

Here, at the burning bush, we see Jesus in the book of Exodus. He is the one and only Mediator between the Godhead and humankind. Each and every time human beings hear directly from God, see God, meet with God, make covenants with God, experience God's presence, and witness His miracles, it is the Mediator, the One we know as Jesus, the Son of God, the Anointed One, the Messiah, whom they encounter. The only exception is when messages are specifically delivered by angels, who identify themselves as such.

How many followers of Jesus fully grasp this? Too many Christians, I believe, tend to look at encounters between man and God in the Old Testament as meetings between man and the Father. They see God in the Hebrew Scriptures as God the Father and see His Son only in the Greek Scriptures. Of course, the Father and Son are one (John 10:30). But relations between God and man come only through the Son (John 8:16) This message of Jesus' eternal nature as the great "I Am," Creator, Savior, and Mediator is affirmed in John 14:6: "Jesus saith unto him, I am the way, the truth, and the life: no man cometh unto the Father, but by me."

If you have never considered it before, it is time: It was Jesus the Messiah, "the LORD God of the Hebrews" (Exodus 3:18), who led the children of Israel out of the land of Egypt. It was Jesus speaking to Moses on Mount Horeb and whispering in his ear when He demanded of the Pharaoh, "Let my people go!"

It was Jesus, too, who stretched out His mighty hand to smite Egypt using all His wonders, which He had warned He would do (Exodus 3:19–20) God does not show us two different personalities of God in the Tanakh and the Greek Scriptures, as some wrongly believe. There is no difference between the personalities of God the Father and God the Son. They are One—inseparable, unchanging, the same yesterday, today, and tomorrow (see Hebrews 13:8). Jesus is the perfect reflection of the Father and His will. If there is one message I want you to take away from this book, that would be it.

I imagine that for some reading this, there will be some skepticism. This is a truth not stated clearly or frequently in our churches. I've provided some scriptural evidence here for you to consider, but I urge you to be like the Bereans, whom I mentioned in the last chapter, who listened to what Paul taught them and then studied the Scriptures daily for themselves to see if what he'd told them was so.

As I wrote in *The Restitution of All Things*, people tend to believe in the traditions of men rather than the clear word of Scripture. It was true of the Pharisees in Jesus' time, and He told them so (Mark 7:8). It is equally true of many today in the church, who believe what they are taught by human teachers and don't dig deeper into

Scripture to put those teachings to the ultimate test of truth.

Exodus 10 tells the story of people who could not save themselves and repeatedly fell short of God's mark for them. For the Hebrew people, this failure was manifest in the physical world.

Without God's intervention, as when they were trapped between the Red Sea and Pharaoh's army bent on their annihilation, they would have been slaughtered. But God parted the sea for them, offering a type of baptism as they crossed through the parted waters (Exodus 14).

In Exodus 12, we see through the first Passover a foreshadowing of Jesus' sacrifice on the cross. God instructed Moses to tell the children of Israel how to protect themselves from the judgment that was to befall Egypt because of Pharaoh's refusal to let His people go: the slaying of the firstborn, both of man and beast. Notice the Passover details in Exodus 12 and their fulfillment in Jesus

- Each family was to sacrifice a lamb (v. 3). Jesus is the Lamb of God (John 1:29).

- The lamb must be without blemish (v. 5). Jesus also had to be—and was—without sin (1 Peter 1:19; Hebrews 4:15).

- The lamb must be slain by "the whole assembly of the congregation" (v. 6). Jesus was sentenced to death on the cross by "the multitude" of "the people" (the assembly) who cried "Crucify him" (Mark 15:8–14).

- The blood of the lamb must be sprinkled on the lintels and doorposts of each dwelling (v. 22). Think of what that blood-spattered door would look like—forming the image of a cross.

- Each inhabitant of the house must feed upon the lamb (v. 4). To be saved, everyone must partake of the Lamb of God (John 6:51–56).

- The lamb must be eaten with bitter herbs and unleavened bread (v. 8). These requirements foreshadow the need for true penitence, obedience, and sincerity through Jesus' offering of salvation.

As much as any other Old Testament book, the gospel themes of redemption are clearly seen in Exodus. Jesus, though unnamed, is pictured throughout the book. God's faithfulness to His people is key to the book as He reveals Himself to them and then provides a path for them to be in relationship with Him.

In 1 Corinthians 5:7, followers of Jesus are instructed, "Purge out . . . the old leaven that ye may be a new lump, as ye [really] are unleavened. For even Christ, our Passover lamb, is sacrificed for us." That's what the feast of unleavened bread is all about (see Exodus 12:17–20).

Both Passover and the feast of unleavened bread were first observed in Exodus. While most Jews who observe it today don't see Jesus in the feast, sadly, neither do most Christians, who don't even observe it because they are not steeped in the imagery and commandments of the Old Testament.

Most significantly, we're told in Exodus 12:24–25: "And ye shall observe this thing for an ordinance to thee and to thy sons for ever. And it shall come to pass, when ye be come to the land which the LORD will give you, according as he hath promised, that ye shall keep this service."

The children of Israel were instructed to make Passover a permanent holy day, so that its greater meaning would not be forgotten by future generations. That meaning came to fulfillment through Messiah's death on the cross on Passover and His resurrection three days later on the feast of firstfruits.

It's in Exodus where we are first shown that salvation from sin does not come without the shedding of blood—a point echoed in Hebrews 9:22. The tenth and final plague upon the Egyptians brought about the death of every firstborn in the land of Egypt—

except for those whose doors were marked by the blood of spotless lambs (12:23). Only these escaped judgment. Thus, the first Passover demonstrated while pointing to a future Passover in which the Lamb of God would be slain for the sins of the whole world.

In Exodus 13:1–2, God instructs Moses to sanctify to Him all the firstborn among the children of Israel throughout their generations. And it would be the firstborn of Mary (Miriam) who would come to offer redemption to the whole world.

Not to put too fine a point on it, but Jesus the Messiah, the Son of God and future King of kings, is all over the book of Exodus, just, as we will see later, He is all over the Tanakh—in every book.

It was Jesus who turned the staff of Moses, and later of Aaron, into a serpent (Exodus 4:3; 7:10). It was Jesus who turned the Nile River into a river of blood (7:20). It was Jesus who performed all the miracles that brought Pharaoh to his knees and then parted the Red Sea, and it was Jesus who provided a cloud to lead the Israelites by day and the pillar of fire by night (8–14).

In Exodus 15, the children of Israel reached Marah, but they could not drink of the waters there, for they were bitter. The Lord showed Moses a tree, which, when he had cast it into the waters, purified them (vv. 23–25). Jesus died on a kind of tree *and* is the fountain of living waters (see 1 Peter 2:24; John 4:10–15), confirmation of that to be fulfilled in the kingdom of God on Earth when He rules and reigns from Jerusalem, pouring out His living waters and wiping away all tears (Revelation 7:17).

§

The ark of the covenant, first seen in Exodus, holds a special fascination in the imagination even today. Every few years, there's some new theory about where it might be found. It went missing after the destruction of the first temple, and the apostle John saw it when he was in the temple of heaven (Revelation 11:19). Popular movies have been made about its mysteries and power. The children of Israel would carry it out before them to war with their enemies.

When it was captured by the Philistines, it brought them a plague of emerods, or hemorrhoids, causing them to send it back to Israel (see 1 Samuel 5–6).

In Exodus it was built by God's people, according to His exacting specifications. On one level, it was built to carry the two tablets of stone upon which were "written with the finger of God" the Ten Commandments (Exodus 31:18). On another level, it is a symbol of Jesus. It was the ark of the *covenant*, and what does the covenant offer? Redemption, restoration, the kingdom.

The ark was made with wood; thus, like the Savior who would enter the world in human form as the seed of the woman, it has an earthly substance. But it is more than wood. Every part of it is covered with pure gold, suggesting Jesus' kingship. Thus, the ark embodies the law, just as Jesus, who fulfills it, does. He also covers us with His shed blood to provide forgiveness for our infractions of the law. If you need more confirmation of the significance of the ark, consider what sits atop its cover—in the center between two angels on either side. It is the "mercy seat" (see Exodus 25:17–22)

The ark was kept inside the tabernacle, or tent, yet another representation of Jesus, we're told in Hebrews 9:11: "But Christ being come an high priest of good things to come, by a greater and more perfect tabernacle, not made with hands, that is to say, not of this building;" Jesus' destiny was to come "camp" with us on this impermanent earth.

Hebrews 8:5 shows this was a foreshadowing of what was to come when Jesus would appear in human form as Messiah: "Who serve unto the example and shadow of heavenly things, as Moses was admonished of God when he was about to make the tabernacle: for, See, saith he, that thou make all things according to the pattern shewed to thee in the mount."

The Synoptic Gospels (Matthew, Mark, and Luke) all tell the story of the "transfiguration" (and John 1:14 is said to allude to it), in which Jesus is joined by Moses and Elijah in glory before three apostles. His face shone like the sun, we're told (Matthew 17:2), much as Moses' did after spending time with God atop Mount Horeb (Exodus 34:29–30). There, high atop another mountain, Jesus spoke with his servants Moses and Elias, or Elijah. Peter suggested making three tabernacles, or tents: one for Jesus, one for Moses, and one for Elijah (Matthew 17:3–4).

Then, in Revelation 21:3, we see the complete fulfillment of this tabernacle foreshadowing: "And I heard a great voice out of heaven saying, Behold, the tabernacle of God is with men, and he will dwell with them, and they shall be his people, and God himself shall be with them, and be their God."

God's mercy and righteousness are found throughout Exodus.

Consider, for instance, what transpired among the children of Israel while Moses was visiting God atop Mount Horeb, absorbing the law and communing with the Creator for forty days.

In Exodus 32, we witness how quickly God's chosen people forgot all they had seen and heard since miraculously leaving Egypt. It was a shocking fall, led, to make matters worse, by Aaron, Moses' brother and the high priest.

> And when the people saw that Moses delayed to come down out of the mount, the people gathered themselves together unto Aaron, and said unto him, Up, make us gods, which shall go before us; for as for this Moses, the man that brought us up out of the land of Egypt, we wot not what is become of him.
>
> And Aaron said unto them, Break off the golden earrings, which are in the ears of your wives, of your sons, and of your daughters, and bring them unto me.
>
> And all the people brake off the golden earrings which were in their ears, and brought them unto Aaron.
>
> And he received them at their hand, and fashioned it with a graving tool, after he had made it a molten calf: and they said, These be thy gods, O Israel, which brought thee up out of the land of Egypt.

And when Aaron saw it, he built an altar before it; and Aaron made proclamation, and said, To morrow is a feast to the LORD.

And they rose up early on the morrow, and offered burnt offerings, and brought peace offerings; and the people sat down to eat and to drink, and rose up to play.

And the LORD said unto Moses, Go, get thee down; for thy people, which thou broughtest out of the land of Egypt, have corrupted themselves: They have turned aside quickly out of the way which I commanded them: they have made them a molten calf, and have worshipped it, and have sacrificed thereunto, and said, These be thy gods, O Israel, which have brought thee up out of the land of Egypt.

And the LORD said unto Moses, I have seen this people, and, behold, it is a stiffnecked people: "Now therefore let me alone, that my wrath may wax hot against them, and that I may consume them: and I will make of thee a great nation (Exodus 32:1–10).

One can only imagine how God felt—betrayed. He considered destroying all the people and making only his servant Moses into His holy nation.

Moses appealed to God for mercy for His people, and it was granted. With whom was Moses interceding? The one and only Mediator between God and man—Jesus. Moses was playing the role of the intercessor by pleading with the ultimate Intercessor (see Hebrews 7:25).

While many participated in the worship of the golden calf, God gave all Israel a second chance. Moses simply asked of his people which of them stood with God. Those who repented of their evil were spared. Some three thousand did not and perished (Exodus 34:26–28).

Just as three thousand rejected repentance in Exodus 34, on a future feast of Shavuot, what most Christians call "Pentecost" or the feast of weeks, three thousand Jews would accept Jesus as their

Messiah, repent, and be saved (Acts 2:41). Shavuot, by the way, commemorates the giving of the law at Sinai.

This is how we see Jesus, the gospel and redemption in the wilderness of Sinai.

Perhaps we see it best in Exodus 34:6–7 when God's attributes are listed: "merciful and gracious, longsuffering, and abundant in goodness and truth, keeping mercy for thousands, forgiving iniquity and transgression and sin, and that will *by no means clear the guilty*" (emphasis added).

There is no disconnect between Moses and Jesus or between the Old Testament and the New. In fact, there is perfect harmony. Again and again, Moses is affirmed in the Greek Scriptures.

When challenged by the Pharisees on the Mosaic rules of marriage and divorce in Matthew 19:7, Jesus explained that nothing in God's perfect will had changed, only that Moses had provided a rule of divorce because of the hardness of mankind's heart. "But from the beginning it was not so," He added. "And I say unto you, Whosoever shall put away his wife, except it be for fornication, and shall marry another, committeth adultery: and whoso marrieth her which is put away doth commit adultery" (vv. 8–9).

Frequently throughout the New Testament, Jesus confronted and harshly criticized the Pharisees for their interpretations of Moses' law, but never the law itself, which He fulfilled to perfection as Messiah. For example, in Matthew 23:1–3, He commanded the people to obey what the Pharisees said when they sat in Moses' seat—at which time they could only recite the Torah—"but do not after their works: for they say, and do not."

A striking example of Jesus' consistency with Moses appears in Luke 16:31, when the Lord hints at His own resurrection, saying: "If they hear not Moses and the prophets, neither will they be persuaded, though one rose from the dead."

In Exodus 16:15, when the children of Israel found themselves hungry during the sojourn through the wilderness, they were miraculously provided with manna from heaven. Moses said: "This is the bread which the LORD hath given you to eat." This was the bread of survival in the flesh. Later, in John 6:32, Jesus explained that He came as the ultimate bread of life from heaven: "Verily, verily, I say unto you, Moses gave you not that bread from heaven; but my Father giveth you the true bread from heaven." That true bread was the kind that provides eternal life.

God is just. God is righteous. There's mercy and forgiveness available to those who sincerely repent. But there is righteous judgment for the unrepentant.

That's what God promises in His future kingdom on Earth, which is part of the gospel sometimes forgotten or overlooked in our considerations of "the restitution of all things," as Peter described it in Acts 3:21. It's the same message found in Exodus—and throughout the Tanakh.

God is loving and good, compassionate and forgiving, merciful and gracious, slow to anger and abounding in love and faithfulness, holy and righteous. But God never leaves the guilty unpunished. God's character doesn't change, either. He's the same yesterday, today and tomorrow.

3

THE GOSPEL IN LEVITICUS

For I am the LORD your God: ye shall therefore sanctify yourselves, and ye shall be holy. —LEVITICUS 11:44

Be holy: for I the LORD your God am holy. —LEVITICUS 19:2

WHEN WAS THE LAST TIME you read Leviticus?

No, I mean, when was the last time you *really* read Leviticus?

Maybe a better question is: When did you last study this middle book of the Torah with two things in mind?

- What is the central theme?

- Where are the connections to the gospel?

Those are excellent questions to ask yourself when you resume your studies of the Old Testament, or, as you use this book to guide you through the Hebrew Scriptures.

Every book in the Bible is there for a reason—a reason beyond learning the historical foundations of the Bible, the cultural framework of our faith, the significance of the rituals, the meaning of the stories.

Most Christians aren't really that familiar with Leviticus. They don't spend time there. They steer clear of it because it seems confusing and dry. It's about the detail of the law, which they believe, because they've been taught, has no consequence for them. They avoid it because they think it's hard to read. And that's a shame.

By contrast, Genesis and Exodus are fascinating collections of stories, many of which are familiar to Christians and non-Christians alike because of extrabiblical literature and Hollywood movies. If we don't approach Leviticus in the right way, it can read like a dry rule book with little relevance to our contemporary life.

But understanding Leviticus—as Jesus and His apostles did— enriches our appreciation and passion for the Gospels, for the complete picture of redemption, for the coming kingdom of God and a true understanding of our Creator.

Is that motivation enough to take a deeper look at this foundational holy book? If not, here's another reason to consider: Leviticus has more direct quotes from God than any other book in the Bible.

As Andrew Bonar, the esteemed theologian and minister of the Free Church of Scotland back in the nineteenth century, wrote, "There is no book in the whole Bible compass of that inspired volume which the Holy Spirit has given us, that contains more of the very words of God than *Leviticus*. It is God that is the direct speaker in almost every page; his gracious words are recorded in the form in which they were spoken. This consideration cannot fail to send us to the study of it with singular interest and attention."[1]

If that's not enough to grab you, let me add this: the book addresses the key question of what it looks like when God dwells with His people. In other words, it's about a tangible time in history when the Creator of the universe lived with His people as an example for us of what that relationship was like and will be in the future when the gospel is fully realized in His kingdom.

Isn't that precisely why we're so fascinated, understandably so, with the four gospel accounts themselves?

In other words, Leviticus is a blueprint for life with God. It's an explanation of why He created the world, the universe, and humankind, and an explanation of why He hasn't given up on any of it because of the fall.

Even more to the point, Leviticus is where we can see the design for redemption—and how Jesus fulfills it. Nowhere can we see more how the sacrifices point to the Redeemer Himself, nor appreciate more how, through Jesus, we can draw near to the Creator as God showed the children of Israel to draw near to Him.

Am I getting your interest?

Yes, it helps to know what to look for in Leviticus.

Now that we have the general theme of the book, it's time for a few more disclaimers before we begin exploring the connections to the gospel of the kingdom.

Another obstacle Christians have when they encounter Leviticus is that it's almost all *law*. For many Christians today, *law*, in the spiritual context, is a bad word. They've been taught to view the law in a negative light and as the opposite of grace. But, as I covered extensively in my previous book, *The Restitution of All Things*, that is a false paradigm—and a dangerous one.

The opposite of law is lawlessness.

Repentance and grace are the cures for breaches of the law, or sins. That is not something we first learn in the New Testament, yet it is affirmed there (1 John 3:3–4) The definition of sin is "transgression of the law." It's something we observe throughout the Bible from the beginning. The only cure is repentance and grace. Every book of the Old Testament, in one way or another, points to the Redeemer. And every righteous person we meet in the Tanakh understood that he or she was indebted to this future Messiah.

There is a consistency throughout the Hebrew and Greek Scriptures. Yet, in a superficial comparison of Leviticus with, say, the book of Luke, one can perceive a stark contrast. That is simply a perception problem contemporary Christians have because they are not in tune with the critical Hebraic foundations of their faith.

One secret to a new appreciation of Leviticus is not trying immediately to understand all the details—of which there are many. That will take much more study. There are answers if you search for them, but the first step in this journey is to comprehend the big picture. The Bible is a complex book, as we should expect from one breathed into existence through God's relationship and direct communication with humankind over thousands of years. It has multiple layers. You can study it for a lifetime and get new meaning and revelation from it under the guidance of the Holy Spirit every time you pick it up.

The big question we should have when we open the book of Leviticus is, how can an all-knowing, perfect, holy Creator God who defines right from wrong live among a sinful and impure people without destroying us in our sin and impurity? Precautions must be taken. Rules must be imposed. Obedience must be absolute. Provisions for mercy need to be provided. But the rewards are staggeringly beyond our mortal comprehension.

With that, let's begin our search for the gospel in the book of Leviticus.

The first seven chapters of Leviticus explain the sacrifices that address sin and enable the children of Israel to maintain their relationship with God, fulfill their destiny as His chosen people, and prosper in both the wilderness and in their future home in the promised land.

Immediately in chapter 1, notice God's repetition of some key descriptive phrases about the animals to be chosen for sacrifice (emphasis is added):

- "If his offering be a burnt sacrifice of the herd, let him offer *a male without blemish*: he shall offer it of his own voluntary will at the door of the tabernacle of the congregation before the LORD" (v. 3).

- "And if his offering be of the flocks, namely, of the sheep, or of the goats, for a burnt sacrifice; he shall bring it *a male without blemish*" (v. 10).

What stands out? The atoning sacrifices must be males without blemish, meaning they must be inspected carefully, just as the sinless Jesus was inspected carefully by the religious authorities of His day, and even by Herod and Pilate, before being sacrificed for the sins of the world. The animals were without sin, of course, but they could not cover the sins of humankind if they had a blemish. They needed to be perfect, in that sense, just as Jesus was perfectly sinless.

But there's more here. Notice that the offerings must be voluntary. If they were coerced, they would be of no effect. If they were brought forward out of a sense of duty or under duress, they would not provide the necessary covering of sin that would permit God to continue relationship with His people.

"And he shall put his hand upon the head of the burnt offering; and it shall be accepted for him to make atonement for him," verse 4 goes on to say. Why would the one making the offering be required to place his hand on the head of the sacrificial animal? It was a symbolic transfer of sin that required a closeness and familiarity between the offering and the offeree.

Only Aaron, the high priest, and his sons could sprinkle the blood and lay the wood on the altar. The killing of the offering must be done in the sight of the high priest, just as Jesus, the ultimate sacrifice, would be killed in the sight and under the supervision of the high priest.

Right from the start, Leviticus is full of imagery and symbolism of the coming Redeemer.

In chapter 2, we learn that when offerings of "fine flour" were made, they must be without leaven. Leaven is symbolic of sin throughout the Bible. Unleavened bread was the kind Jesus and His apostles ate at the Passover meal before His death on the cross. These "unleavened wafers" (v. 4) would also be anointed with oil, just as the future kings of Israel, including Jesus, were (see Matthew 26:6–13). The priests were instructed to lay frankincense on these offerings, just as the wise men would lay frankincense at the feet of the young Jesus in Bethlehem (Leviticus 2:1–2; Matthew 2:11).

The offerings were also required to be salted (Leviticus 2:13), recalling what Jesus said in Mark 9:49–50: "For every one shall be salted with fire, and every sacrifice shall be salted with salt. Salt is good: but if the salt have lost his saltness, wherewith will ye season it? Have salt in yourselves, and have peace one with another."

The next section of Leviticus, chapters 8 through 10, deals with the priesthood that leads worship and intercedes on the behalf of the whole congregation of Israel. Moses and Aaron did exactly as they were told and nothing more. But in chapter 10, we see what happens when Aaron's sons, Nadab and Abihu, improvise.

> And Nadab and Abihu, the sons of Aaron, took either of them his censer, and put fire therein, and put incense thereon, and offered strange fire before the LORD, which he commanded them not. And there went out fire from the LORD, and devoured them, and they died before the LORD. Then Moses said unto Aaron, This is it that the LORD spake, saying, I will be sanctified in them that come nigh me, and before all the people I will be glorified. And Aaron held his peace (vv. 1–3).

The lesson here is that we serve a holy God who does not sanction improvisation with his meticulously clear and specific instructions. It was a lesson not to mix the holy with the unholy or profane v. 10)

In Leviticus 11–16, the Lord gives the instructions on dealing with impurity, including an annual ceremony to remove all sin from the congregation. These chapters include the dietary laws and the nature of clean and unclean. While these teachings are often scoffed at by Christians today, there is every reason to believe, according to the prophecies of the coming kingdom, that they will be in full force when Jesus reigns on His throne in Jerusalem. If I am right, and these teachings were followed by Jesus and His apostles through the first century, and will be observed again after the "restitution of all things," this becomes an issue about which all believers would be advised to pray for wisdom and discernment.

Have the definitions of holiness and purity changed? If so, we need to ask, who changed them? Those are questions you might ask yourself as you discover, or rediscover, the book of Leviticus.

God cares a lot about our purity and holiness. And it's Him we must please, not ourselves.

Those who call themselves Christians sometimes look at the Bible and pick and choose what they like and leave the rest. Some might look at Leviticus as a relic of the past. Heretics of the past, like Marcion, suggested the entire Old Testament was the creation of a different god than the one who inspired the New Testament. I have even heard of pastors today who teach that. Of course, then we must ask ourselves why we see Jesus so clearly in prophecy, foreshadowing, and even personal appearances all over the Hebrew Scriptures.

Much of this confusion comes from how we view Leviticus.

But the law as recorded in Leviticus is what taught the children of Israel how to live in relationship with God, who had entered into covenant with them and lived in their midst. The gospel, meanwhile, is about the same thing. Jesus tells us to make the kingdom of God first in our lives. The kingdom of God is the time in which we will, once again, have the opportunity to live in relationship with God, who made covenant with us and will live in our midst as King of kings, Lord of lords and our High Priest.

If Leviticus is irrelevant to our lives now, do you think it will be then? Remember: it's the blueprint for living in real relationship with God.

Even Jesus referred to the law of Leviticus directly when He healed a man of leprosy. You'll remember the story from Mark 1:40–44:

> And there came a leper to him, beseeching him, and kneeling down to him, and saying unto him, If thou wilt, thou canst make me clean. And Jesus, moved with compassion, put forth his hand, and touched him, and saith unto him, I will; be thou clean. And as soon as he had spoken, immediately the leprosy departed from him, and he was cleansed. And he straitly charged him, and forthwith sent him away; and saith unto him, See thou say nothing to any man: but go thy way, *shew thyself to the priest, and offer for thy cleansing those things which Moses commanded, for a testimony unto them.* (Emphasis added)

Where does Moses offer specific commands about the cleansing of leprosy? In Leviticus 13. The entire chapter is devoted to this subject. Did Jesus think Leviticus outdated? It doesn't appear so.

In fact, His entire life on earth in human form was spent guided by the commandments of Leviticus, beginning with His birth. In Luke 2:21, we see that He was circumcised when He was eight days old. That's when He was named Yehoshua, or Yeshua, which means "salvation," as the angel Gabriel had instructed.

Next, in Luke 2:22–24, we find that Mary is observing another Leviticus instruction: "And when the days of her purification according to the law of Moses were accomplished, they brought him to Jerusalem, to present him to the Lord; (As it is written in the law of the LORD, Every male that openeth the womb shall be called holy to the Lord;) And to offer a sacrifice according to that which is said in the law of the Lord, A pair of turtledoves, or two young pigeons."

In John 8, Jesus is confronted by a mob, led by the Pharisees and scribes, about to stone a woman caught in adultery: "Now Moses in the law commanded us, that such should be stoned: but what sayest thou?" they asked. And Jesus said, "He that is without sin among you, let him first cast a stone at her" (vv. 2–7). Where is the commandment found that prescribes death for the sin of adultery? Leviticus 20:10.

Leviticus 17:11–27 is the heart and soul of the book. It is a series of laws that direct the children of Israel in living like a "kingdom of priests and a holy nation" (Exodus 19:6).

In Leviticus 17:11, we find this key verse that explains the necessity of blood sacrifice for the atonement of sin: "For the life of the flesh is in the blood: and I have given it to you upon the altar to make an atonement for your souls: for it is the blood that maketh an atonement for the soul."

Read that verse again carefully, because there's something there you might not have noticed.

This is both law and prophecy. Yes, on the one hand, God gave us the sacrificial system to atone for sins. But look at the way this is phrased—with a dual meaning: "I have given it to you upon the altar to make an atonement for your souls." God was not just commanding His people to shed animal blood for atonement; He was also saying that He Himself had already shed His own blood for the atonement of all sin. It's reminiscent of that incomparable verse in Genesis in which Abraham tells his son Isaac, whom he is about to sacrifice, that "My son, God will provide *himself* a lamb for a burnt offering" (Genesis 22:8; emphasis added). This too is one of the most remarkable and overlooked foreshadowings of the coming Messiah, Redeemer, and Savior in the Old Testament.

When I see things like this in the Bible, it confirms that this is a supernaturally authored book—from cover to cover, beginning to end. It recalls what the apostle John wrote about Jesus in Revelation 13:8, calling Him the *"the Lamb slain from the foundation of the world."*

In God's economy, Christ's death had already taken place at the foundation of the world—the end from the beginning.

≥●

Even many people who have never read the Bible know Jesus instructed us to "love our neighbors as ourselves." Was that a new commandment? No, it is found in Leviticus 19:18: "Thou shalt not avenge, nor bear any grudge against the children of thy people, but thou shalt love thy neighbour as thyself: I am the LORD."

It has always been a tough law to follow. Jesus reiterated it, of course, in Matthew 5:43–48, but, as usual, He didn't lower the bar. He *raised* it.

> Ye have heard that it hath been said, Thou shalt love thy neighbour, and hate thine enemy. But I say unto you, Love your enemies, bless them that curse you, do good to them that hate you, and pray for them which despitefully use you, and persecute you; That ye may be the children of your Father which is in heaven: for he maketh his sun to rise on the evil and on the good, and sendeth rain on the just and on the unjust. For if ye love them which love you, what reward have ye? do not even the publicans the same? And if ye salute your brethren only, what do ye more than others? do not even the publicans so? Be ye therefore perfect, even as your Father which is in heaven is perfect.

Some Christians think Jesus came to make it easier to gain entry into His kingdom, but consistently He seemingly did just the opposite, which explains why He says few find their way. He didn't just proclaim, "Love thy neighbor." He commanded that we love our *enemies*. Moreover, he commanded *perfection*. We can only really appreciate some of this by knowing the Old Testament, which not only provided the foundation for the gospel, but has as much or more to say about the promise of the coming kingdom as do the Greek scriptures.

Leviticus's prescription to love they neighbor as thyself is also pretty sweeping, extending from family matters to business matters to courts of law to proper treatment of the poor and disadvantaged. It means sharing the gospel, pursuing reconciliation, extending mercy and seeking justice—in other words, living as we will be expected to live in God's kingdom.

Are you starting to get excited about what you can actually find in Leviticus?

There's more. To me, one of the most special elements of this book is found in Leviticus 23. If you are looking for Jesus in the Old Testament, He's all over the feasts of the Lord—from the Sabbath to Passover, to the feast of unleavened bread to firstfruits to Shavuot, the feast of trumpets, Yom Kippur and the feast of tabernacles. My friend Mark Biltz calls them "God's Day-Timer," and that's accurate. They show us a timeline of the past, present and future. They occurred on God's calendar on historic days long ago and will occur again on magnificently victorious days still ahead.

And they are all about Jesus and His kingdom to come. Jesus is the Lord of the Sabbath (Matthew 12:8). He is the ultimate Passover Lamb (John 1:29). He rose from the dead during the feast of first-fruits (2Timothy 2:6). He poured out the Holy Spirit as Comforter on Shavuot, or Pentecost (Acts 2). And likewise, the perceptive will see that the fall feasts will be fulfilled in like fashion when He returns to usher in His kingdom and the restoration of all things.

4

THE GOSPEL IN NUMBERS

The LORD *bless thee, and keep thee: the* LORD *make his face shine upon thee, and be gracious unto thee: the* LORD *lift up his countenance upon thee, and give thee peace. And they shall put my name upon the children of Israel; and I will bless them.'—*NUMBERS 6:24–27

I shall see him, but not now: I shall behold him, but not nigh: there shall come a Star out of Jacob, and a Sceptre shall rise out of Israel, and shall smite the corners of Moab, and destroy all the children of Sheth. And Edom shall be a possession, Seir also shall be a possession for his enemies; and Israel shall do valiantly. Out of Jacob shall come he that shall have dominion, and shall destroy him that remaineth of the city. —NUMBERS 24:17–19

"NUMBERS" It's a strange title for a book of the Bible. What is this—a math book?

Not at all. The English name for the fourth book of the Torah, or Pentateuch, comes from second numbering of the people The Lord

41

told Moses, "Take ye the sum of all the congregation of the children of Israel, after their families, by the house of their fathers, with the number of their names, every male by their polls; from twenty years old and upward, all that are able to go forth to war in Israel: thou and Aaron shall number them by their armies" (Numbers 1:2–3).

But Numbers, or as the book is called in Hebrew, "In the Wilderness," is much more than a genealogy or a census. It continues the Torah theme of the consequences of faithfulness versus unfaithfulness. More than other books, Numbers illustrates what happens when God's people do not act in faith.

Despite the fact that those "numbered" in this book include only men capable of fighting the wars that will face the children of Israel, it also reveals that in God's economy, everyone counts—all His people—defying the notion that the Bible is a book celebrating patriarchy and inequality.

Numbers 5 makes this point repeatedly and emphatically: "Speak unto the children of Israel, When a man or woman shall commit any sin that men commit, to do a trespass against the LORD, and that person be guilty; then they shall confess their sin which they have done: and he shall recompense his trespass with the principal thereof, and add unto it the fifth part thereof, and give it unto him against whom he hath trespassed" (Numbers 5:6–7).

The rules apply equally. God judges each individual—man and woman alike. There is salvation and justice for all. And He is no respecter of persons in judgment, as we will read later (Acts 10:34; Romans 2:11; Ephesians 6:9; Colossians 3:25; James 2:1; and 1 Peter 1:17).

The children of Israel faced not only the special challenges of the wilderness, but the kind that people face in any community. What happens when men and women are unfaithful to their spouses? What happens when they are *suspected* of being unfaithful to their spouses?

Numbers 5:12–31 deals with this "spirit of jealousy." In other cultures, a man might be able to issue a divorce for such suspicion.

He might even feign such suspicion to marry another. Not so among the children of Israel. God Himself would judge the truth and the hearts of those involved. A woman could not be condemned on a husband's word alone. Thus, each individual is, first and foremost, accountable to God.

This legislation, which we see for the first time in the book of Numbers, reminds us of how Jesus judged the woman about to be stoned to death for adultery in John 8. The woman's accusers were not following the law first found in Numbers. They were not in compliance with the process of adjudication laid out in specific detail, a system of justice that would require God to act supernaturally for the woman to be convicted of the accused offense. Thus, we see the gospel message of mercy and forgiveness explained in Numbers and we see Numbers revealed in the actions of Jesus, who wrote with his finger in the earth before telling the woman she was forgiven and to sin no more. Could it be Jesus was writing the law of Numbers 5 on the ground? Perhaps we will have to wait for the gospel to be fulfilled in the kingdom to completely understand.

Thus, Numbers teaches humanity to trust in God's ultimate justice and faithfulness, not man's. It is man's unbelief and unfaithfulness that will result in our destruction. This is a familiar refrain throughout all four gospel accounts—something Jesus reminds us about over and over.

But there are more than just hints, glimpses, and subtle foreshadowing of the Messiah, the restoration of all things, and the future kingdom of God in the book of Numbers, and nowhere more so than in what we know of as the Aaronic blessing in Numbers 6:24–27: "The LORD bless thee, and keep thee: the LORD make his face shine upon thee, and be gracious unto thee: The LORD lift up his countenance upon thee, and give thee peace. And they shall put my name upon the children of Israel, and I will bless them."

That's not just a blessing; it's a prophecy. For putting God's name upon the children of Israel with His blessing is exactly what every prophet of the Bible says will happen in His coming kingdom. In turn, the entire world will be blessed. That's the ultimate gospel message. There's forgiveness. There's atonement. And there's peace, justice, and an Edenic-style restoration of the world as God intended it to be from the beginning.

In Numbers 8:7; 19:7–9; 19:13; and 19:17–21, we see the cleansing power of water—more than a mere hint of the living water of John 4:10–11; John 7:38; and Revelation 7:17.

Then in Numbers 20, the congregation of the children of Israel came to the desert of Zin, where there was no water. Once again, as we witnessed in Exodus, God's unfaithful people, who had witnessed so many miracles on this journey, accused Moses of leading them into the desert to die: "And wherefore have ye made us to come up out of Egypt, to bring us in unto this evil place? it is no place of seed, or of figs, or of vines, or of pomegranates; neither is there any water to drink," they said (v. 5).

One could imagine Moses getting tired and angry about being blamed at every turn by his flock for leading them out of bondage in Egypt. And it was here in this place that his anger with the people was displayed, costing him personally the chance to enter the promised land.

In Numbers 20:8, God instructed Moses: "Take [your] rod, and gather thou the assembly together, thou, and Aaron thy brother, and speak ye unto the rock before their eyes; and it shall give forth his water, and thou shalt bring forth to them water out of the rock: so thou shalt give the congregation and their beasts drink."

But Moses took his rod and struck the rock twice in anger.

In Numbers 20:12, God gives Moses the bad news: "Because ye believed me not, to sanctify me in the eyes of the children of Israel, therefore ye shall not bring this congregation into the land which I have given them."

What went wrong here?

Moses did not obey God's instructions to the letter. In Exodus 17:6, a similar event occurred. The children of Israel found themselves in the desert without water. God instructed Moses to strike the rock with his rod. Here in Numbers 20, God instructed Moses to "speak" to the rock.

Interestingly, throughout the Bible, who is characterized as the Rock?

- In Deuteronomy 32:18, we're told of "the Rock that begat thee."

- In Deuteronomy 32:4, we're told, "[The LORD] is the Rock, his work is perfect: for all his ways are judgment: a God of truth and without iniquity, just and right is he."

- In 1 Samuel 2:2, Hannah prayed, "There is none beside thee: neither is there any rock like our God."

- In 2 Samuel 22:2–3, we read: "The LORD is my rock, and my fortress, and my deliverer; the God of my rock; in him will I trust: he is my shield, and the horn of my salvation, my high tower, and my refuge, my saviour; thou savest me from violence."

- In 2 Samuel 22:32, we're asked, "For who is God, save the LORD? and who is a rock, save our God?" Similarly, Psalm 18:31 asks, "For who is God save the LORD? or who is a rock save our God?"

- In 2 Samuel 22:47, we're told: "The LORD liveth; and blessed be my rock; and exalted be the God of the rock of my salvation." Psalms 18:46 repeats the refrain: "The LORD liveth; and blessed be my rock; and let the God of my salvation be exalted."

- In 2 Samuel 23:3, David wrote, "The God of Israel said, the Rock of Israel spake to me, He that ruleth over men must be just, ruling in the fear of God."

- Psalm 18:2, says, "The LORD is my rock, and my fortress, and my deliverer; my God, my strength, in whom I will trust; my buckler, and the horn of my salvation, and my high tower."

Get the picture?

God is our Rock. *He rocks.*

There's a time for striking the Rock, as Jesus was stricken to atone for our sins, and a time for speaking to the Rock, in prayer in repentance. That is the underlying lesson of Moses' encounters with the Rock that provides living waters.

It didn't take long for the children of Israel to lose their faith in the Rock, again. As they approached the land of Edom in Numbers 21:4–5, they became "discouraged because of the way. And the people spake against God, and against Moses, Wherefore have ye brought us up out of Egypt to die in the wilderness? for there is no bread, neither is there any water; and our soul loatheth this light bread," meaning the bread that God had been miraculously providing each day. So, God gave them something else to worry about: "fiery serpents" to bite them—some fatally (v. 6).

Yet, He also, once again, showed mercy after the people repented.

> Therefore the people came to Moses, and said, We have sinned, for we have spoken against the LORD, and against thee; pray unto the LORD, that he take away the serpents from us. And Moses prayed for the people. And the LORD said unto Moses, Make thee a fiery serpent, and set it upon a pole: and it shall come to pass, that every one that is bitten, when he looketh upon it, shall live. And Moses made a serpent of brass, and put it upon a pole, and it came to pass, that if a serpent had bitten any man, when he beheld the serpent of brass, he lived (vv. 7–9).

Now picture a serpent on a pole. What would that look like? You don't have to think too hard, because that image is still very much a part of our medical practice today. You've seen it many times. Today it is known as the "rod of Asclepius," so named by the Greeks for their false god of healing and medicine. It is often seen at hospitals and the offices of doctors and medical insurance companies.

No one can tell me, however, that the origin of that symbol is not the brass serpent on the pole in the book of Numbers. More significantly, it is a picture of Jesus on the cross.

Am I imagining this? No, because Jesus Himself made this connection in one of the most familiar and loved portions of the gospel of John. We all know John 3:16, right? "For God so loved the world, that he gave his only begotten Son, that whosoever believeth in him should not perish, but have everlasting life." The verses immediately preceding that say, "And as Moses lifted up the serpent in the wilderness, *even so must the Son of man be lifted up*: that whosoever believeth in him should not perish, but have eternal life" (vv. 14–15; emphasis added).

Stunning. Once again we see the gospel shining through in the Old Testament. But it gets better. It gets even easier to see in Numbers 24.

As the army of Israel was making its way to the promised land, the neighboring nations were understandably alarmed at this sight. No one had ever seen an entire nation on the move like this—millions of men, women, and children headed to a former homeland none of them had known because Israel had been away in Egypt for nearly four hundred years. When Israel had left, it was one extended family, the family of Jacob and his children and grandchildren. As they returned, they represented a formidable force.

This did not go unnoticed by Balak, the king of the Moabites. It's a fascinating story that ends with one of the most famous and meaningful prophecies of the coming kingdom of God: the restitution of all things, the gospel message at its fullest: "And Balak the son of Zippor saw all that Israel had done to the Amorites. And Moab was sore afraid of the people, because they were many: and Moab was distressed because of the children of Israel. And Moab said unto the elders of Midian, Now shall this company lick up all that are round about us, as the ox licketh up the grass of the field" (Numbers 22:2–4).

So Balak enlisted the help of a mysterious prophet named Balaam, asking him to place a curse upon the children of Israel. Balaam knew God. He spoke to God. He heard from God. Whatever power he had was given to him by God. But he was not an Israelite, nor did he have any loyalty to them.

Balak, meanwhile, promised him great wealth if he would stop the children of Israel on their God-directed march through Moab to Canaan. Balaam, however, knew he could not do anything without God's permission.

He didn't have to wait long to find out what God thought about His desire to curse the children of Israel.

"Though shalt not curse the people," God told Balaam, "for they are blessed" (Numbers 22:12).

But the princes of Balak continued to plead with Balaam for help. Balaam was of two minds. He knew he was powerless if not in the will of God, but the riches Balak had promised were tempting and calling him. So one morning he got up early and saddled his ass, with the intention of seeing the princes of Moab again.

But God sent an angel of the Lord to block his way. The ass saw the angel in front of him, with his sword raised, though Balaam did not. Balaam struck the ass, but she would not proceed.

> And the LORD opened the mouth of the ass, and she said unto Balaam, What have I done unto thee, that thou hast smitten me these three times? And Balaam said unto the ass, Because thou hast mocked me: I would there were a sword in mine hand, for now would I kill thee. And the ass said unto Balaam, Am not I thine ass, upon which thou hast ridden ever since I was thine unto this day? was I ever wont to do so unto thee? and he said, Nay. Then the LORD opened the eyes of Balaam, and he saw the angel of the LORD standing in the way, and his sword drawn in his hand: and he bowed down his head, and fell flat on his

face. And the angel of the LORD said unto him, Wherefore hast thou smitten thine ass these three times? behold, I went out to withstand thee, because thy way is perverse before me: And the ass saw me, and turned from me these three times: unless she had turned from me, surely now also I had slain thee, and saved her alive. And Balaam said unto the angel of the LORD, I have sinned; for I knew not that thou stoodest in the way against me: now therefore, if it displease thee, I will get me back again. And the angel of the LORD said unto Balaam, Go with the men: but only the word that I shall speak unto thee, that thou shalt speak. So Balaam went with the princes of Balak (Numbers 22:21–35).

Balak was eager to see Balaam when he arrived, but Balaam told him he could only speak the words God would allow him to speak. Balaam spoke these words: "How shall I curse, whom God hath not cursed? or how shall I defy, whom the LORD hath not defied? For from the top of the rocks I see him, and from the hills I behold him: lo, the people shall dwell alone, and shall not be reckoned among the nations. Who can count the dust of Jacob, and the number of the fourth part of Israel? Let me die the death of the righteous, and let my last end be like his!" (23:8–10)

"What hast thou done unto me?" Balaam spat. "I took thee to curse mine enemies, and, behold, thou hast blessed them altogether" (23:11)

Balaam responded that he could only speak what the Lord allowed him to say. Later, he added:

God is not a man, that he should lie; neither the son of man, that he should repent: hath he said, and shall he not do it? or hath he spoken, and shall he not make it good? Behold, I have received commandment to bless: and he hath blessed; and I cannot reverse it. He hath not beheld iniquity in Jacob, neither hath he seen perverseness in Israel: the LORD his God is with him, and the shout of a king is among them. God brought them out of Egypt;

he hath as it were the strength of an unicorn. Surely there is no enchantment against Jacob, neither is there any divination against Israel: according to this time it shall be said of Jacob and of Israel, What hath God wrought! Behold, the people shall rise up as a great lion, and lift up himself as a young lion: he shall not lie down until he eat of the prey, and drink the blood of the slain (Numbers 23:19–24).

Balaam's prophecies get worse and worse for Balak and Moab, culminating with a remarkable one that explains the coming of the Messiah and His kingdom:

How goodly are thy tents, O Jacob, and thy tabernacles, O Israel! As the valleys are they spread forth, as gardens by the river's side, as the trees of lign aloes which the LORD hath planted, and as cedar trees beside the waters. He shall pour the water out of his buckets, and his seed shall be in many waters, and his king shall be higher than Agag, and his kingdom shall be exalted. God brought him forth out of Egypt; he hath as it were the strength of an unicorn: he shall eat up the nations his enemies, and shall break their bones, and pierce them through with his arrows. He couched, he lay down as a lion, and as a great lion: who shall stir him up? Blessed is he that blesseth thee, and cursed is he that curseth thee (Numbers 24:5–9).

Then, to Balak's great consternation, Balaam went on to explain what the children of Israel would do to the people of Moab and its neighbors "in the latter days": "I shall see him, but not now: I shall behold him, but not nigh: there shall come a Star out of Jacob, and a Sceptre shall rise out of Israel, and shall smite the corners of Moab, and destroy all the children of Sheth. And Edom shall be a possession, Seir also shall be a possession for his enemies; and Israel shall do valiantly. Out of Jacob shall come he that shall have dominion, and shall destroy him that remaineth of the city" (Numbers 24:14, 17–19)

Jesus is that Star who would come out of Jacob and it is He who shall have dominion over the whole word when He returns.

What a remarkable prediction from a non-Hebrew prophet!

Again, the apostle Peter tells us in Acts 3:21 that all the holy prophets from the beginning of the world spoke of this time of ultimate fulfillment of God's kingdom on Earth. And here is one reluctant prophet who did so in dramatic and vivid fashion.

It's the gospel. And it's right there in the book of Numbers.

5

THE GOSPEL IN DEUTERONOMY

The LORD thy God will raise up for thee a Prophet from the midst of thee, of thy brethren, like unto me; unto him ye shall hearken.
—DEUTERONOMY 18:15

THE GREAT BIBLE SCHOLAR DANIEL BLOCK calls the book of Deuteronomy "the gospel according to Moses"[1] which gives us a hint of what we should expect to find in a serious study of the last book of the Torah, or, as many Christians call it, the Pentateuch.

And while it is commonly referred to as one of the books of the law, what we are actually reading in Deuteronomy are the urgent *teachings* of Moses, who knew his time on earth and with his people was coming to an end.

The word *remember* is used more than a dozen times for a reason. Deuteronomy represents Moses's last chance to impress upon the congregation what was most important for them to not forget. In

Deuteronomy, Moses was providing his last long sermon—or, perhaps, three different teachings. While Leviticus has more direct quotes from God than any other book in the Bible, Deuteronomy has more direct quotes from Moses. It is also the book from which Jesus quoted more than any other. Thus, Block calls it "Jesus' favorite book."[2]

So, what is "the gospel according to Moses"? It should be a very familiar one to those steeped in the four Gospels of the New Testament because it is the same message of grace and redemption we see there and, in fact, what we see in all the books of Moses and, for that matter, in every other Old Testament book.

That's what may be a surprise to Christians who believe there's something "new" in the New Testament besides the arrival of the long-anticipated Messiah.

It's the same message. It's the same gospel. It's the same commandments. It's the same God, and the same mercy and forgiveness based on repentance and grace.

We often refer to Moses as "the lawgiver" and to Deuteronomy as "the second law." Yet, the Hebrew word *Torah* is more precisely defined as "teaching" or "instruction." And Moses and the narrator of his death provide only one title for him: "prophet" (Deuteronomy 18:18; 34:10) If we think about the role of Moses, clearly he did not have the authority to legislate. Only God had that power.

Right from the start in Deuteronomy, the mission of the book is explained this way: "Moses spake unto the children of Israel, according unto all that the LORD had given him in commandment unto them" (1:3).

Deuteronomy has been compared with the gospel of John because of its presentation in sweeping theological terms. Like John, it starts with a review of creation and the redemption for the fall of man, and Israel's role in it. Here's an example:

> For ask now of the days that are past, which were before thee, since the day that God created man upon the earth, and ask from the one side of heaven unto the other, whether there hath been

any such thing as this great thing is, or hath been heard like it? Did ever people hear the voice of God speaking out of the midst of the fire, as thou hast heard, and live? Or hath God assayed to go and take him a nation from the midst of another nation, by temptations, by signs, and by wonders, and by war, and by a mighty hand, and by a stretched out arm, and by great terrors, according to all that the LORD your God did for you in Egypt before your eyes? Unto thee it was shewed, that thou mightest know that the LORD he is God; there is none else beside him. Out of heaven he made thee to hear his voice, that he might instruct thee: and upon earth he shewed thee his great fire; and thou heardest his words out of the midst of the fire. And because he loved thy fathers, therefore he chose their seed after them, and brought thee out in his sight with his mighty power out of Egypt; To drive out nations from before thee greater and mightier than thou art, to bring thee in, to give thee their land for an inheritance, as it is this day. Know therefore this day, and consider it in thine heart, that the LORD he is God in heaven above, and upon the earth beneath: there is none else. Thou shalt keep therefore his statutes, and his commandments, which I command thee this day, that it may go well with thee, and with thy children after thee, and that thou mayest prolong thy days upon the earth, which the LORD thy God giveth thee, for ever (Deuteronomy 4:32–40).

Another thing these two books have in common is the way they both call on Israel to respond to God's grace with sincerity, passion, and love. So, let's take a walk through what the Lord gave Moses for us in this powerful, foundational book and its relationship to the gospel of the kingdom of God.

In Deuteronomy 1:11, Moses says parenthetically: "(The LORD God of your fathers make you a thousand times so many more as ye are, and bless you, as he hath promised you!)" This is not just a blessing. It's not just a wish. It's a prediction of a time about which all the prophets from creation onward spoke. It's the time when Israel will no longer be the tail, but the head, and a King based in Jerusalem will rule over not just Israel but the entire world. It's about the time of restoration—the kingdom of God on earth.

Again, we don't always *think* of the gospel in those terms, but it is in indeed the heart and soul of what Jesus preached.

How many times did Jesus mention the gospel of the coming kingdom in the New Testament? By my count, fifty-four times in Matthew alone. Moses dealt extensively with this future period, winding glimpses between his promises of blessing and curses to come based on the obedience or disobedience of his flock upon entering the promised land. But the stakes are higher than just the difference between rewards and punishments. In Deuteronomy 4, Moses explains obedience to the commandments he is giving the children of Israel are a matter of life and death.

> Now therefore hearken, O Israel, unto the statutes and unto the judgments, which I teach you, for to do them, *that ye may live*, and go in and possess the land which the Lord God of your fathers giveth you. Ye shall not add unto the word which I command you, neither shall ye diminish ought from it, that ye may keep the commandments of the Lord your God which I command you. Your eyes have seen what the Lord did because of Baalpeor: for all the men that followed Baalpeor, the Lord thy God hath destroyed them from among you. But ye that did cleave unto the Lord your God are *alive* every one of you this day (4:1–4, emphasis added).

Jesus Himself reprimanded continuously the religious authorities of His day for adding to the Word of God through their traditions and teachings of men. This represented what I called in my previous book, *The Restitution of All Things*, "the great error of the Pharisees." It also depicted, inarguably, the central conflict in all four Gospels. Here, Moses was warning his people not to fall into the very grave error Jesus would address so frequently in the four Gospels, neither adding to the commandments nor diminishing them in any way. Thus, Moses was not just reiterating a commandment; he was prophesying of a future collective sin that will befall his people before the Messiah comes.

In Chapter 4, Moses continued to remind his people how fortunate they were to be chosen of God to bring spiritual light and truth to the world: "For what nation is there so great, who hath God so nigh unto them, as the LORD our God is in all things that we call upon him for?" (v. 7)

Predicting their shortcomings in keeping the commandments and the punishments that will befall them, Moses reminded them that grace is always close to them—even in the latter days that represent complete restoration and the full realization of God's covenant with them: "When thou art in tribulation, and all these things are come upon thee, even in the latter days, if thou turn to the LORD thy God, and shalt be obedient unto his voice . . ." (Deuteronomy 4:30).

It surprises some Christians to learn that forgiveness, repentance, and grace were always available before the time of Jesus' death and resurrection in the first century. That realization in no way diminishes the atoning sacrifice Jesus made when He took upon Himself all the sins of the world. In fact, Jesus' works were not only foreordained from the beginning, but "finished from the foundation of the world" (Hebrews 4:3). Likewise, consider what Revelation 13:8 tells us: the Lamb, the Messiah Jesus, was "slain from the foundation of the world."

In Deuteronomy 5:9–10, Moses warns against idolatry as a form of adultery, but promises mercy to those that "love me and keep my commandments." This should be familiar to those who have pondered the repetition of Jesus' own words in the gospel of John:

- "If ye love me, keep my commandments" (14:15).

- "He that hath my commandments, and keepeth them, he it
  is that loveth me: and he that loveth me shall be loved of my
  Father, and I will love him, and will manifest myself to him"
  (14:21).

- "If ye keep my commandments, ye shall abide in my love; even
  as I have kept my Father's commandments, and abide in his
  love" (15:10).

In Matthew 22:34–40, one of the Pharisees, a lawyer, asked
Jesus "which is the great commandment in the law." Jesus responded,
"Thou shalt love the Lord thy God with all thy heart, and with all
thy soul, and with all thy mind. This is the first and great commandment. And the second is like unto it, Thou shalt love thy neighbour
as thyself. On these two commandments hang all the law and the
prophets." This is a direct reference to what Jews know today as the
Shema, found in Deuteronomy 6. It is the heart of the covenant
between God and Israel: "Hear, O Israel: The LORD our God is one
LORD: And thou shalt love the LORD thy God with all thine heart,
and with all thy soul, and with all thy might" (vv. 4–5). Jesus wasn't
adding to the law or reinterpreting the commandments. In addition to the Shema, He was citing Leviticus 19:18's commandment:
"Thou shalt love thy neighbour as thyself."

During Jesus' forty days of fasting in the wilderness, He was
tempted by Satan. Three times in that confrontation, he cited Deuteronomy. In Matthew 4:3–4, "when the tempter came to him, he
said, If thou be the Son of God, command that these stones be made
bread. But he answered and said, It is written, Man shall not live by
bread alone, but by every word that proceedeth out of the mouth of
God." In Deuteronomy 8:3, Moses says the manna the children of
Israel were provided throughout their wilderness journey was designed
to show them "that man doth not live by bread only, but by every
word that proceedeth out of the mouth of the LORD doth man live."

"Then the devil taketh him up into the holy city, and setteth him on a pinnacle of the temple, and saith unto him, If thou be the Son of God, cast thyself down: for it is written, He shall give his angels charge concerning thee: and in their hands they shall bear thee up, lest at any time thou dash thy foot against a stone. Jesus said unto him, It is written again, Thou shalt not tempt the Lord thy God" (Matthew 4:5–7). Jesus' response was from Deuteronomy 6:16.

In Matthew 4:8–10, the devil tries a different approach: "Again, the devil taketh him up into an exceeding high mountain, and sheweth him all the kingdoms of the world, and the glory of them; and saith unto him, All these things will I give thee, if thou wilt fall down and worship me. Then saith Jesus unto him, Get thee hence, Satan: for it is written, Thou shalt worship the Lord thy God, and him only shalt thou serve." Jesus' response this time is from Deuteronomy 6:13.

Five times in Deuteronomy, Moses refers to the prophetic destiny of His people as one that will stand "above all the nations on the earth" (14:2; 15:6; 17:6; 26:19; 28:1). This is very much a gospel message as well, though often missed by some Christians who do not have a full appreciation of the kingdom of God as articulated so profoundly and clearly by Peter in Acts 3 as "the restitution of all things."

The apostles were all expecting Jesus to assume His rightful throne as an heir to King David, for He was preaching the "gospel of the kingdom" (Matthew 4:23). But that kingdom is to come only upon the Messiah's return to earth in the latter days, when He will heal the earth and rule and reign over all the nations from Jerusalem. That's when Israel will truly become a "holy people unto the LORD thy God" (Deuteronomy 7:6; 14:12). That is the gospel of the kingdom.

Romans 2:29 and Acts 7:51 discuss circumcision of the heart. For many Christians, who do not know their Old Testament, this may seem like another "new" concept of the New Testament. Yet Moses advised his people to allow God to "circumcise thine heart" so they could "love the

LORD thy God with all thine heart, and with all thy soul, that thou mayest live" (Deuteronomy 30:6). The point? While physical circumcision is an outward sign of the covenant between God and His people, salvation comes from deep within when we allow Jesus to transform our natural hearts of stone (Ezekiel 36:26).

Previously, in chapter 3, we looked at the story of the woman caught in adultery in John 8 to examine the actual law that was broken. In Deuteronomy, we see the much-overlooked model for executing that law. You recall the story. In John 8:3–7, the scribes and Pharisees bring a woman to Jesus, saying "Master, this woman was taken in adultery, in the very act. Now Moses in the law commanded us, that such should be stoned: but what sayest thou?"

Jesus, of course, answers, "He that is without sin among you, let him first cast a stone at her." In Deuteronomy 17:6, we see why Jesus so adjudicated this case:

- Why was only the woman "caught in the act" being punished? The law requires punishment for both parties in adultery.

- And as for casting the first stone, the law prescribed those to be thrown by the hands of the two or more witnesses. Thus, where were the witnesses?

So, while some Christians today believe Jesus may have been softening the law or even overturning it by His actions, indeed He was holding the accusers to the letter of the law.

Of course, one of the most memorable verses in Deuteronomy is the prophecy Moses offered of the coming Messiah: "The LORD thy God will raise up unto thee a Prophet from the midst of thee, of thy brethren, like unto me; unto him ye shall hearken" (Deuteronomy 18:15). It's a picture of Jesus—truly man, but not merely man. He appears as like Moses, but greater than he (Hebrews 3:3). He's one of the brethren who can compassionately understand our weaknesses and temptations and willingly lay down His life for us—if only we will listen to Him.

Think about the parallels between Moses and Jesus: Moses was born amid conflict and oppression, facing a death sentence from a jealous tyrant. Both Moses and Jesus survived miraculously under God's protection. Both did so in Egypt, one in hiding as a prince, the other in obscurity. Both went through a period of deep seclusion. Both eventually came out of Egypt prepared for their heavenly missions. When they did, they both faced rejection and derision. Yet, signs and wonders proved their anointing.

Moses had to die before the people could pass Jordan's waters. Jesus had to die before His people could obtain salvation. Moses mediated between heaven and earth and Jesus serves as our great intercessor.

Those are the similarities. But there is infinite difference, with Moses offering a foreshadowing of the ultimate Savior-Redeemer.

But there is more, in Deuteronomy 18:16–19. This future Prophet whom God would raise up from among their brethren would speak and appear to the children of Israel in a different way than they had witnessed at Sinai (Horeb), for the people had asked not to hear the thundering voice and the great fire that accompanied Him. They were frightened by it: "And the LORD said unto me, They have well spoken that which they have spoken. I will raise them up a Prophet from among their brethren, like unto thee, and will put my words in his mouth; and he shall speak unto them all that I shall command him. And it shall come to pass, that whosoever will not hearken unto my words which he shall speak in my name, I will require it of him." This is so clearly a messianic prophecy about the coming of Jesus, who came in meekness, like Moses.

Jesus became the perfect atoning sacrifice as the One who followed the law perfectly, the very laws He Himself gave Moses. If there is any doubt, we have two New Testament verses to confirm this.

- ACTS 3:22 "For Moses truly said unto the fathers, A prophet shall the Lord your God raise up unto you of your brethren, like unto me; him shall ye hear in all things whatsoever he shall say unto you."

• ACTS 7:37 "This is that Moses, which said unto the children of Israel, A prophet shall the Lord your God raise up unto you of your brethren, like unto me; him shall ye hear."

As we move on to Deuteronomy 21:23, Moses proclaims in both teaching and prophecy another gospel allusion: anyone who is hung on a tree is under God's curse. It's a picture of Jesus hung on the cross, cursed, not because of His own actions, but by taking on the sins of His fallen creation. He came to bear the curse on behalf of humankind. There's the gospel—in the blink of an eye—in Deuteronomy.

Galatians 3:10 reminds us, "For as many as are of the works of the law are under the curse: for it is written, Cursed is every one that continueth not in all things which are written in the book of the law to do them."

৯

Have you ever wondered what was going on in Matthew 12:1–8, where Jesus and His disciples walk through a corn field on the Sabbath and munch on ears of corn because they were hungry?

The Pharisees, who apparently were stalking Him, accused Jesus and His disciples of breaking the Sabbath. Of course, they were not. Jesus could not break the law or He would not be the perfect atoning sacrifice who led a sinless life. Nowhere does the law suggest that this kind of activity is forbidden. The law only states that no "work" can be done on the Sabbath (Exodus 20:10; 23:12; Deuteronomy 5:14). This was not work. In fact, the Pharisees were referring to one of those non-scriptural, man-made commandments that Deuteronomy warns against. There's something relevant to this point in Deuteronomy 23:25: "When thou comest into the standing corn of thy neighbour, then thou mayest pluck the ears with thine hand; but thou shalt not move a sickle unto thy neighbour's standing corn." While this is not a commandment dealing with Sabbath activity, it is the only commandment you will find in Scripture dealing with snacking in a corn field. Notice, though, the contrast delineated between casually plucking ears of corn with one's hands and harvesting with a sickle. That was the distinction in Jesus' case. Had Jesus and the disciples been "working" on the Sabbath, or "stealing" from their neighbor, the Pharisees' accusation would have had scriptural merit. But neither of these suggestions was true. In fact, Scripture affirms the specific activity in which Jesus and the disciples were taking part: simply eating, because they were hungry.

&

Deuteronomy 28 paints a vivid picture of the future kingdom in language reminiscent of the Sermon on the Mount in Matthew 5:

> And it shall come to pass, if thou shalt hearken diligently unto the voice of the LORD thy God, to observe and to do all his commandments which I command thee this day, that the LORD thy God will set thee on high above all nations of the earth: And all these blessings shall come on thee, and overtake thee, if thou shalt hearken unto the voice of the LORD thy God. Blessed shalt thou be in the city, and blessed shalt thou be in the field. Blessed shall be the fruit of thy body, and the fruit of thy ground, and the fruit of thy cattle, the increase of thy kine, and the flocks of thy sheep. Blessed shall be thy basket and thy store. Blessed shalt thou be when thou comest in, and blessed shalt thou be when thou goest out. The LORD shall cause thine enemies that rise up against thee to be smitten before thy face: they shall come out against thee one way, and flee before thee seven ways. The LORD shall command the blessing upon thee in thy storehouses, and in all that thou settest thine hand unto; and he shall bless thee in the land which the LORD thy God giveth thee. The LORD shall establish thee an holy people unto himself, as he hath sworn

unto thee, if thou shalt keep the commandments of the LORD thy God, and walk in his ways. And all people of the earth shall see that thou art called by the name of the LORD; and they shall be afraid of thee. And the LORD shall make thee plenteous in goods, in the fruit of thy body, and in the fruit of thy cattle, and in the fruit of thy ground, in the land which the LORD sware unto thy fathers to give thee. The LORD shall open unto thee his good treasure, the heaven to give the rain unto thy land in his season, and to bless all the work of thine hand: and thou shalt lend unto many nations, and thou shalt not borrow. And the LORD shall make thee the head, and not the tail; and thou shalt be above only, and thou shalt not be beneath; if that thou hearken unto the commandments of the LORD thy God, which I command thee this day, to observe and to do them: And thou shalt not go aside from any of the words which I command thee this day, to the right hand, or to the left, to go after other gods to serve them (Deuteronomy 28:1–14).

And what are the keys to this kingdom? "Hearken diligently unto the voice of the LORD thy God, to observe and to do all his commandments." That is how the children of Israel will be set high above all the nations of the earth when all is restored. The key is to not turn right or left or go after other gods to serve them, but to live by faith that God knows what is best for you and wants the best for you, including everlasting life.

Another kingdom verse is Deuteronomy 29:29: "The secret things belong unto the LORD our God: but those things which are revealed belong unto us and to our children for ever, that we may do all the words of this law." Note the words *for ever.* Moses was not just laying out a plan for a better life in the promised land. He was offering his children the keys to eternal life.

Before the children of Israel ever enter the promised land, we see in Deuteronomy 30:2–15 the extraordinary prophecy by Moses of the regathering of Israel that follows its turning away from the ways of God. It's another glimpse of the restoration of all things. It's the gospel of the kingdom of God.

Perhaps one of the most astonishing prophecies in Deuteronomy is one seldom cited, found in Deuteronomy 32:21: "They have moved me to jealousy with that which is not God; they have provoked me to anger with their vanities: and I will move them to jealousy with those which are not a people; I will provoke them to anger with a foolish nation."

What does this mean? What is the significance? Who is it that "are not a people" that move the children of Israel to jealousy? Who is this "foolish nation"? Paul answered this question in Romans: "I say then, Have they stumbled that they should fall? God forbid: but rather through their fall salvation is come unto the Gentiles, for to provoke them to jealousy" (11:11).

That is who Moses was referring to in Deuteronomy—the Gentiles who turn to Jesus the Messiah. Just as the children of Israel brought them to the light by carrying the torch of the Scriptures, the holy oracles of God, so, in turn, do those "which are not a people," a "foolish nation," provoke the original chosen people to return to the covenant.

In Deuteronomy 30:14, Moses proclaims: "The word is very nigh unto thee, in thy mouth, and in thy heart, that thou mayest do it." And who is the Word? John tells us in the very beginning of his gospel. The Word is God. In Jesus we know the Word became flesh (1:14). The Word was very near the children of Israel as they made their way through the wilderness under His watchful eye and ear, speaking to them both directly and through Moses.

Paul made reference to this key verse in Romans 10:6–9:

But the righteousness which is of faith speaketh on this wise, Say not in thine heart, Who shall ascend into heaven? (that is, to bring Christ down from above:) Or, Who shall descend into the deep? (that is, to bring up Christ again from the dead.) But what saith it? The word is nigh thee, even in thy mouth, and in thy heart: that is, the word of faith, which we preach; that if thou shalt confess with thy mouth the Lord Jesus, and shalt believe in thine heart that God hath raised him from the dead, thou shalt be saved.

A few chapters later, in Deuteronomy 33:7, as Moses bids his flock farewell as they were about to enter the promised land, leaving him behind, he offers blessings to all the Hebrew tribes, including Judah—through which the future Messiah will enter the world. "And this is the blessing of Judah: and he said, Hear, LORD, the voice of Judah, and bring him unto his people: let his hands be sufficient for him; and be thou an help to him from his enemies." Judah is the royal tribe; to this tribe belong the throne, the scepter and the authority of future kings, including the God-man Jesus, "the Lion of the tribe of Judah." So, Moses' inspired blessing to Judah should be of special note—and it is.

"Hear, LORD, the voice of Judah," Moses said. He was invoking God to hear the prayers and petitions of Judah in the future. Jesus serves many roles: God, King, High Priest, Redeemer, Savior. But during His earthly ministry, His life was marked by prayer. He even taught His followers how to pray. Jesus prayed to His Father in John 11:42: "I knew that thou hearest me always." In fact, His power during this ministry was based on His prayers, the connection He maintained with His Father in heaven.

Moses' blessing continues: "And bring him unto his people: let his hands be sufficient for him; and be thou an help to him from his enemies." Again, this strikes me as a profound prophecy fulfilled through the coming of the Messiah who was brought unto his people, whose hands were sufficient to bear the cross, and who conquered His enemies through death and resurrection.

The gospel in Deuteronomy? Absolutely. From beginning to end, it's a story of holiness, stewardship, obedience, justice, love, and restoration.

6

THE GOSPEL IN JOSHUA

Moses my servant is dead; now therefore arise —JOSHUA 1:2

And Israel served the LORD all the days of Joshua, and all the days of the elders that overlived Joshua, and which had known all the works of the LORD, that he had done for Israel. —JOSHUA 24:31

THERE'S MORE THAN A HINT of Jesus in the main character of this book.

For one, Joshua, the main character, a seemingly flawless one, shares the actual Hebrew name of the Messiah.

The name Jesus, as it is rendered in the Greek Scriptures, is actually *Yeshua*, or, more formally, *Yehoshua* in Hebrew. Joshua, too, would rightly be pronounced "Yeshua." The very name means "salvation," or "the Lord saves." It's important to know that going into a discussion of the book of Joshua because the successor to Moses as the leader of the children of Israel is most definitely a messianic type—a victorious leader cleaving to the God of Israel who, like Jacob's beloved son Joseph, Elijah, and very few other figures in the Bible, is never rebuked by God.

As Moses' young protégé in the wilderness, Joshua, along with his friend Caleb, was among the twelve spies chosen to recon the promised land. Only Joshua and Caleb brought back a favorable report, while the other ten showed their lack of faith in God by telling the congregation the children of Israel were no match for the bigger, stronger, better-fortified inhabitants of Canaan.

Thus, only Joshua and Caleb, from that entire generation of Israelites, including Moses, would ever cross the Jordan to inherit the land of milk and honey that awaited them.

Throughout this book that chronicles God's deliverance of the land to His people, Joshua is a picture of courage and faith who, like Moses, hears directly from the Lord and dutifully passes on His instructions to the people.

But that's not to suggest Joshua is any more than a glimmer of Jesus, an obedient mortal, a faithful steward of what God had given him, a courageous warrior, or God's chosen vehicle for delivering the land into the hands of His people as He had promised.

Some suggest in the person of Joshua a contrast —Joshua leading a physical fulfillment of God's promise, with Jesus leading a spiritual fulfillment of His kingdom. But that interpretation neglects the reality of the coming kingdom on earth that Jesus Himself, along with all the prophets, promised, which Jesus is still to deliver in this physical world in the form of the restoration of all things. Furthermore, Jesus, in His first coming, eschewed physical comfort and endured unspeakable torture and an agonizing death to overcome the sins of the world—which renders the physical-spiritual comparison inadequate.

While Joshua undoubtedly holds a place in the spiritual hall of fame, there is no question One greater than he has come, conquered death, and will return again to do mightier works still.

Nevertheless, perhaps it's best to say Joshua is a model of faith and courage for followers of Jesus.

The book of Joshua consists of two sections. The first part, chapters 1–12, provide the history of the conquest of the land. This section contains the familiar stories of the crossing of the Jordan, the walls of Jericho, and the day the sun stood still. The second section deals with the distribution of the land among the tribes and Joshua's poignant farewell to his people and his death.

Now let's walk through this book in search of Jesus and the gospel of the kingdom.

In chapter 1, God speaks to Joshua, described as Moses' minister, as he and the children of Israel arrive at the bank of the Jordan River near the determined crossing point of Gilgal. He says:

> Moses my servant is dead; now therefore arise, go over this Jordan, thou, and all this people, unto the land which I do give to them, even to the children of Israel. Every place that the sole of your foot shall tread upon, that have I given unto you, as I said unto Moses. From the wilderness and this Lebanon even unto the great river, the river Euphrates, all the land of the Hittites, and unto the great sea toward the going down of the sun, shall be your coast. There shall not any man be able to stand before thee all the days of thy life: as I was with Moses, so I will be with thee: I will not fail thee, nor forsake thee. Be strong and of a good courage: for unto this people shalt thou divide for an inheritance the land, which I sware unto their fathers to give them. Only be thou strong and very courageous, that thou mayest observe to do according to all the law, which Moses my servant commanded thee: turn not from it to the right hand or to the left, that thou mayest prosper withersoever thou goest (vv. 2–7).

He was also told not to let this law "depart out of thy mouth," but to meditate on it day and night—good advice that Joshua followed for the rest of his life—"for then thou shalt make thy way prosperous, and then thou shalt have good success," and "thy God is with thee whithersoever thou goest."

Before the congregation of millions crossed the Jordan, Joshua dispatched two spies to stake out the city of Jericho. There, in chapter 2, God led them to the house of Rahab, a harlot, who provided some great intelligence, shelter for the night, and a cover story for the king.

Here's what Rahab told the two Israelite spies:

> I know that the LORD hath given you the land, and that your terror is fallen upon us, and that all the inhabitants of the land faint because of you. For we have heard how the LORD dried up the water of the Red sea for you, when ye came out of Egypt; and what ye did unto the two kings of the Amorites, that were on the other side Jordan, Sihon and Og, whom ye utterly destroyed. And as soon as we had heard these things, our hearts did melt, neither did there remain any more courage in any man, because of you: for the LORD your God, he is God in heaven above, and in earth beneath. Now therefore, I pray you, swear unto me by the LORD, since I have shewed you kindness, that ye will also shew kindness unto my father's house, and give me a true token: And that ye will save alive my father, and my mother, and my brethren, and my sisters, and all that they have, and deliver our lives from death (vv. 9–13).

The deal was struck. The spies left, according to her instructions, and returned with their good report to Joshua.

Now it was time to cross the Jordan without getting wet.

As soon as the feet of the priests bearing the Ark of the Covenant dipped into the water, the Jordan River stopped flowing, allowing the congregation to pass over on dry land, just like the miracle at the Red Sea.

The manna ceased. The congregation celebrated Passover in the promised land. And then Joshua met a "man" he did not recognize.

He had his sword drawn, so Joshua asked, "Art thou for us, or for our adversaries?" (Joshua 5:13)

"And he said, Nay; but as captain of the host of the LORD am I now come. And Joshua fell on his face to the earth, and did worship, and said unto him, What saith my Lord unto his servant? And the captain of the LORD's host said unto Joshua, Loose thy shoe from off thy foot; for the place whereon thou standest is holy. And Joshua did so" (vv. 14–15).

We learn nothing more about this strange encounter in Scripture, but many commentaries, including the esteemed Matthew Henry's, concludes that this appearance is a Christophany—an appearance of Jesus in human form in the Old Testament. What's the evidence?

Think back to Exodus 3:2–6, when Moses encountered the burning bush:

> And *the angel of the LORD* appeared unto him in a flame of fire out of the midst of a bush: and he looked, and, behold, the bush burned with fire, and the bush was not consumed. And Moses said, I will now turn aside, and see this great sight, why the bush is not burnt. And when the LORD saw that he turned aside to see, God called unto him out of the midst of the bush, and said, Moses, Moses. And he said, Here am I. And he said, Draw not nigh hither: *put off thy shoes from off thy feet, for the place whereon thou standest is holy ground.* Moreover he said, *I am the God of thy father, the God of Abraham, the God of Isaac, and the God of Jacob. And Moses hid his face; for he was afraid to look upon God.* (Emphasis added)

Notice that Moses' encounter was "the angel of the LORD," but the voice he heard identified Himself as God. Also, pay attention to God's instructions to Moses: "Put off thy shoes from off thy feet, for the place whereon thou standest is holy ground"—the same instructions Joshua received from "the captain of the LORD's host."

Jesus' early disciple Stephen, before he was martyred, recounted the story of Moses' encounter, recorded in Acts 7:30–35. We also know from Luke 24 that some of the early disciples who encountered the risen Jesus were actually taught to see references to Him throughout the Hebrew Scriptures (v. 27) causing their hearts to burn within them (v. 32). Would this have been one of those many passages about Jesus? I believe so. In fact, it only makes sense that all such encounters between men and God are with Jesus—the Creator of heaven and earth (John 1:3). (See Chapter 2 for more on why Moses' encounter with God was most assuredly with the person of Jesus.)

So here in Joshua we not only see the gospel, but we actually find Jesus making a cameo appearance. It stands to reason He was there, sword in hand, to go to battle in Jericho, and perhaps subsequent conflicts.

Though we don't have any further visual reports of Jesus in Joshua, Joshua 6 has "the Lord" counseling the leader of the Israelites with instructions on taking Jericho. You know the story. They would parade around the city one time for six days. On the seventh day, they would compass the city seven times with the priests blowing their shofars.

"And it shall come to pass, that when they make a long blast with the ram's horn, and when ye hear the sound of the trumpet, all the people shall shout with a great shout; and the wall of the city shall fall down flat, and the people shall ascend up every man straight before him," the Lord explained (Joshua 6:5).

It happened exactly that way. And Rahab and her family were saved. This foreigner was adopted into the congregation of Israel with open arms and lived among the people for the rest of her life (v. 25).

The next time we hear about her is in the New Testament, in Matthew 1, the genealogy of Jesus the Messiah. That's right, this foreign harlot found her way into the lineage of her future Savior. She was the mother of Boaz, the husband of the famous Ruth. (More on that later, in chapter 8.)

It's pure speculation, but it's entirely possible that Jesus the Messiah was there at Jericho not just to encourage Joshua to victory but to physically protect Rahab, the great-great-grandmother of David, the future king of Israel, and, twenty-eight generations later, Jesus' earthly stepfather, Joseph.

Just as remarkable, in Luke 3, Boaz, the son of Rahab and the husband of Ruth, and, of course, King David also found their way into the genealogy of Mary, the mother of Jesus.

But there's more.

One of the meanings of the name Rahab is "proud." Yet Rahab humbled herself before the two spies and confessed the God of Abraham, Isaac, and Jacob as "God in heaven above, and in earth beneath" (Joshua 2:11). In other words, she and all the people of Jericho were aware of the miraculous events that took place during the exodus and were, thus, fearful when the children of Israel arrived at their doorstep. All had a chance to repent and escape judgment, but as far as we know, only Rahab did. She got the good news of the gospel, while others just trembled in fear of God's army on the march. But repentance was open to all.

It wasn't a surprise that the Israelis were coming. The people of Canaan had had forty years to think about it, reflect on it, consider the implications. Yet, only one woman in all of Jericho, plus her immediate family, were saved, despite all of Jericho knowing of the miracles of God associated with the children of Israel and their generation-long trek through the wilderness.

Why didn't more surrender given what they knew? Why did only one woman choose God—entering into the kingdom hall of fame as a result?

It reminds me of what Jesus said in Matthew 7:13: "Enter ye in at the strait gate: for wide is the gate, and broad is the way, that leadeth to destruction, and many there be which go in thereat."

1

THE GOSPEL IN JUDGES

And also all that generation were gathered unto their fathers: and there arose another generation after them, which knew not the LORD, nor yet the works which he had done for Israel. And the children of Israel did evil in the sight of the LORD, and served Baalim. —JUDGES 2:10–11

So let all thine enemies perish, O LORD: but let them that love him be as the sun when he goeth forth in his might. And the land had rest forty years. —JUDGES 5:31

FROM MY EXPERIENCE, the book of Judges seems foreign, strange, and hard to understand for many Christians. It was like that for me for many years after I began following the Lord. It shouldn't be that way. It should be familiar. Why?

Because the time of the judges actually represents a nearly perfect reflection of our world today.

It begins with the death of Joshua, a righteous, God-fearing disciple of Moses who obeyed God and accomplished his mission of delivering the children of Israel into the promised land.

Joshua had won the beachhead, to put it in military parlance, by conquering Jericho. In his parting sermon to the people, he told them: "And if it seem evil unto you to serve the LORD, choose you this day whom ye will serve; whether the gods which your fathers served that were on the other side of the flood, or the gods of the Amorites, in whose land ye dwell: but as for me and my house, we will serve the LORD" (Joshua 24:15).

The people responded appropriately in the next verse: "God forbid that we should forsake the LORD, to serve other gods."

Joshua further warned: "If ye forsake the LORD, and serve strange gods, then he will turn and do you hurt, and consume you, after that he hath done you good." And the people said, "Nay; but we will serve the Lord" (vv. 20–21)

After Joshua's passing, things got off to a good start. The opening words of Judges show the people asking God for direction in their mission of driving out the Canaanites and the others living in the land upon whom God had pronounced judgment.

In Judges 1, we see Judah successful in battles against the Canaanites and Perizzites. The tribe of Joseph was also initially successful. But other tribes could not or would not drive out their enemies, as instructed, to claim the land God had promised them. Something was holding them back.

Then we learn the children of Israel chose, against the clear commandments of the Lord, to allow these pagans to remain in the land and pay tribute.

There was another problem. There arose in Israel a generation that knew not the Lord, "nor yet the works which He had done for Israel." Worse yet, we're told in Judges 2:12–15:

And they forsook the LORD God of their fathers, which brought them out of the land of Egypt, and followed other gods, of the gods of the people that were round about them, and bowed themselves unto them, and provoked the LORD to anger. And they forsook the Lord, and served Baal and Ashtaroth. And the anger of the LORD was hot against Israel, and he delivered them into the hands of spoilers that spoiled them, and he sold them into the hands of their enemies round about, so that they could not any longer stand before their enemies. Whithersoever they went out, the hand of the LORD was against them for evil, as the LORD had said, and as the LORD had sworn unto them: and they were greatly distressed.

Welcome to the age of the judges. But is the world of the Judges really so different from our world today? Is it unusual for the knowledge of God and righteousness to be lost in a single generation? Doesn't it seem that every generation must learn the hard lessons their fathers before them learned? Isn't it true only a remnant actually embrace those lessons? Isn't that the kind of world Jesus the Messiah Himself entered—a generation under judgment, under occupation, under a curse?

Yet, God offered mercy and raised up a series of judges to deliver His people. And the Lord was with those judges.

"And it came to pass, when the judge was dead, that they returned, and corrupted themselves more than their fathers, in following other gods to serve them, and to bow down unto them; they ceased not from their own doings, nor from their stubborn way" (Judges 2:19).

So, God left them to their own devices. He left them to their own gods—Baal and Ashtaroth. He left them to be oppressed by their enemies.

When their cries for deliverance would come, God would raise up new judges. "And yet they would not hearken unto their judges, but they went a whoring after other gods, and bowed themselves unto them: they turned quickly out of the way which their fathers walked in, obeying the commandments of the LORD; but they did not do so" (Judges 2:17).

But as always, God maintains His outstretched arm of mercy. And ultimately, God's outstretched arm of mercy represents the very essence of the gospel message. It was our Messiah and Savior who would stretch out both His arms on the cross for us.

Still, many have looked hard for the gospel in Judges and not seen it—and not preached from this book. Even the book of Hebrews, in its famous chapter 11 review of examples of salvation by faith in the Hebrew Scriptures seems, almost humorously, to dodge the issue of where it is found in Judges. But it really doesn't. Instead it explains precisely why the lessons of the book are there for us.

> Now faith is the substance of things hoped for, the evidence of things not seen. For by it the elders obtained a good report. Through faith we understand that the worlds were framed by the word of God, so that things which are seen were not made of things which do appear. By faith Abel offered unto God a more excellent sacrifice than Cain, by which he obtained witness that he was righteous, God testifying of his gifts: and by it he being dead yet speaketh. By faith Enoch was translated that he should not see death; and was not found, because God had translated him: for before his translation he had this testimony, that he pleased God. But without faith it is impossible to please him: for he that cometh to God must believe that he is, and that he is a rewarder of them that diligently seek him. By faith Noah, being warned of God of things not seen as yet, moved with fear, prepared an ark to the saving of his house; by the which he condemned the world, and became heir of the righteousness which is by faith. By faith Abraham, when he was called to go out into a place which he should after receive for an inheritance, obeyed; and he went out, not knowing whither he went. By faith he sojourned in the land of promise, as in a strange country,

dwelling in tabernacles with Isaac and Jacob, the heirs with him of the same promise: For he looked for a city which hath foundations, whose builder and maker is God. Through faith also Sara herself received strength to conceive seed, and was delivered of a child when she was past age, because she judged him faithful who had promised. Therefore sprang there even of one, and him as good as dead, so many as the stars of the sky in multitude, and as the sand which is by the sea shore innumerable. These all died in faith, not having received the promises, but having seen them afar off, and were persuaded of them, and embraced them, and confessed that they were strangers and pilgrims on the earth. For they that say such things declare plainly that they seek a country. And truly, if they had been mindful of that country from whence they came out, they might have had opportunity to have returned.

But now they desire a better country, that is, an heavenly: wherefore God is not ashamed to be called their God: for he hath prepared for them a city. By faith Abraham, when he was tried, offered up Isaac: and he that had received the promises offered up his only begotten son, of whom it was said, That in Isaac shall thy seed be called: Accounting that God was able to raise him up, even from the dead; from whence also he received him in a figure. By faith Isaac blessed Jacob and Esau concerning things to come. By faith Jacob, when he was a dying, blessed both the sons of Joseph; and worshipped, leaning upon the top of his staff. By faith Joseph, when he died, made mention of the departing of the children of Israel; and gave commandment concerning his bones. By faith Moses, when he was born, was hid three months of his parents, because they saw he was a proper child; and they were not afraid of the king's commandment. By faith Moses, when he was come to years, refused to be called the son of Pharaoh's daughter; choosing rather to suffer affliction with the people of God, than to enjoy the pleasures of sin for a season; esteeming the reproach of Christ greater riches than the treasures in Egypt: for he had respect unto the recompence of the reward. By faith he forsook Egypt, not fearing the wrath of the king: for he endured, as seeing him who is invisible. Through faith he kept the passover, and the sprinkling of blood, lest he that destroyed the firstborn should touch them. By faith they passed through the Red sea as by dry land: which the Egyptians assaying to do were drowned. By faith the walls of Jericho fell down, after they were compassed about seven days. By faith the harlot Rahab perished not with them that believed not, when she had received the spies with peace. And what shall I more say? for the time would fail me to tell of Gedeon, and of Barak, and of Samson, and of Jephthae; of David also, and Samuel, and of the prophets: who through faith subdued kingdoms, wrought righteousness, obtained promises, stopped the mouths of lions (vv. 1–33).

Yes, we all remember Gedeon (Gideon), Barak, Samson and maybe even Jephthae (Jephthah) and Ehud from the book of Judges, but little else, it seems, because seldom is the gospel preached from this book in churches today. Yet the gospel of the kingdom is surely found in Judges—in glimpses, in foreshadows, in inferences.

Look what Gideon, Barak, Deborah, Samson, and Jephthah did in their faith, quenching the violence of fire and escaping the edge of the sword. Out of weakness they were made strong, waxing valiant in fight and turning to fight the armies of the aliens, as Hebrews 11:34 explains.

It's right there in plain view, explicated in the Greek Scriptures, yet seldom preached from the pulpits that find the book of Judges perhaps too dark.

Though one principle of the gospel of the kingdom is hardly hidden in Judges, and that is the principle of God, not man nor judge, as the Deliverer of His people. It's a principle found repeatedly in the stories of Gideon, Barak, and the other heroes and heroines of the faith. It was not their word, but their faith and trust in the Lord as Deliverer. God delivered His people from seemingly hopeless situations in surprising ways and by using unlikely warriors.

The book of Judges, more than many other historical Scriptures, calls to mind the "post- Christian" times in which we are living, surrounded by nonbelievers, also known in the Bible as "pagans." This is what happens when believers don't use the power, light, and anointing they have been given to take dominion over their communities and countries.

Few books in the Bible, in fact, reveal as much human depravity and the weakness of human nature, which points us to the coming king and the Savior of the world.

What is the gospel truly about? It's about the predilection of humanity to fall into sin, followed by judgment, cries for help, and deliverance. That's the story of Judges. And it's the story of the gospel. It's the story of grace abounding more than sin.

But Gideon, Barak, Deborah, Samson, and Jephthah were temporary deliverers, imperfect saviors and mere candles in the wind compared to Jesus, the King of kings and Savior of the world. They could not forgive sin or atone for it for all time. That would require One who never tasted of sin, who never yielded to it and who would give His life as an atonement for the transgressions of the whole world. However, these judges are role models for us—they are the kind of people God wants us to be, sinners saved by faith and grace and champions for the kingdom of God, subduing kingdoms, reflecting His righteousness, accepting His promises, and stopping the mouths of lions.

8

THE GOSPEL IN RUTH

Now it came to pass in the days when the judges ruled, that there was a famine in the land. —RUTH 1:1

And Ruth said, Intreat me not to leave thee, or to return from following after thee: for whither thou goest, I will go; and where thou lodgest, I will lodge: thy people shall be my people, and thy God my God. —RUTH 1:16

THE BOOK OF RUTH is not only an amazingly uplifting story; it is literature so great that it testifies to its higher inspiration, drawing from the Torah that precedes it and foreshadowing the prophetic fulfillment that follows it.

Among the accomplishments of this twenty-five-hundred-word book are the following:

- It illustrates that not only are Gentiles, those of nations other than Israel, open to the promises of salvation through adoption, but they can and do sometimes, spectacularly and supernaturally, play a part in the redemption of God's chosen, Hebrew people through their faith.

- It illustrates the miraculous, just, and perfect nature of the law of Moses.

- It illustrates how the Redeemer-to-come works—not outside of the law, but within even some of the most seemingly arcane details foreign today to most Christians.

- It illustrates how a life led by faith leads to redemption and glory beyond our imaginations.

- It illustrates how if we first seek the kingdom of God in our lives, all other blessings will follow.

The book of Ruth is seemingly a short, four-act play, but it is rich in meaning and beautifully constructed, and the more we learn about the Bible and the way God works in our lives, the more profound it becomes.

We meet Ruth as the daughter-in-law of Elimelech and Naomi, Bethlehemites who left Israel with their two sons for Moab in a time of famine. We should first note that the family was not "called" out of the land, like other Israelites of the past—Jacob and his family or Joseph and Mary after the birth of Jesus. There's no hint that Elimelech and Naomi sought God's direction about leaving Israel for the cursed, idol-worshipping kingdom of Moab.

How was Moab cursed? There were actually two different curses.

In Numbers 24:17, as we recall from chapter 4, Balaam pronounced this messianic prophecy, whose full realization is still in the future: "I shall see him, but not now: I shall behold him, but not nigh: there shall come a Star out of Jacob, and a Sceptre shall rise out of Israel, *and shall smite the corners of Moab, and destroy all the children of Sheth*" (emphasis added). This is a curse that extends to the messianic era and will result in judgment, though I would note that already today, Moab, modern-day Jordan, is a parched land, teeming with refugees and with scarcely enough fresh water to support a population half its size. It's hard to imagine this would be a land to which anyone would flee seeking refuge from a famine.

There was another curse in Deuteronomy 23:3–4: we see that a Moabite "shall not enter into the congregation of the LORD; *even to their tenth generation shall they not enter into the congregation of the LORD for ever:* Because they met you [Israel] not with bread and with water in the way, when ye came forth out of Egypt; and because they hired against thee Balaam the son of Beor of Pethor of Mesopotamia, to curse thee" (emphasis added). So how did Ruth become a famous member of the congregation of the Lord? The Bible is always precise. By the time of Ruth and Naomi, this curse had run its course, beyond the tenth generation. Therefore, it was not prohibited for a Moabite to enter into the congregation of the Lord forever.

Nevertheless, this history from the Torah demonstrates that the decision by Elimelech and his sons to flee to Moab was probably not one made in prayer and the leading of the Lord.

While in Moab, Elimelech died, leaving Naomi left with her two sons, Mahlon and Chilion, who married women from Moab—Orpah and Ruth—and they continued living there for ten years. Then Mahlon and Chilion died, leaving Naomi with her two daughters-in-law. Life in what we today call the Middle East could be harsh for women, and more so for widows, around 1300 BC, especially outside of Israel. This is still true today.

Knowing the three women might be reduced to begging, Naomi told her daughters-in-law she planned to return to Bethlehem because "the LORD had visited His people in giving them bread." The three began the journey together (Ruth 1:6).

But Naomi had second thoughts about her daughters-in-law, telling them: "Go, return each to her mother's house: the LORD deal kindly with you, as ye have dealt with the dead, and with me. The LORD grant you that ye may find rest, each of you in the house of her husband. Then she kissed them; and they lifted up their voice, and wept" (vv. 8–9).

Both sought to continue with her, but Naomi was persistent. They wept. Orpah kissed Naomi and turned back "unto her people, and unto her gods" (v. 15) but Ruth cleaved to Naomi, uttering these familiar words: "Intreat me not to leave thee, or to return from following after thee: for whither thou goest, I will go; and where thou lodgest, I will lodge: thy people shall be my people, and thy God my God: Where thou diest, will I die, and there will I be buried: the LORD do so to me, and more also, if ought but death part thee and me" (vv. 16–17). And Ruth's decision was not merely a sentimental one for a mother-in-law she loved, but a statement of faith in the God of Israel.

When they arrived in Bethlehem, at the beginning of the barley harvest, Naomi's old neighbors remembered her, but she said to them: "Call me not Naomi, call me Mara: for the Almighty hath dealt very bitterly with me. I went out full and the LORD hath brought me home again empty: why then call ye me Naomi, seeing the LORD hath testified against me, and the Almighty hath afflicted me?" (vv. 20–21).

In Ruth 2:1, we learn that "Naomi had a kinsman of her husband's, a mighty man of wealth, of the family of Elimelech; and his name was Boaz." Since it was harvesttime, Ruth suggested, "Let me now go to the field, and glean ears of corn after him in whose sight I shall find grace. And [Naomi] said unto her, Go, my daughter" (v. 2). Again, it was an act of faith that she would find grace in the sight of Boaz.

Let me interrupt the story here because "gleaning" is something today's believers might not fully understand. Think of it as God's set-aside provision for the poor and the stranger. We first learn in

Leviticus 19:10 that it was a merciful commandment of the law that when harvesting was done, the corners of the fields were to be left unharvested as provision for foreigners and those in dire need.

"And, behold, Boaz came from Bethlehem, and said unto the reapers, The LORD be with you. And they answered him, The LORD bless thee," we're told.

> Then said Boaz unto his servant that was set over the reapers, Whose damsel is this? And the servant that was set over the reapers answered and said, It is the Moabitish damsel that came back with Naomi out of the country of Moab: And she said, I pray you, let me glean and gather after the reapers among the sheaves: so she came, and hath continued even from the morning until now, that she tarried a little in the house. Then said Boaz unto Ruth, Hearest thou not, my daughter? Go not to glean in another field, neither go from hence, but abide here fast by my maidens: Let thine eyes be on the field that they do reap, and go thou after them: have I not charged the young men that they shall not touch thee? and when thou art athirst, go unto the vessels, and drink of that which the young men have drawn (2:4–9).

Boaz recognized this Moabite "stranger" as "my daughter" on account of his in-law relationship with Naomi, giving her special protection and consideration. The story continues:

> Then she fell on her face, and bowed herself to the ground, and said unto him, Why have I found grace in thine eyes, that thou shouldest take knowledge of me, seeing I am a stranger? And Boaz answered and said unto her, It hath fully been shewed me, all that thou hast done unto thy mother in law since the death of thine husband: and how thou hast left thy father and thy mother, and the land of thy nativity, and art come unto a people which thou knewest not heretofore. The LORD recompense thy work, and a full reward be given thee of the LORD God of Israel, under

whose wings thou art come to trust. Then she said, Let me find favour in thy sight, my lord; for that thou hast comforted me, and for that thou hast spoken friendly unto thine handmaid, though I be not like unto one of thine handmaidens. And Boaz said unto her, At mealtime come thou hither, and eat of the bread, and dip thy morsel in the vinegar. And she sat beside the reapers: and he reached her parched corn, and she did eat, and was sufficed, and left. And when she was risen up to glean, Boaz commanded his young men, saying, Let her glean even among the sheaves, and reproach her not: And let fall also some of the handfuls of purpose for her, and leave them, that she may glean them, and rebuke her not. So she gleaned in the field until even, and beat out that she had gleaned: and it was about an ephah of barley. And she took it up, and went into the city: and her mother in law saw what she had gleaned: and she brought forth, and gave to her that she had reserved after she was sufficed (2:10–18).

There is much to "glean" from this in the spiritual sense of the word.

Note Ruth's graciousness and appreciation for the acts of kindness by Boaz. Note Boaz's eagerness not just to follow the letter of the law but the spirit of it as well. He acknowledged Ruth's adoption into the house of Israel and her trust in the Lord. This was more than an act of charity by Boaz; it was an act of evangelism and encouragement of Ruth's decision to join the people of promise.

Keep all this in mind, because many modern commentators completely misinterpret what comes next in the story of Ruth because they don't understand the Torah and the culture of ancient Israel. Chapter 3 of Ruth can be confusing for Christians who view it through the lens of their own modern, worldly culture and without the benefit of diligent study of the Old Testament, especially the books of Moses.

I've read and heard many recent teachings on the book of Ruth that have suggested Naomi was scheming to get Boaz and Ruth together, perhaps even inappropriately. Some have even gone so far as to suggest Ruth was trying to seduce Boaz into a sinful moral compromise or perhaps did so successfully. So, it's important to look at what comes next in light of the law and the actual text of Ruth.

In Chapter 3, Naomi begins by telling Ruth: "My daughter, shall I not seek rest for thee, that it may be well with thee? And now is not Boaz of our kindred, with whose maidens thou wast?" (vv. 1–2). Naomi was expressing love and compassion for her daughter-in-law, explaining that Boaz had accepted her as one of his own kindred. She went on to give her clear instructions about what she was to do next.

"Behold, he winnoweth barley to night in the threshingfloor. Wash thyself therefore, and anoint thee, and put thy raiment upon thee, and get thee down to the floor: but make not thyself known unto the man, until he shall have done eating and drinking. And it shall be, when he lieth down, that thou shalt mark the place where he shall lie, and thou shalt go in, and uncover his feet, and lay thee down; and he will tell thee what thou shalt do" (vv. 2–4).

There are a few key Torah verses you need to familiarize yourself with before fully appreciating these instructions and what follows:

- **EXODUS 22:22–24** "Ye shall not afflict any widow, or fatherless child. If thou afflict them in any wise, and they cry at all unto me, I will surely hear their cry; and my wrath shall wax hot, and I will kill you with the sword; and your wives shall be widows, and your children fatherless."

- **DEUTERONOMY 10:17–19** "For the LORD your God is God of gods, and Lord of lords, a great God, a mighty, and a terrible, which regardeth not persons, nor taketh reward: He doth execute the judgment of the fatherless and widow, and loveth the stranger, in giving him food and raiment. Love ye therefore the stranger: for ye were strangers in the land of Egypt."

- DEUTERONOMY 24:17–19 "Thou shalt not pervert the judgment of the stranger, nor of the fatherless; nor take a widow's raiment to pledge: But thou shalt remember that thou wast a bondman in Egypt, and the LORD thy God redeemed thee thence: therefore I command thee to do this thing. Cursed be he that perverteth the judgment of the stranger, fatherless, and widow. And all the people shall say, Amen."

- Review Leviticus 25:25–55 for more details on the laws of kinsman-redeemers—or, in Hebrew, "go-els."

In Boaz we see a righteous, God-fearing man familiar with the law of Moses. This is demonstrable through his treatment, compassion, and respect for Naomi and Ruth. He was eager to do these things as a kinsman to them. We also see a son of Israel who practiced what is called in Hebrew *chesed*, most commonly translated as "loving-kindness."

There's another key Torah passage I need to introduce at this point: Deuteronomy 25:5–6: "If brethren dwell together, and one of them die, and have no child, the wife of the dead shall not marry without unto a stranger: her husband's brother shall go in unto her, and take her to him to wife, and perform the duty of an husband's brother unto her. And it shall be, that the firstborn which she beareth shall succeed in the name of his brother which is dead, that his name be not put out of Israel."

This might seem strange to us today, but it was God's law, and God's ways are not our ways (Isaiah 55:8). How important was this commandment in ancient Israel's culture? So important that it included public humiliation for those unwilling to exercise it, as stated in Deuteronomy 25:7–10:

And if the man like not to take his brother's wife, then let his brother's wife go up to the gate unto the elders, and say, My husband's brother refuseth to raise up unto his brother a name in Israel, he will not perform the duty of my husband's brother. Then the elders of his city shall call him, and speak unto him: and if he stand to it, and say, I like not to take her; Then shall his brother's wife come unto him in the presence of the elders, and loose his shoe from off his foot, and spit in his face, and shall answer and say, So shall it be done unto that man that will not build up his brother's house. And his name shall be called in Israel, The house of him that hath his *shoe loosed*. (Emphasis added; this detail will be explained later in the story.)

But now, let the next phase of Ruth's story unfold. It would be best, at this point, to review the actual text, which, too often today, is misunderstood by pastors and teachers who see behavior that is not in evidence. Following Naomi's instructions, let's pick up the story in Ruth 3:6–18:

And she went down unto the floor, and did according to all that her mother in law bade her. And when Boaz had eaten and drunk, and his heart was merry, he went to lie down at the end of the heap of corn: and she came softly, and uncovered his feet, and laid her down. And it came to pass at midnight, that the man was afraid, and turned himself: and, behold, a woman lay at his feet. And he said, Who art thou? And she answered, I am Ruth thine handmaid: spread therefore thy skirt over thine handmaid; for thou art a near kinsman. And he said, Blessed be thou of the LORD, my daughter: for thou hast shewed more kindness in the latter end than at the beginning, inasmuch as thou followedst not young men, whether poor or rich. And now, my daughter, fear not; I will do to thee all that thou requirest: for all the city of my people doth know that thou art a virtuous woman. And now it is true that I am thy near kinsman: howbeit there is a kinsman nearer than I. Tarry this night, and it shall be in the morning, that if he will perform unto thee the part of a kinsman, well; let him do the kinsman's part: but if he will not do the part of a kinsman to thee, then will I do the part of a kinsman to thee, as the Lord liveth: lie down until the morning. And she lay at his feet until the morning: and she rose up before one could know another. And he said, Let it not be known that a woman came into the floor. Also he said, Bring the vail that thou hast upon thee, and hold it. And when she held it, he measured six measures of barley, and laid it on her: and she went into the city. And when she came to her mother in law, she said, Who art thou, my daughter? And she told her all that the man had done to her. And she said, These six measures of barley gave he me; for he said to me, Go not empty unto thy mother in law. Then said she, Sit still, my daughter, until thou know how the matter will fall: for the man will not be in rest, until he have finished the thing this day.

Let's review exactly what happened that night:

- She waited until Boaz was asleep, uncovered his feet, and lay down there.

- When Boaz awoke and asked who was there, she said, "I am Ruth thine handmaid: spread therefore thy skirt over thine handmaid; for though art a near kinsman."

- Boaz graciously and eagerly accepted her request to be her husband and kinsman- redeemer or, in Hebrew, *go-el*, but explained there was one kinsman closer than he who must first be offered the opportunity.

- She was told to lie down until the morning.

- Ruth lay at his feet and arose early, before anyone else arrived.

The details are plain and precise. Yet, many modern commentators suggest a sexual liaison actually took place. It clearly did not.

The story concludes in Ruth 4 when Boaz finds the unnamed nearest kinsman and publicly offers him the chance to purchase the property of Naomi and Ruth. While he was more than willing to buy the property, he could not do so without marring his own inheritance. So, he gave permission to Boaz to redeem it, symbolizing this by *plucking off his shoe*, as stated in Deuteronomy 25:10.

Boaz said to the elders and others gathered:

> Ye are witnesses this day, that I have bought all that was Elimelech's, and all that was Chilion's and Mahlon's, of the hand of Naomi. Moreover, Ruth the Moabitess, the wife of Mahlon, have I purchased to be my wife, to raise up the name of the dead upon his inheritance, that the name of the dead be not cut off from among his brethren, and from the gate of his place: ye are witnesses this day. And all the people that were in the gate, and the elders, said, We are witnesses. The LORD make the woman that is come into thine house like Rachel and like Leah, which two did build the house of Israel: and do thou worthily in Ephratah, and be famous in Bethlehem: And let thy house be like the house of Pharez, whom Tamar bare unto Judah, of the seed which the LORD shall give thee of this young woman (Ruth 4:9–12).

Ruth became Boaz's wife, and the women of Bethlehem rejoiced for Naomi, exclaiming that her daughter-in-law was "better to thee than seven sons" (4:15). Their son was named Obed. He became the father of Jesse, who in turn became the father of David. Boaz and Ruth, then, are the great-grandparents of King David, and, of course, and David's line leads directly through the generations to Jesus, who will, one day in the future, sit on David's throne as King of Israel and King of kings.

What are the lessons to be drawn from this story?

- There is value in keeping the law zealously and eagerly.

- We are all brothers and sisters who worship the one true God.

- It's a testimony to the power of mercy and generosity.

- Jesus, a direct descendant of Boaz and Ruth, is the ultimate *go-el*, or Redeemer for all—Jew and gentile alike.

We have a "Jesus-type" in Boaz. We have a remarkable birth in Bethlehem that leads directly to the line of David and to Jesus. Bread is a theme, with Naomi's family leaving Bethlehem, the "city of bread," to sojourn to Moab only to suffer calamities that force her and one daughter-in- law to return. Bethlehem is famously the birthplace of Jesus. And Jesus is the bread of life (John 6:35).

Thus, Jesus and the Gospels are all over the book of Ruth.

9

THE GOSPEL IN I SAMUEL

And the LORD *said unto Samuel, How long wilt thou mourn for Saul, seeing I have rejected him from reigning over Israel? fill thine horn with oil, and go, I will send thee to Jesse the Bethlehemite: for I have provided me a king among his sons.* —1 SAMUEL 16:1

The adversaries of the LORD *shall be broken to pieces; out of heaven shall he thunder upon them: the* LORD *shall judge the ends of the earth; and he shall give strength unto his king, and exalt the horn of his anointed.*
—1 SAMUEL 2:10

HAVE YOU EVER FOUND YOURSELF laughing at or crying with characters in the Scriptures, Old Testament or New?

It's tempting to do, but perhaps unwise. I've heard many teachings over the years that mock the shortsightedness of those portrayed in the Bible, including some of the most anointed figures, people like Abraham, David, and certain apostles, like Peter.

I'm convinced the errors of these great personalities are chronicled for a reason other than amusement or sympathy. They are there to show their humanity, I believe, in part, so that we can relate to their actions and their words and comprehend that we, too, are fallen souls in need of redemption, who still see only glimpses of the truth "through a glass, darkly" (1 Corinthians 13:12)

In 1 Samuel, we see the story of a judge, priest, and prophet who leads the transition of the children of Israel through one epoch, the time of the judges, to another, the era of the kings—with a foreshadowing of yet another future period, the messianic age of the King of kings.

The time of the judges—from Joshua to Samuel —was characterized by periods of peace and prosperity, when Israel was walking with God, to periods of war and famine, when Israel walked away from God. As the last judge, Samuel brought the children of Israel back from serving other gods to walking with the one true God.

But the elders of Israel were not content. And as Samuel grew old, they cried out to him to "make us a king to judge us like all the nations" (1 Samuel 8:5).

The children of Israel had been intentionally and purposely set apart from all the other nations, and Samuel was displeased with this demand. So, he prayed to the Lord. God's answer was direct:

Hearken unto the voice of the people in all that they say unto thee: for they have not rejected thee, but they have rejected me, that I should not reign over them. According to all the works which they have done since the day that I brought them up out of Egypt even unto this day, wherewith they have forsaken me, and served other gods, so do they also unto thee. Now therefore hearken unto their voice: howbeit yet protest solemnly unto them, and shew them the manner of the king that shall reign over them (1 Samuel 8:7–9).

It's the story of biblical Israel in nutshell: God's chosen people embrace Him and God's chosen people reject Him. When they embrace Him, they are blessed. When they reject Him, they are cursed. When they are blessed by God, they love their distinction among the nations of the world. But, when they are cursed, they want to be like "all the other nations."

The omnipotent Creator knew this would be the case from before the fall of humankind, and it was all part of His redemption plan from the beginning. With the aid of this knowledge of this historical backdrop, there's a temptation for today's believers to think they might have made wiser choices than those in ancient Israel. But would we? Clearly, God knows humanity better than we know ourselves. He knows what is best for us, better than we know for ourselves. And that is one of the great lessons of 1 Samuel.

The Lord told Samuel to warn the children of Israel how a mortal king would reign over them:

- "He will take your sons, and appoint them for himself, for his chariots, and to be his horsemen; and some shall run before his chariots."

- "And he will appoint him captains over thousands, and captains over fifties; and will set them to ear his ground, and to reap his harvest, and to make his instruments of war, and instruments of his chariots."

- "And he will take your daughters to be confectionaries, and to be cooks, and to be bakers."

- "And he will take your fields, and your vineyards, and your olive-yards, even the best of them, and give them to his servants."

- "And he will take the tenth of your seed, and of your vineyards, and give to his officers, and to his servants."

- "And he will take your menservants, and your maidservants, and your goodliest young men, and your asses, and put them to his work."

- "He will take the tenth of your sheep: and ye shall be his servants."

"And ye shall cry out in that day because of your king which ye shall have chosen you; and the LORD will not hear you in that day," he concluded (1 Samuel 8:11–18).

"Nevertheless, the people refused to obey the voice of Samuel; and they said, Nay; but we will have a king over us; that we also may be like all the nations; and that our king may judge us, and go out before us, and fight our battles" (vv. 19–20).

So, God told Samuel to make them a king. And of course, this was all part of His ultimate plan of redemption—to make His own Son the King of kings, ruling and reigning from Jerusalem over all the people of the earth. Later in this book, as Samuel prepares to anoint David as king, from whom Jesus will later descend as God's heir to the throne, God tells Samuel, "Fill thine horn with oil, and go, I will send thee to Jesse the Bethlehemite: for I have provided *me* a king among his sons" (16:1). (Note the added emphasis on the word "me," as this would be the king God provided for Himself and His own purposes. The language reminds me of another very famous verse: Genesis 22:8, in which Abraham tells his own son, Isaac: "My son, God will provide *himself* a lamb for a burnt offering" (emphasis added).

But first, the children of Israel must experience for themselves the hardships that would come as a result of their own choices—just as people today must experience the suffering of doing what seems right in our own eyes.

Let's walk through 1 Samuel chapter by chapter to see what other hints of the gospel we may find.

In Chapter 1, we meet Hannah, the wife of Elkanah, who we learn in the first verse is "an Ephrathite" (v. 1) What is an "Ephrathite"? Way back in Genesis 35:19, we learn that "Ephrath," or "Ephrata," was the ancient name of Bethlehem. Like another very special woman from Bethlehem centuries later, Hannah would experience a miraculous birth.

Hannah was unable to bear a child. This grieved her greatly. At this time, the center of worship in Israel was in Shiloh. This is where the high priest, Eli, resided and where the annual sacrifices took place. While Hannah was there with her husband for the holy days, she was praying fervently to the Lord for a child, while Eli observed.

> And she vowed a vow, and said, O LORD of hosts, if thou wilt indeed look on the affliction of thine handmaid, and remember me, and not forget thine handmaid, but wilt give unto thine handmaid a man child, then I will give him unto the LORD all the days of his life, and there shall no razor come upon his head. And it came to pass, as she continued praying before the LORD, that Eli marked her mouth. Now Hannah, she spake in her heart; only her lips moved, but her voice was not heard: therefore Eli thought she had been drunken. And Eli said unto her, How long wilt thou be drunken? put away thy wine from thee. And Hannah answered and said, No, my lord, I am a woman of a sorrowful spirit: I have drunk neither wine nor strong drink, but have poured out my soul before the LORD. Count not thine handmaid for a daughter of Belial: for out of the abundance of my complaint and grief have I spoken hitherto. Then Eli answered and said, Go in peace: and the God of Israel grant thee thy petition that thou hast asked of him. And she said, Let thine handmaid find grace in thy sight. So the woman went her way, and did eat, and her countenance was no more sad (1 Samuel 1:11–18).

Shortly after, Hannah bore a son and named him Samuel. She expressed her intent to her husband to bring him to Shiloh to live under Eli's care after he was weaned—a sacrifice of her own son, if you will, to the service of the Lord.

Years later, she did just that. Presenting Samuel to Eli, Hannah said: "Oh my lord, as thy soul liveth, my lord, I am the woman that stood by thee here, praying unto the LORD. For this child I prayed; and the LORD hath given me my petition which I asked of him: Therefore also I have lent him to the LORD; as long as he liveth he shall be lent to the LORD. And he worshipped the LORD there" (1 Samuel 1:26–28).

Hannah offered a heartfelt and prophetic prayer while there:

My heart rejoiceth in the LORD, mine horn is exalted in the LORD: my mouth is enlarged over mine enemies; because I rejoice in thy salvation. There is none holy as the LORD: for there is none beside thee: neither is there any rock like our God. Talk no more so exceeding proudly; let not arrogancy come out of your mouth: for the LORD is a God of knowledge, and by him actions are weighed. The bows of the mighty men are broken, and they that stumbled are girded with strength. They that were full have hired out themselves for bread; and they that were hungry ceased: so that the barren hath born seven; and she that hath many children is waxed feeble. The LORD killeth, and maketh alive: he bringeth down to the grave, and bringeth up. The LORD maketh poor, and maketh rich: he bringeth low, and lifteth up. He raiseth up the poor out of the dust, and lifteth up the beggar from the dunghill, to set them among princes, and to make them inherit the throne of glory: for the pillars of the earth are the LORD's, and he hath set the world upon them. He will keep the feet of his saints, and the wicked shall be silent in darkness; for by strength shall no man prevail. The adversaries of the LORD shall be broken to pieces; out of heaven shall he thunder upon them: the LORD shall judge the ends of the earth; and he shall give strength unto his king, and exalt the horn of his anointed (1 Samuel 2:1–10).

Does this prayer seem familiar to you? It bears striking resemblance to the one offered by Mary, often referred to traditionally as the *Magnificat*. She uttered this prayer in Luke 1:46–55 in the presence of her cousin Elisabeth, who also had a miraculous birth of a child, who would be known as John the Baptist.

> And Mary said, My soul doth magnify the Lord, And my spirit hath rejoiced in God my Saviour. For he hath regarded the low estate of his handmaiden: for, behold, from henceforth all generations shall call me blessed. For he that is mighty hath done to me great things; and holy is his name. And his mercy is on them that fear him from generation to generation. He hath shewed strength with his arm; he hath scattered the proud in the imagination of their hearts. He hath put down the mighty from their seats, and exalted them of low degree. He hath filled the hungry with good things; and the rich he hath sent empty away. He hath helped his servant Israel, in remembrance of his mercy; As he spake to our fathers, to Abraham, and to his seed for ever.

Do you notice the striking resemblances in construction and content? Both are prayers of thanksgiving, love, joy, mercy, and the future promise of the good news of redemption.

And what do the prayers by both Hannah and Mary reveal? A profound understanding of "the gospel of the kingdom"—a future time in which all justice will be served.

Next, we learn that Eli's two sons and heirs to the high priesthood were corrupt and "knew not the LORD" (1 Samuel 2:12). Eli watched the sinful behavior of his sons and warned them, but they didn't listen. Meanwhile, by contrast, "the child Samuel grew on, and was in favour both with the LORD, and also with men" (1 Samuel 2:26).

Then "there came a man of God unto Eli," with a warning. We don't know if it was a prophet or an angel, but he was clearly speaking for God. He told Eli that his sons would both die in one day and added cryptically what sounds like the prophetic words of the LORD: "And I will raise me up a faithful priest, that shall do according to that which is in mine heart and in my mind: and I will build him a sure house; and he shall walk before mine anointed for ever" (vv. 27–28, 34–35).

This is clearly a reference to a future "faithful priest" from Bethlehem, who will rule and reign in His house in Jerusalem forever. Though, immediately, it became clear to Eli that his adopted son, Samuel, likely also of the tribe of Judah, would serve as his heir in the priesthood—as well as a prophet and judge.

The young prophet began ministering "unto the LORD before Eli. And the word of the LORD was precious in those days; there was no open vision" (3:1). This suggests that Eli was not hearing directly from the Lord, but the Holy Spirit began speaking to Samuel.

One night, after Samuel had lain down in his bed, in the temple of God, the Lord called him. Thinking that it was Eli who had called him, Samuel responded, "Here am I," and ran to him. This happened three times.

"And Eli perceived that the Lord had called the child. Therefore Eli said unto Samuel, Go, lie down: and it shall be, if he call thee, that thou shalt say, Speak, LORD; for thy servant heareth. So Samuel went and lay down in his place, and the next time the Lord called Samuel, he responded, "Speak; for thy servant heareth" (3:8–10).

> And the LORD said to Samuel, Behold, I will do a thing in Israel, at which both the ears of every one that heareth it shall tingle. In that day I will perform against Eli all things which I have spoken concerning his house: when I begin, I will also make an end. For I have told him that I will judge his house for ever for the iniquity which he knoweth; because his sons made themselves vile, and he restrained them not. And therefore I have sworn unto the house of Eli, that the iniquity of Eli's house shall not be purged with sacrifice nor offering for ever. And Samuel lay until the morning, and opened the doors of the house of the LORD. And Samuel feared to shew Eli the vision. Then Eli called Samuel, and said, Samuel, my son. And he answered, Here am I. And he said, What

is the thing that the LORD hath said unto thee? I pray thee hide it not from me: God do so to thee, and more also, if thou hide any thing from me of all the things that he said unto thee. And Samuel told him every whit, and hid nothing from him. And he said, It is the LORD: let him do what seemeth him good.

And Samuel grew, and the LORD was with him, and did let none of his words fall to the ground. And all Israel from Dan even to Beersheba knew that Samuel was established to be a prophet of the LORD. And the LORD appeared again in Shiloh: for the LORD revealed himself to Samuel in Shiloh by the word of the LORD (3:11–21).

And thus Samuel became the prophet to all Israel at this time.

In chapter 4, Israel goes out to fight, with the ark of the covenant in tow, its dreaded enemy the Philistines. But because of the presence of sin in the camp—namely, Eli's sons, Hophni and Phinehas—the battle was a rout. The Philistines killed Eli's sons in one day, as prophesied, and captured the ark.

When Eli got the word, he fell back in his chair and broke his neck. His mantle as judge of Israel for forty years, thus, fell upon Samuel.

The Philistines soon found the presence of the ark of the covenant did not bring them good fortune. Instead, when it was brought into the presence of Dagon, their false god, the idol would fall on its face. The Philistines would put their idol upright again, only to find Dagon bowing to the ark again the next day. Then the Philistines found themselves plagued with hemorrhoids.

Fearful that they were cursed because of the ark, they placed it on a cart pulled by cattle and set it in the direction of the Israelis— along with an offering of golden hemorrhoids and mice. (I'm not joking. Read it for yourself.) When the ark arrived in Bethshemesh, it did not bring the inhabitants any better fortune than it had brought the Philistines. When they looked upon the ark, more than fifty thousand were struck dead.

Finally, the ark was brought to the house of Abinadab, where his son, Eleazar, was properly sanctified to keep it for the next twenty years.

Meanwhile, Samuel was coming into his own as the new judge of Israel. He understood the real problem the nation was experiencing. He called a meeting of the house of Israel and explained, "If ye do return unto the LORD with all your hearts, then put away the strange gods and Ashtaroth from among you, and prepare your hearts unto the LORD, and serve him only: and he will deliver you out of the hand of the Philistines. Then the children of Israel did put away Baalim and Ashtaroth, and served the LORD only" (1 Samuel 7:3–4).

Samuel called another meeting in Mizpeh, where he would pray for nation. While they were gathered, the Philistines planned an attack. But the Lord confused the attackers and they were routed by the children of Israel. They would no longer plague Israel during Samuel's days. There was also peace with the Amorites.

But Samuel had an Eli problem. His two sons were no-goodniks. And all Israel recognized it. So the elders, apparently not trusting God, hatched a plan to ensure the blessings they were experiencing would continue once Samuel died—and they told Samuel to give them a king.

The man chosen by God was Saul. He was the tallest man in all Israel, of the tribe of Benjamin. All went well with Saul and Israel during his first two years as king. The Lord was with him. But at a critical moment, he did not follow Samuel's instructions. Strike 1.

Then, Saul's son Jonathan took the initiative in a battle with the Philistines. Meanwhile, Saul arbitrarily issued a decree that no man should eat until evening, an edict not heard by his son. Hungered after the battle, Jonathan dipped his hand in honey to refresh himself. Saul ordered him to be killed. (Thankfully, the people interceded on Jonathan's behalf.) Strike 2.

Finally, the Lord, through the prophet Samuel, ordered Saul to attack and slay all of the Amalekites, including their flocks and herds. But Saul chose not to kill the animals and spared the life of Agag the king. Strike 3.

Samuel's words explained the judgment: "For rebellion is as the sin of witchcraft, and stubbornness is as iniquity and idolatry. Because thou hast rejected the word of the LORD, he hath also rejected thee from being king. . . . And Samuel came no more to see Saul until the day of his death: nevertheless Samuel mourned for Saul: and the LORD repented that he had made Saul king over Israel" (1 Samuel 15:23, 35). By then, Samuel had already told Saul that his kingdom would not continue. "The LORD hath sought him *a man after his own heart,*" he said, "and the LORD hath commanded him to be captain over his people, because thou hast not kept that which the LORD commanded *thee*" (13:14; emphasis added).

God directed Samuel to find that man after God's own heart and anoint him as king. Samuel would find him in Bethlehem, one of the sons of a man named Jesse. When Samuel arrived and stated his mission, Jesse called for his sons. The prophet examined seven sons. One of them was particularly handsome and impressive, but God rejected all of them, saying, "Look not on his countenance, or on the height of his stature; because I have refused him: for the LORD seeth not as man seeth; for man looketh on the outward appearance, but the LORD looketh on the heart" (16:7)

There was one more son, the youngest, out tending the sheep. His name was David. And when Samuel looked at him, the Lord said, "Arise, anoint him: for this is he. Then Samuel took the horn of oil, and anointed him in the midst of his brethren: and the Spirit of the LORD came upon David from that day forward" (16:12–13).

Meanwhile, the spirit of the Lord departed from Saul and an evil spirit troubled him. His servants came up with an idea: find a harpist to play for the king whenever the evil spirit descends on the king. You know the rest. That young harpist was David.

These events were taking place around the time when the army of Israel and the army of the Philistines were facing off in battle by the valley of Elah. The Philistines had sent out their champion, a giant named Goliath, to taunt and challenge Israel. "Send out your best warrior," he said. "If he can kill me, we will be your servants. But if I kill him, you will be our servants." This went on for forty days, and no one from Israel volunteered to take on Goliath.

When David returned to the camp from Bethlehem and heard Goliath's jeers, he asked, "What shall be done to the man that killeth this Philistine, and taketh away the reproach from Israel? for who is this uncircumcised Philistine, that he should defy the armies of the living God?" (17:26).

The rest is history. The teenage shepherd slew Goliath. But in doing so, he raised a spirit of jealousy in Saul that would plague the secretly anointed king for the rest of his life.

Saul was afraid of David because the spirit of God was with him, while it had departed from Saul himself. In time, Saul tried to ensnare David by giving him his daughter, Michal, to marry. He then urged his son Jonathan and his servants to kill David. And Saul repeatedly tried to kill David himself, with his own javelin.

For years Saul pursued David relentlessly as he hid in the wilderness. David had to find refuge for his father and mother in Moab. David himself actually went to live with the Philistines, even joining their army.

Eventually, Saul and his sons, including David's beloved friend Jonathan, were killed in a battle with the Philistines. And thus, the door was finally opened for David to assume the throne God intended him to inherit. That throne of David, by the way, will one day serve as the throne of Jesus: "He shall be great, and shall be called the Son of the Highest: and the Lord God shall give unto him the throne of his father David: And he shall reign over the house of Jacob for ever; and of his kingdom there shall be no end" (Luke 1:32–33).

10

THE GOSPEL IN II SAMUEL

Moreover I will appoint a place for my people Israel, and will plant them,
that they may dwell in a place of their own, and move no more; neither shall
the children of wickedness afflict them any more, as beforetime.
—2 SAMUEL 7:10

And when thy days be fulfilled, and thou shalt sleep with thy fathers, I will
set up thy seed after thee, which shall proceed out of thy bowels, and I will
establish his kingdom. —2 SAMUEL 7:12

WE'RE ALL TEMPTED. We're all sinners. We all fall. Even David, the great champion we met in 1 Samuel, a man after God's own heart, who was destined to fulfill His will (Acts 13:22), was susceptible to falling into temptation in profound ways that would prevent him from accomplishing a greater personal destiny.

That is the great story line of 2 Samuel.

David was a strong warrior. He was at his best when he was overcoming crises, relying on God for direction, surviving against all odds, living on the run in the wilderness, defeating powerful enemies in times of great stress. He was at his worst when, by all appearances, he was at the top of his game—in power, the world at his feet, prosperous, perhaps even bored, seemingly facing no great or imminent danger. Sound familiar? It's true of so many of us, which is why God needs to remind us of our own human frailty with testing.

It was in one of those latter times that David fell into a temptation familiar to so many—if not all.

Though he had been anointed as king by Samuel at God's instructions much earlier, David began his reign over Judah at the age of thirty—approximately the same age at which Jesus began His earthly ministry. Seven years later, David united all Israel under his leadership as king reigning in Jerusalem—placing him in the unique position from which he would serve as the progenitor of the Messiah. He would reign thirty-three years before his death.

It was during this latter half of his life, when he had the world at his feet, that David faced his biggest character challenges.

David's greatest victories came when he sought God's direction. Each and every time he did so, he was rewarded with victory. Each and every time he did not, he fell short. It's true of most of us, which makes David a biblical character to whom we can relate as fallen human beings.

The spiritual crescendo of 2 Samuel comes in chapter 7:

And it came to pass, when the king sat in his house, and the LORD had given him rest round about from all his enemies; that the king said unto Nathan the prophet, See now, I dwell in an house of cedar, but the ark of God dwelleth within curtains. And Nathan said to the king, Go, do all that is in thine heart; for the LORD is with thee. And it came to pass that night, that the word of the LORD came unto Nathan, saying, Go and tell my servant David, Thus saith the LORD, Shalt thou build me an house for me to dwell in? Whereas I have not dwelt in any house since the time that I brought up the children of Israel out of Egypt, even to this day, but have walked in a tent and in a tabernacle. In all the places wherein I have walked with all the children of Israel spake I a word with any of the tribes of Israel, whom I commanded to feed my people Israel, saying, Why build ye not me an house of cedar? Now therefore so shalt thou say unto my servant David, Thus saith the LORD of hosts, I took thee from the sheepcote, from following the sheep, to be ruler over my people, over Israel: And I was with thee whithersoever thou wentest, and have cut off all thine enemies out of thy sight, and have made thee a great name, like unto the name of the great men that are in the earth. Moreover I will appoint a place for my people Israel, and will plant them, that they may dwell in a place of their own, and move no more; neither shall the children of wickedness afflict them any more, as beforetime, And as since the time that I commanded judges to be over my people Israel, and have caused thee to rest from all thine enemies. Also the LORD telleth thee that he will make thee an house. *And when thy days be fulfilled, and thou shalt sleep with thy fathers, I will set up thy seed after thee, which shall proceed out of thy bowels, and I will establish his kingdom. He shall build an house for my name, and I will stablish the throne of his kingdom for ever. I will be his father, and he shall be my son. If he commit iniquity, I will chasten him with the rod of men, and with the stripes of the children of men: But my mercy shall not depart away from him, as I took it from Saul, whom I put away before thee. And thine house and thy kingdom shall be established for ever before thee: thy throne shall be established for ever.* According to all these words, and according to all this vision, so did Nathan speak unto David (vv. 1–17; emphasis added).

For his faithfulness during the first half of David's life, God was making a great irrevocable promise to him. God would be Solomon's father, just as He was and is Jesus' Father.

- Both Solomon and Jesus would build houses for His name.

- Through Solomon's throne (and David's), God would establish His kingdom forever.

- Solomon (and David, as we will see later in Samuel 2) would be chastened for his iniquity.

- God's mercy would not depart from Solomon, as He had removed it from Saul.

This is same throne and kingdom about which Jesus spoke so often. It's the great hope for Israel and the entire world, a kingdom of justice, mercy, peace, prosperity and life not seen since the garden of Eden before the fall. It's the kingdom about which John the Baptist preached, saying, "Repent ye: for the kingdom of heaven is at hand" (Matthew 3:2). It's the "restitution of all things" about which Peter spoke (Acts 3:21). It's the kingdom of heaven on earth to which Jesus referred often throughout His ministry (Matthew 4:17). In fact, it's the restoration to which *all* the prophets from creation forward referred (Acts 3:24).

And it's right there in 2 Samuel.

David willingly accepted this blessing in a prayer that extends through the end of the chapter.

But four chapters later, David will succumb to human, fleshly temptation will put the covenant to the test.

He was the king. He was living in his palace. He was no longer commanding his own army on the front lines of battle. He was living the good life. But David was restless, and when he awakened in the night and went for a walk on the palace roof, he saw a "woman very beautiful to look upon" washing herself (2 Samuel 2:2).

He didn't turn away. Instead, he found out who she was and summoned her to his house. Then, the Bible tells us, "he lay with her," knowing she was married to Uriah the Hittite, one of his faithful

THE GOSPEL IN EVERY BOOK OF THE OLD TESTAMENT

warriors, who was fighting for his adopted nation of Israel (v. 4).

Bathsheba conceived, and this is where the sinful plot thickens. David had already committed the grave sin of adultery—and now he was about to compound the offense.

As chapter 11 continues, we read that David sent his right-hand man, Joab, to get Uriah to return from the war front to see the king. David asked Uriah about how the battle was going, then sent him away with food, assuming he would go home and sleep with his wife. Even if Bathsheba didn't get pregnant, when her child by David was born, Uriah would assume it was his own. See, David was *hoping* to cover his own sin.

But Uriah did not go home. Instead, he slept at the door of the king's house with David's servants. When David found out, he summoned Uriah again and asked him why he did not sleep in his own house.

Uriah's explanation demonstrates his own character: "The ark, and Israel, and Judah, abide in tents; and my lord Joab, and the servants of my lord, are encamped in the open fields; shall I then go into mine house, to eat and to drink, and to lie with my wife? as thou livest, and as thy soul liveth, I will not do this thing" (2 Samuel 11:11).

David's scheming continued. He ordered Uriah to stay in Jerusalem another day and feast with the king. They ate, drank, and got drunk, but still Uriah did not go home to be with his wife, Bathsheba. Again, the sinful plot thickens.

Next, David wrote a letter to Joab, ordering him to arrange for Uriah to be killed in battle. He even personally handed the sealed letter to Uriah to deliver.

Thus, Uriah and other valiant men with him, were killed by special arrangement of the king. When Bathsheba's mourning for her husband was concluded, David married her.

"But the thing that David had done displeased the LORD" (11:27).

A bigger understatement you will not find in the Bible. God's anointed king, this man "after his own heart" (1 Samuel 13:14), broke at least five of the Ten Commandments by allowing himself to fall to the lust of his eyes. Like Eve in the Garden, David "saw" something that looked "good" but was forbidden. Then he "took" it (2 Samuel 11:4; see Genesis 3:6). This great man of faith fell, just like Adam and Eve. It's more than a coincidence when you see this pattern from Genesis repeated here. It demonstrates the susceptibility of us all to stumbling badly.

In David's case, he coveted his neighbor's wife, breaking commandment 10. He also stole his neighbor's wife, violating commandment 8. He committed adultery, breaking commandment 7. And finally, he murdered Uriah (breaking commandment 6).

He also dragged others into his sin by ordering them to become complicit.

But to make matters worse, he did not repent until he was confronted with his grave sin by Nathan the prophet.

In the next chapter, God, speaking through Nathan, confronts David with what seems like a parable of a man who commits much less egregious sins than his own.

> There were two men in one city; the one rich, and the other poor. The rich man had exceeding many flocks and herds: But the poor man had nothing, save one little ewe lamb, which he had bought and nourished up: and it grew up together with him, and with his children; it did eat of his own meat, and drank of his own cup, and lay in his bosom, and was unto him as a daughter.
>
> And there came a traveller unto the rich man, and he spared to take of his own flock and of his own herd, to dress for the wayfaring man that was come unto him; but took the poor man's lamb, and dressed it for the man that was come to him (2 Samuel 12:1–4).

David's anger was immediately kindled against the rich man in the story. "As the LORD liveth," he huffed, "the man that hath done this thing shall surely die: And he shall restore the lamb fourfold, because he did this thing, and because he had no pity."

> And Nathan said to David, Thou art the man. Thus saith the LORD God of Israel, I anointed thee king over Israel, and I delivered thee out of the hand of Saul; and I gave thee thy master's house, and thy master's wives into thy bosom, and gave thee the house of Israel and of Judah; and if that had been too little, I would moreover have given unto thee such and such things. Wherefore hast thou despised the commandment of the LORD, to do evil in his sight? thou hast killed Uriah the Hittite with the sword, and hast taken his wife to be thy wife, and hast slain him with the sword of the children of Ammon. Now therefore the sword shall never depart from thine house; because thou hast despised me, and hast taken the wife of Uriah the Hittite to be thy wife. Thus saith the LORD, Behold, I will raise up evil against thee out of thine own house, and I will take thy wives before thine eyes, and give them unto thy neighbour, and he shall lie with thy wives in the sight of this sun. For thou didst it secretly: but I will do this thing before all Israel, and before the sun (2 Samuel 12:5–12).

Then and only then did David repent.

He would not die for his sin, but the baby Bathsheba would bear would not live. Yet, another son would one day be born to David and Bathsheba: Solomon, whose descendants would include Jesus the Messiah, thus fulfilling the Davidic covenant.

In the meantime, all of the familial and personal trials David would endure throughout his personal and family life had their genesis in this series of sins that he committed when he was powerful, prosperous, restless, and, possibly, a little bored. What does Jesus tell us in Matthew 19:24? "It is easier for a camel to go through the eye of a needle, than for a rich man to enter into the kingdom of God."

When Peter questioned Jesus about how anyone will make it

into the kingdom, He responded, "With men this is impossible; but with God all things are possible" (Matthew 19:26). He went on to promise, "Verily I say unto you, That ye which have followed me, in the regeneration when the Son of man shall sit in the throne of his glory, ye also shall sit upon twelve thrones, judging the twelve tribes of Israel" (v. 28). Here he was referring right back to the Davidic covenant of 2 Samuel 7. Indeed, the apostles will one day sit upon twelve thrones, judging the twelve tribes of Israel, in a very real kingdom on earth and centered in Israel.

Can we find the gospel in 2 Samuel? Of course, we can. For it is those of us who believe in Jesus, the son of David and of Solomon, who will be saved for all eternity and will live in His kingdom.

11

THE GOSPEL IN I KINGS

*And he said, L*ORD *God of Israel, there is no God like thee, in heaven above,*
or on earth beneath, who keepest covenant and mercy with thy servants that
walk before thee with all their heart: —1 KINGS 8:23

*And let these my words, wherewith I have made supplication before the L*ORD*,*
*be nigh unto the L*ORD *our God day and night, that he maintain the cause of*
his servant, and the cause of his people Israel at all times, as the matter shall
*require: That all the people of the earth may know that the L*ORD *is God, and*
that there is none else. —1 KINGS: 8:59–60

THE BOOK OF I KINGS is a history of Israel from just before the
death of David to the death of King Ahab, providing an overview
of Israel's rulers, from the best to the worst. It contains some famous
Bible stories, from the rise of Solomon, in all his wisdom, wealth, and
power, to the sudden and mysterious appearance of Elijah, who calls

down fire from heaven, humiliating and judging the prophets of Baal.

Not many have written before about glimpses of the gospel in this historical book. Yet they are there, indeed. On a grand scale, we see in Solomon the king whose reign most closely foreshadows the peace and prosperity prophesied for a united Israel in the future kingdom of God.

In 1 Kings 2:12, we're told, after the passing of King David, "Then sat Solomon upon the throne of David his father; and his kingdom was established greatly." Indeed, it was. No other king of Israel, including his father David, would bring such accomplishment and splendor to the office. He reigned for forty years, like his father, all of that time in Jerusalem. David had to conquer Jerusalem before he could set up the kingdom there. Solomon built the temple, whereas God had told David he could not. Solomon's reign was peaceful and exceedingly prosperous, far outshining David's reign. Solomon's wisdom, power, and wealth were the envy of other nations, presaging, in a limited way, the prophesied millennial reign of Israel's ultimate Redeemer-King, Jesus.

Solomon started out strong, though there was evidence of weakness from the beginning, we learn in 1 Kings 3:3: "And Solomon loved the LORD, walking in the statutes of David his father: *only he sacrificed and burnt incense in high places*" (emphasis added).

The Torah is clear about these *high places*, or hilltop shrines built for worship of idols.

- LEVITICUS 26:30 "And I will destroy your high places, and cut down your images, and cast your carcases upon the carcases of your idols, and my soul shall abhor you."

- NUMBERS 33:52 "Then ye shall drive out all the inhabitants of the land from before you, and destroy all their pictures, and destroy all their molten images, and quite pluck down all their high places,"

- **DEUTERONOMY 12:2** "Ye shall utterly destroy all the places, wherein the nations which ye shall possess served their gods, upon the high mountains, and upon the hills, and under every green tree."

And these represent just a few among dozens of Old Testament references to "high places."

The high places were where the pagans worshipped. God commanded them to be destroyed. But God gave Solomon grace. He also began speaking to him—even while he was in one of those high places, making sacrifices. In a dream, He asked Solomon what he would like for God to give him.

Solomon's answer pleased the Lord. This was Solomon's response:

Thou hast shewed unto thy servant David my father great mercy, according as he walked before thee in truth, and in righteousness, and in uprightness of heart with thee; and thou hast kept for him this great kindness, that thou hast given him a son to sit on his throne, as it is this day. And now, O LORD my God, thou hast made thy servant king instead of David my father: and I am but a little child: I know not how to go out or come in. And thy servant is in the midst of thy people which thou hast chosen, a great people, that cannot be numbered nor counted for multitude. Give therefore thy servant an understanding heart to judge thy people, that I may discern between good and bad: for who is able to judge this thy so great a people? (1 Kings 3:6–9)

Because Solomon did not ask for a long life, riches, honor, or the lives of his enemies, God granted him the wisdom he sought—as well as the rest.

Here's the picture of the kingdom under Solomon's leadership:

Judah and Israel were many, as the sand which is by the sea in multitude, eating and drinking, and making merry. And

Solomon reigned over all kingdoms from the river unto the land of the Philistines, and unto the border of Egypt: they brought presents, and served Solomon all the days of his life. For he had dominion over all the region on this side the river, from Tiphsah even to Azzah, over all the kings on this side the river: and he had peace on all sides round about him. And Judah and Israel dwelt safely, every man under his vine and under his fig tree, from Dan even to Beersheba, all the days of Solomon. And Solomon had forty thousand stalls of horses for his chariots, and twelve thousand horsemen (1 Kings 4:21–26).

Not before or since was there as much glory to be found in the kingdom of Israel. It will only be surpassed when the Messiah returns.

In fact, the Gospels point to that glory, including allusions by the future king whose glory would surpass it. In Matthew 6:28–29. Jesus makes reference to Solomon's splendor: "And why take ye thought for raiment? Consider the lilies of the field, how they grow; they toil not, neither do they spin: And yet I say unto you, That even Solomon in all his glory was not arrayed like one of these." In Matthew 12:42, Jesus again referenced Solomon's stature, but, by contrast, concluded, "Behold, a greater than Solomon is here."

People came from all over the world to marvel at Solomon's accomplishments and to hear his wisdom. Nowhere in Scripture does it suggest any other king of Israel had such global appeal— except for one future king, Jesus. Zechariah 14:16 prophesies that all nations will go up to Jerusalem from year to year to worship this future King of kings.

But Solomon's biggest accomplishment was building the temple. It took thirteen years. And while it would fall into disrepair after his death, it would be rebuilt. And it would be that rebuilt temple that Jesus, the future King, would visit before its destruction in judgment for rejecting Him.

Solomon's temple became the seat of the ark of the covenant, containing the Ten Commandments, which had previously been kept in the City of David in David's palace. At the ceremony marking the presence of the ark in the temple, Solomon, on his knees, with arms stretched heavenward, offered a magnificent prayer, commemorated in 1 Kings 8:23–53:

> LORD God of Israel, there is no God like thee, in heaven above, or on earth beneath, who keepest covenant and mercy with thy servants that walk before thee with all their heart: Who hast kept with thy servant David my father that thou promisedst him: thou spakest also with thy mouth, and hast fulfilled it with thine hand, as it is this day.
>
> Therefore now, LORD God of Israel, keep with thy servant David my father that thou promisedst him, saying, There shall not fail thee a man in my sight to sit on the throne of Israel; so that thy children take heed to their way, that they walk before me as thou hast walked before me.
>
> And now, O God of Israel, let thy word, I pray thee, be verified, which thou spakest unto thy servant David my father.
>
> But will God indeed dwell on the earth? behold, the heaven and heaven of heavens cannot contain thee; how much less this house that I have builded?
>
> Yet have thou respect unto the prayer of thy servant, and to his supplication, O LORD my God, to hearken unto the cry and to the prayer, which thy servant prayeth before thee to day: That thine eyes may be open toward this house night and day, even toward the place of which thou hast said, My name shall be there: that thou mayest hearken unto the prayer which thy servant shall make toward this place. And hearken thou to the supplication of thy servant, and of thy people Israel, when they shall pray toward this place: and hear thou in heaven thy dwelling place: and when thou hearest, forgive.
>
> If any man trespass against his neighbour, and an oath be laid upon him to cause him to swear, and the oath come before

thine altar in this house: then hear thou in heaven, and do, and judge thy servants, condemning the wicked, to bring his way upon his head; and justifying the righteous, to give him according to his righteousness.

When thy people Israel be smitten down before the enemy, because they have sinned against thee, and shall turn again to thee, and confess thy name, and pray, and make supplication unto thee in this house: then hear thou in heaven, and forgive the sin of thy people Israel, and bring them again unto the land which thou gavest unto their fathers.

When heaven is shut up, and there is no rain, because they have sinned against thee; if they pray toward this place, and confess thy name, and turn from their sin, when thou afflictest them: then hear thou in heaven, and forgive the sin of thy servants, and of thy people Israel, that thou teach them the good way wherein they should walk, and give rain upon thy land, which thou hast given to thy people for an inheritance.

If there be in the land famine, if there be pestilence, blasting, mildew, locust, or if there be caterpiller; if their enemy besiege them in the land of their cities; whatsoever plague, whatsoever sickness there be; what prayer and supplication soever be made by any man, or by all thy people Israel, which shall know every man the plague of his own heart, and spread forth his hands toward this house: then hear thou in heaven thy dwelling place, and forgive, and do, and give to every man according to his ways, whose heart thou knowest; (for thou, even thou only, knowest the hearts of all the children of men;) that they may fear thee all the days that they live in the land which thou gavest unto our fathers.

Moreover concerning a stranger, that is not of thy people Israel, but cometh out of a far country for thy name's sake;

(For they shall hear of thy great name, and of thy strong hand, and of thy stretched out arm;) when he shall come and pray toward this house; hear thou in heaven thy dwelling place, and do according to all that the stranger calleth to thee for: that all people of the earth may know thy name, to fear thee, as do thy people Israel; and that they may know that this house, which I have builded, is called by thy name.

If thy people go out to battle against their enemy, whithersoever thou shalt send them, and shall pray unto the LORD toward the city which thou hast chosen, and toward the house that I have built for thy name: then hear thou in heaven their prayer and their supplication, and maintain their cause.

If they sin against thee, (for there is no man that sinneth not,) and thou be angry with them, and deliver them to the enemy, so that they carry them away captives unto the land of the enemy, far or near; yet if they shall bethink themselves in the land whither they were carried captives, and repent, and make supplication unto thee in the land of them that carried them captives, saying, We have sinned, and have done perversely, we have committed wickedness; and so return unto thee with all their heart, and with all their soul, in the land of their enemies, which led them away captive, and pray unto thee toward their land, which thou gavest unto their fathers, the city which thou hast chosen, and the house which I have built for thy name: then hear thou their prayer and their supplication in heaven thy dwelling place, and maintain their cause, and forgive thy people that have sinned against thee, and all their transgressions wherein they have transgressed against thee, and give them compassion before them who carried them captive, that they may have compassion on them: for they be thy people, and thine inheritance, which thou broughtest forth out of Egypt, from the midst of the furnace of iron: that thine eyes may be open unto the supplication of thy servant, and unto the supplication of thy people Israel, to hearken unto them in all that they call for unto thee. For thou didst separate them from among all the people of the earth, to be thine inheritance, as thou spakest by the hand of Moses thy servant, when thou broughtest our fathers out of Egypt, O LORD God.

It was this remarkable prayer that prompted the Lord to speak to Solomon for the second time, His word recorded in 1 Kings 9:3–9:

I have heard thy prayer and thy supplication, that thou hast made before me: I have hallowed this house, which thou hast built, to put my name there for ever; and mine eyes and mine heart shall be there perpetually. And if thou wilt walk before me, as David thy father walked, in integrity of heart, and in uprightness, to do according to all that I have commanded thee, and wilt keep my statutes and my judgments: Then I will establish the throne of thy kingdom upon Israel for ever, as I promised to David thy father, saying, There shall not fail thee a man upon the throne of Israel. But if ye shall at all turn from following me, ye or your children, and will not keep my commandments and my statutes which I have set before you, but go and serve other gods, and worship them: Then will I cut off Israel out of the land which I have given them; and this house, which I have hallowed for my name, will I cast out of my sight; and Israel shall be a proverb and a byword among all people: And at this house, which is high, every one that passeth by it shall be astonished, and shall hiss; and they shall say, Why hath the LORD done thus unto this land, and to this house? And they shall answer, Because they forsook the LORD their God, who brought forth their fathers out of the land of Egypt, and have taken hold upon other gods, and have worshipped them, and served them: therefore hath the LORD brought upon them all this evil.

Solomon accomplished much more in the years to come, but he still had a vulnerability that led to his fall. We learn about it in 1 Kings 11:1–13:

But king Solomon loved many strange women, together with the daughter of Pharaoh, women of the Moabites, Ammonites, Edomites, Zidonians, and Hittites: of the nations concerning which the LORD said unto the children of Israel, Ye shall not go in to them, neither shall they come in unto you: for surely they will turn away your heart after their gods: Solomon clave unto these in love. And he had seven hundred wives, princesses, and three hundred concubines: and his wives turned away his heart. For it came to pass, when Solomon was old, that his wives turned away his heart after other gods: and his heart was not perfect with the LORD his God, as was the heart of David his father. For Solomon went after Ashtoreth the goddess of the Zidonians, and after Milcom the abomination of the Ammonites. And Solomon did evil in the sight of the LORD, and went not fully after the LORD, as did David his father. Then did Solomon build an high place for Chemosh, the abomination of Moab, in the hill that is before Jerusalem, and for Molech, the abomination of the children of Ammon. And likewise did he for all his strange wives, which burnt incense and sacrificed unto their gods. And the LORD was angry with Solomon, because his heart was turned from the LORD God of Israel, which had appeared unto him twice, and had commanded him concerning this thing, that he should not go after other gods: but he kept not that which the Lord commanded. Wherefore the LORD said unto Solomon, Forasmuch as this is done of thee, and thou hast not kept my covenant and my statutes, which I have commanded thee, I will surely rend the kingdom from thee, and will give it to thy servant. Notwithstanding in thy days I will not do it for David thy father's sake: but I will rend it out of the hand of thy son. Howbeit I will not rend away all the kingdom; but will give one tribe to thy son for David my servant's sake, and for Jerusalem's sake which I have chosen.

How could the wisest man on the planet, who had communicated directly with the God of the universe, have chosen so poorly? How could he go from offering such a heartfelt prayer of thanksgiving to the Lord, and then chase after other gods? This is what happens when we allow ourselves to be led into temptation. As a result, the kingdom would be divided. Never again, until the restoration to be brought about in the future by Jesus, will Israel experience the peace, prosperity, and justice of Solomon's reign. Good kings would follow. Bad kings would follow. There would be peace and there would be war. But the kingdom would not achieve and has not achieved the heights of glory and splendor established during Solomon's time to this day.

While Solomon's rule set the standard for the zenith of the Israel's kingdom, we meet another king in this book, Ahab, who represented the nadir. His weakness, too, was female temptation. In his case, just one particular woman: Jezebel. But before we get there, let's explore the amazingly heroic character Elijah—a man who never sees death, is discussed in all four Gospel accounts, and shows up with Moses on a mountaintop to meet with Jesus, as witnessed by two apostles and chronicled in the books of Matthew and Mark.

Elijah is compared in the Gospels with John the Baptist. In addition, Elijah, we're told by the prophet Malachi, will play yet another key, future role in the restoration of all things when God sends him back to earth before "the coming of the great and dreadful day of the LORD," when "he shall turn the heart of the fathers to the children, and the heart of the children to their fathers, lest [God] come and smite the earth with a curse" (Malachi 4:5–6).

Elijah was a prophet who lived in complete obedience to the Lord and fully trusted Him. As a faithful servant living in a time of judgment, drought, and famine for Israel, he recognized that God sets the times and places for His showdowns with evil. Elijah was instructed to hide east of the Jordan, where he would live by faith with miraculous sustenance provided by ravens by a brook. Once the brook dried up, he was instructed to visit widow in Zarephath who, God assured him, would provide food and shelter.

When he arrived in Zarephath, hungry and thirsty, the widow had nothing. In fact, she and her son were preparing to eat their last meager meal before becoming victims of the famine. She told Elijah,

"As the LORD thy God liveth, I have not a cake, but an handful of meal in a barrel, and a little oil in a cruse: and, behold, I am gathering two sticks, that I may go in and dress it for me and my son, that we may eat it, and die" (1 Kings 17:12).

The man of faith assured the widow that the grain she had left would last until the end of the drought and famine and told her to go ahead and make the meal—for him. We learn from the rest of her story that because of her obedience, God multiplied her meal and her oil, feeding her and her son until the famine was over. Interestingly, we see Jesus in the gospel accounts feeding multitudes with a few fish and loaves of bread.

Later, the widow's son became sick and died. She then said to Elijah in 1 Kings: 17:18: "What have I to do with thee, O thou man of God? art thou come unto me to call my sin to remembrance, and to slay my son?" Through prayer, Elijah raised the son from death, foreshadowing yet another of the miracles performed by Jesus. But there is one particularly striking parallel between this story and the story found in Luke 7:11–14. There Jesus had compassion for a widow in Capernaum whose son had died and was being carried out of the town for burial. Jesus told the widow not to weep. Then He touched the bier upon which the dead man was being carried and said, "Young man, I say unto thee, Arise. And he that was dead sat up, and began to speak. And he [Jesus] delivered him to his mother." And that's exactly what Elijah did in 1 Kings 17:23—he not only raised the dead son; he delivered him to his mother.

Then came Elijah's call from the Lord to confront Ahab, the most wicked king of Israel who, with his wife, Jezebel, served the pagan gods Baal and Asherah. Elijah told Ahab to gather the 450 prophets of Baal and the 400 prophets of Asherah for a challenge on Mount Carmel before all the people to determine whose god is real.

In 1 Kings 18:21, Elijah said to the multitude gathered for the spectacle: "How long halt ye between two opinions? if the LORD be God, follow him: but if Baal, then follow him. And the people answered him not a word."

A sacrifice was prepared, but no fire was to be kindled. The pagan prophets were challenged to call on their gods to provide the fire. They called on their gods from early morning until noon without even a puff of smoke to encourage them. They continued through the rest of the day, cutting themselves in desperation, shouting for their gods to act, all to no avail.

Then it was Elijah's turn. He prepared his own altar, and his own sacrifice. Then he soaked the wood three times with water, so there could be no chance of any coincidental spontaneous combustion. At last, he called on the Lord: "LORD God of Abraham, Isaac, and of Israel, let it be known this day that thou art God in Israel, and that I am thy servant, and that I have done all these things at thy word. Hear me, O LORD, hear me, that this people may know that thou art the LORD God, and that thou hast turned their heart back again" (I Kings 18:36–37).

Fire came down from heaven and consumed the sacrifice, as well as all the water in the trenches around it. Now the people had proof whose god was real. They captured all the false prophets and killed them.

But what about Ahab, the evilest king in Israel's history, according to 1 Kings 21:25–26? Jezebel, who had turned Ahab's heart to false gods, was eaten by dogs. But God spared Ahab. Why? Because when confronted by God with all he had done, Ahab humbled himself (1 Kings 21:29).

God respects repentance, as we're told in 2 Corinthians 7:10. He respected it when King David did evil in his sight. And He respected it despite Ahab's abominable betrayals. It's that simple act of repentance that Jesus preached unceasingly throughout His earthly ministry, Repentance unto salvation is found all over the Gospels. But it is found throughout the Old Testament as well—even in the extreme example of Ahab.

12

THE GOSPEL IN II KINGS

And he answered, Fear not: for they that be with us are more than they that be with them. —2 KINGS 6:16

For so it was, that the children of Israel had sinned against the LORD their God, which had brought them up out of the land of Egypt, from under the hand of Pharaoh king of Egypt, and had feared other gods, and walked in the statutes of the heathen, whom the LORD cast out from before the children of Israel, and of the kings of Israel, which they had made. —2 KINGS 17:7–8

ONE MIGHT EXPECT after Elijah's demonstration of the total power of the one true God on Mount Carmel that Israel would run from idolatry and false gods. Unfortunately, that wasn't the case.

The mostly tragic story of 2 Kings is the pattern of rulers in both the northern kingdom of Israel and the southern kingdom of

Judah doing what the writers of 1 and 2 Kings referred to as "evil in the sight of the Lord"—that is, worshipping other gods, accommodating them, compromising with them, and failing to turn away from them with their hearts to devote themselves to the Creator of all things. (See, for example 1 Kings 11:6; 14:22; 15:26, 34; and 2 Kings 3:2). It's a long history of rebellion against God, with exceptional, but spectacular, moments of miraculous victory when rulers and prophets responded in faithfulness. Ultimately, though, this book ends with both kingdoms in exile.

What might that sweeping, mostly bleak historical panorama have to do with the gospel of truth, hope, and redemption? Think about it. Israel died for its sins in 2 Kings. Both kingdoms, Israel and Judah, were destroyed for their overwhelming serial rejection of God over generations. By contrast, the gospels of Matthew, Mark, Luke, and John tell the story of the long-promised Messiah coming and dying in the place of the reconstituted nation of Israel, offering salvation and ultimate restoration to the remnant—Jew and Gentile alike—who would return to God's covenant.

Meanwhile, within the framework of some 265 years, we see triumphs of faith that parallel those detailed in the New Testament books—from Elijah to Elisha to the Shunamite woman of faith to Naaman, to Hezekiah and Josiah.

In the opening verses of chapter 1, we meet, once again, the mysterious Elijah the Tishbite, one of the epic stars of 1 Kings. Elijah was, without doubt, one of the most interesting characters and prophets in the Bible—and one of the most enigmatic.

If you doubt me, identify from which Hebrew tribe he came. Tell me who his parents were, what his lineage was. He springs upon the scene in 1 Kings 17:1, identified only as "Elijah the Tishbite, who was of the inhabitants of Gilead."

What is a Tishbite? There's much debate about that.

Some biblical scholars suggest a Tishbite was someone from Tishbe who lived in Gilead. Others suggest a Tishbite was a "stranger," meaning a sojourner, a non-Hebrew who lived among the Hebrews, adopting the covenant and walking in obedience to the Torah. But in the Bible, the word "Tishbite" is only associated with Elijah. So, where was Tishbe? It was thought to be in Upper Galilee, though the historian Josephus, in *Antiquities of the Jews*, suggests it was in Gilead (8:13, 2). Others associate the name Tishbe with el-Ishtib, a place south of the Sea of Galilee. Where was Gilead? It was on the east side of the Jordan and associated with the tribes of Manasseh, Gad, and Reuben.

So add up the mysteries:

- Was Elijah from Tishbe or el-Ishtib?

- Did "Tishbite" refer to someone born in Tishbe or el-Ishtib, or to a stranger?

- Did Elijah belong to a specific tribe?

- What was his lineage?

These details may not be important to casual readers of the Bible, but Elijah is a very significant character in both the Hebrew and Greek scriptures, as you will see. He plays a major, ongoing role. The mysteries surrounding him continued through Jesus' time and will linger into the future kingdom of God. And the mysteries about his genealogy make him all the more interesting and enigmatic.

Think about it. The pedigrees of major biblical characters are usually well established. Noah, Abraham, Jacob, Moses, Samuel, David, Jesus—there's a tremendous amount of detail about their family histories and where they came from. Not so with Elijah. Why the mystery? Could it be that he was, indeed, a sojourner—someone like Abraham, who was called by God out of the pagan world?

Whatever the case, he burst upon the scene in the time of the wicked King Ahab and Queen Jezebel to call them to account for their evil, which included forsaking the commandments, killing the prophets of God, and communing with the prophets of Baal.

Elijah raised the dead. He judged the prophets of Baal. He was whisked from the earth in a whirlwind.

Later, we hear about the mysterious man at the end of the book of Malachi, the last book of the Hebrew Scriptures, where we are told: "Remember ye the law of Moses my servant, which I commanded unto him in Horeb for all Israel, with the statutes and judgments. Behold, I will send you Elijah the prophet before the coming of the great and dreadful day of the Lord: And he shall turn the heart of the fathers to the children, and the heart of the children to their fathers, lest I come and smite the earth with a curse" (4:4–6).

It seems Elijah is to have a pivotal role in the coming of the Messiah, specifically in reminding a future generation of the importance of the law of Moses.

Lo and behold, in the Gospels, as mentioned earlier, John the Baptist is directly compared by Jesus with Elijah (Matthew 11:14). And some in Israel believed Jesus Himself to be Elijah or Jeremiah or one of the other prophets (Matthew 16:13–14; Mark 6:14–15; 8:27–28; Luke 9:18–19). Then, later, when Jesus took Peter, James, and John to a high mountain and they witnessed what we call "the transfiguration," Moses and Elijah were there with them (Matthew 17:1–3; Mark 9:2–4).

But Jesus tells us something else about Elijah. When asked why the scribes said that Elijah must come first, before the Redeemer, He answered in Matthew 17:11: "Elijah truly shall first come, and restore all things."

Hear that? *Restore all things.* That's a very big future role in the kingdom for Elijah. For more on how he will do that, see my book, *The Restitution of All Things.*

In the opening verses of 2 Kings, we're told that Moab rebelled against Israel after the death of the wicked king Ahab. The new king, Ahaziah, meanwhile, fell down in his palace and was concerned about whether he would recover. Did he ask God or consult one of His prophets? No, he sent his messengers to inquire of "Baalzebub the god of Ekron" (1:2).

An angel of the Lord then told Elijah, "Arise, go up to meet the messengers of the king of Samaria, and say unto them, Is it not because there is not a God in Israel, that ye go to enquire of Baalzebub the god of Ekron?" (v. 3). The angel then informed Elijah that the king was not going to make it.

Before the king's messengers had a chance to consult their false god, they ran into Elijah, who gave them the bad news just before they entered the king's chambers. When they stood by the king's bedside, Ahaziah wondered why his messengers were back so fast. They explained that they had encountered a man who gave them the grim message that he was going to die. "What manner of man was he?" the king asked.

"He was an hairy man, and girt with a girdle of leather about his loins," they said. "And he said, It is Elijah the Tishbite" (vv. 7–8).

So, the king summoned one of his captains with fifty men to bring Elijah to meet with him. Elijah's response was to bring fire down from heaven to consume them. So the king dispatched another captain with fifty men to summon Elijah. They met with the same fate. Once again, the king sent another captain with fifty men. But this time, the third captain begged Elijah for his life, falling on his knees and saying to him: "O man of God, I pray thee, let my life, and the life of these fifty thy servants, be precious in thy sight." And this time, the angel of the Lord told Elijah, "Go down with him: be not afraid of him. And he arose, and went down with him unto the king" to deliver the bad news in person (vv. 13, 15).

"Thus saith the LORD," Elijah said to Ahaziah. "Forasmuch as thou hast sent messengers to enquire of Baalzebub the god of Ekron, is it not because there is no God in Israel to enquire of his word? therefore thou shalt not come down off that bed on which thou art gone up, but shalt surely die." And so, Ahaziah died (vv. 16–17).

It's an interesting story and, no doubt, one with which Jesus' closest followers were familiar. We read in Luke 9:51–56 about a time when they were traveling to Jerusalem and were not well received in a village of Samaritans. "And when his disciples James and John saw this, they said, Lord, wilt thou that we command fire to come down from heaven, and consume them, even as Elias [Elijah] did? But he turned, and rebuked them, and said, Ye know not what manner of spirit ye are of. For the Son of man is not come to destroy men's lives, but to save them. And they went to another village."

Elijah, you see, lived in a time of judgment. Jesus came in time of offering salvation and mercy. Of course, the prophetic Scriptures are clear that He will come again in a time of judgment to usher in His kingdom. And Elijah will come first, just as John the Baptist did, presaging Jesus' earthly ministry.

Again, Elijah is notable for, among other things, being one of the few people mentioned in the Bible who flew through the sky. He was taken up "by a whirlwind into heaven" (2 Kings 2:11) Before this happened, however, his "mantle," both physical and spiritual, was given to a successor, Elisha. Aware of what was about to happen, Elisha clung to Elijah, allowing him to witness more miracles and request of Elijah a double portion of the spirit God had given him.

Thus, Elisha inherited Elijah's position as the leading prophet of his time—full of faith, power, and zeal—performing many miracles, some similar to what we see in the Gospels:

- In 2 Kings 4:1–7, we meet a widow in distress because her prophet-husband had died, leaving her with nothing. Her two sons faced becoming bondmen as a result. Elisha instructed her to take her only possession, a pot of oil, and pour it into as many vessels as she could gather from her neighbors. The oil was multiplied exponentially, just as we saw Jesus multiply loaves and fishes and turn water to wine (Matthew 14:13–21; Mark 8:1–9). The widow was able to pay her debt and live with her sons. And in 2 Kings 4:42–44, Elisha actually multiplied food, as Jesus would later do.

- In 2 Kings 4:8–37, we meet another woman of faith, a Shunammite, who provided food to Elisha whenever he came to her town. Recognizing Elisha as a "holy man of God," she prevailed upon her husband to provide for him a bed, a table, a stool, and a candlestick—a suitable resting place for Elisha, so he would no longer just pass by. Elisha asked her what he could do for her in return. She suggested that nothing was necessary. But Elisha learned she was childless. Thus, Elisha promised her a son, and it came to pass. When the child was grown, though, he became ill and died. In faith, the mother summoned Elisha, who resurrected the dead child, presaging similar miracles performed by Jesus in the Gospels (see Mark 5:21-43; Luke 7:11–17).

And then there is the powerful story of Naaman in 2 Kings 5.

Naaman was the second in command after the king in Syria. The Bible calls him a "great man," "honourable," and "a mighty man of valor." We're also told that because of Naaman, "the LORD had given deliverance to Syria." But he also had the disease of leprosy (v. 1).

We're next told about a little girl from Israel who found herself serving Naaman's wife. This "little maid" from Israel turned out to be an important player in this drama. It was she who suggested that Naaman could be cured of leprosy if he would see the prophet Elisha (vv. 2–3).

When Naaman arrived at Elisha's house, the prophet sent a messenger with this prescription: "Go and wash in Jordan seven times, and thy flesh shall come again to thee, and thou shalt be clean" (v. 10).

Naaman was angry that Elisha didn't come out personally to see him. And he had doubts about following the advice that would cure him, suggesting that the rivers of Damascus were better than the waters of Israel. But Naaman's servants interceded, persuading him that he had nothing to lose.

When Naaman had dipped himself in the Jordan seven times, his flesh became clean. He returned to Elisha and said: "Behold, now I know that there is no God in all the earth, but in Israel: now therefore, I pray thee, take a blessing of thy servant" (v. 15). Naaman was offering a great reward. But Elisha would not accept it. Naaman then made something of a pledge of faith: "Thy servant will henceforth offer neither burnt offering nor sacrifice unto other gods, but unto the LORD. In this thing the LORD pardon thy servant, that when my master goeth into the house of Rimmon to worship there, and he leaneth on my hand, and I bow myself in the house of Rimmon: when I bow down myself in the house of Rimmon, the LORD pardon thy servant in this thing" (vv. 17–18).

Naaman was an extraordinary case, as Jesus Himself reminds us in Luke 4:27, saying, "And many lepers were in Israel in the time of Eliseus [Elisha] the prophet; and none of them was cleansed, saving Naaman the Syrian."

In Matthew 8, we learn of a man cured of leprosy by Jesus. But the Lord didn't tell him to bathe in the Jordan seven times. Instead he simply said, "Be thou clean" (v. 3). That's probably what Naaman was expecting to hear. Interestingly, this New Testament story is immediately followed by one with remarkable similarities to the story of Naaman. It's the story of a Roman centurion who asked Jesus to heal his servant who was sick with palsy. Jesus offered to go and heal him. But the soldier responded differently than Naaman: "Lord, I am not worthy that thou shouldest come under my roof: but speak the word only, and my servant shall be healed. For I am a man under authority, having soldiers under me: and I say to this man, Go, and he goeth; and to another, Come, and he cometh; and to my servant, Do this, and he doeth it."

Jesus marveled at these words and proclaimed, "Verily I say unto you, I have not found so great faith, no, not in Israel" (Matthew 8:7–10).

What's the common denominator in these two stories? Outsiders. In both stories, Gentiles—non-Jews, non-Hebrews, non-Israelis— were coming to faith in the God of Israel long before the apostles would figure out that the long-awaited Messiah had come to offer salvation to the whole world—even Gentiles.

Salvation to all people wasn't a completely new idea in the New Testament. It was first introduced in the Hebrew Scriptures. And it's a significant component of what we know as *the gospel*.

13

THE GOSPEL IN 1 CHRONICLES

Then shall the trees of the wood sing out at the presence of the LORD, because
he cometh to judge the earth. —1 CHRONICLES 16:33

Thine, O LORD is the greatness, and the power, and the glory, and the victory,
and the majesty: for all that is in the heaven and in the earth is thine; thine
is the kingdom, O LORD, and thou art exalted as head above all.
—1 CHRONICLES 29:11

WRITTEN ABOUT 450 YEARS BEFORE the birth of the Messiah, this historical book covers the same periods as the books of Samuel and the books of Kings. The two books of Chronicles focus more attention on the priesthood, with 1 Chronicles written after the exile to assist those returning to Israel in understanding how to worship God.

The book is full of genealogical detail from Adam through the sons of Jacob-Israel, with special attention paid to the descendants of Judah, through which David and the coming Messiah would be born. In fact, the theme of 1 Chronicles is thoroughly gospel-like in the pattern that it unveils—sin, repentance, forgiveness, restoration.

Perhaps one of the most familiar elements Christians will find in this book if they haven't visited it recently are the two verses that led to one of the biggest blockbuster books in Christian publishing history, *The Prayer of Jabez*. By reading two verses, 1 Chronicles 4:9–10, I believe you will learn everything you need to know about this honorable Bible character and his one- sentence prayer for blessing that was granted by a sovereign and merciful God: "And Jabez was more honourable than his brethren: and his mother called his name Jabez, saying, Because I bare him with sorrow. And Jabez called on the God of Israel, saying, Oh that thou wouldest bless me indeed, and enlarge my coast, and that thine hand might be with me, and that thou wouldest keep me from evil, that it may not grieve me! And God granted him that which he requested."

This prayer is worth reading, indeed. It's worth reflection and study, as is everything, jot and tittle, in Scripture. But it is not a magical incantation we are to invoke for blessings for ourselves. God frowns on formulaic prayers for personal prosperity, and there is no evidence to suggest the 9 million people who bought the book have enlarged their financial portfolios as a result.

My advice? If you really want to be blessed, read all of Scripture, regularly and in context. That means the Old Testament, or Tanakh, as it is more properly known in the Hebrew and Greek Scriptures. Study it. This practice may not bring riches in this world, but it will surely give you hope that God is firmly in control and will prepare your heart and mind for what awaits us in the next. Perhaps even more importantly, it will allow you to share the most valuable good news of salvation, redemption, and restoration ever revealed to humankind with those you love, strangers and enemies alike. That's why I wrote this book, as a simple introduction to how the Hebrew and Greek Scriptures represent one totally integrated, inerrant book with a common theme inspired by the same, unchanging Creator.

Does that mean the gospel can be found in 1 Chronicles, along with every other book in Hebrew Scripture? Yes, I believe it does. Just read through 1 Chronicles 16:6–36 and appreciate David's psalm of thanksgiving after bringing the ark of the covenant to the City of David. It's a song we could and should be singing still in the twenty-first century as a timeless praise to the Lord:

> Give thanks unto the LORD, call upon his name, make known his deeds among the people. Sing unto him, sing psalms unto him, talk ye of all his wondrous works. Glory ye in his holy name: let the heart of them rejoice that seek the LORD. Seek the LORD and his strength, seek his face continually. Remember his marvellous works that he hath done, his wonders, and the judgments of his mouth; O ye seed of Israel his servant, ye children of Jacob, his chosen ones. He is the LORD our God; his judgments are in all the earth. Be ye mindful always of his covenant; the word which he commanded to a thousand generations; Even of the covenant which he made with Abraham, and of his oath unto Isaac; and hath confirmed the same to Jacob for a law, and to Israel for an everlasting covenant, saying, Unto thee will I give the land of Canaan, the lot of your inheritance; when ye were but few, even a few, and strangers in it. And when they went from nation to nation, and from one kingdom to another people; he suffered no man to do them wrong: yea, he reproved kings for their sakes, saying, Touch not mine anointed, and do my prophets no harm. Sing unto the LORD, all the earth; shew forth from day to day his salvation. Declare his glory among the heathen; his marvellous works among all nations. For great is the LORD, and greatly to be praised: he also is to be feared above all gods. For all the gods of the people are idols: but the LORD made the heavens. Glory and honour are in his presence; strength and gladness are in his place. Give unto the LORD, ye kindreds of the people, give unto the LORD glory and strength. Give unto the LORD the glory due

unto his name: bring an offering, and come before him: worship the LORD in the beauty of holiness. Fear before him, all the earth: the world also shall be stable, that it be not moved. Let the heavens be glad, and let the earth rejoice: and let men say among the nations, The LORD reigneth. Let the sea roar, and the fulness thereof: let the fields rejoice, and all that is therein. Then shall the trees of the wood sing out at the presence of the LORD, because he cometh to judge the earth. O give thanks unto the LORD; for he is good; for his mercy endureth for ever. And say ye, Save us, O God of our salvation, and gather us together, and deliver us from the heathen, that we may give thanks to thy holy name, and glory in thy praise. Blessed be the LORD God of Israel for ever and ever.

Here David spoke of things we still speak about today: the day the Lord returns to judge the earth and establish His kingdom upon David's throne, foreshadowing Jesus' own words in Matthew 25. Is it any wonder, despite all of David's faults, that God found him to be a man after His own heart, full of love for the Lord and the spirit of repentance? We see this again in 1 Chronicles 21:13, after Satan tempted David to call for a census of the nation of Israel, probably as a matter of pride as a military leader who was vanquishing his enemies. God gave David a choice of punishments—one in which his enemies would, for a short time, exact vengeance, and another at the hands of the Lord. David chose the latter: "Let me fall now into the hand of the LORD; for very great are his mercies: but let me not fall into the hand of man" (1 Chronicles 21:13). He showed great wisdom and trust, as well as a penitent heart.

Maybe you don't see the direct connection between you, a modern-day Christian, living more than two thousand years after the first coming of the Messiah, and the nation of Israel in ancient times. But understand that we, believers and followers of Jesus, are part of Israel too. We are coheirs with messianic Jews of the past and future. It's through the adoption into that congregation of promise, made possible by Jesus' sacrifice on the cross and victory through resurrection, that we experience this new citizenship. As Paul wrote in Romans 11, we are like branches grafted in to that good olive tree, which represents the nation of Israel and whose roots and trunk represent Jesus the Messiah. With Israel back in the land after an absence of two millennia, it shouldn't be so hard for us to understand.

Now, let's focus on chapter 17, which reiterates the Davidic covenant, which we know will be literally fulfilled by the return of the Messiah, a miraculous descendant of Israel's second king, being both a Son of David and a father to Him. In 1 Chronicles 17:11–14, the prophet Nathan quotes the Lord in telling David what is to come after his death. This prophecy applies perfectly to both the immediate future, in which Solomon would take the throne, and the future when Jesus will assume it:

> And it shall come to pass, when thy days be expired that thou must go to be with thy fathers, that I will raise up thy seed after thee, which shall be of thy sons; and I will establish his kingdom. He shall build me an house, and I will stablish his throne for ever. I will be his father, and he shall be my son: and I will not take my mercy away from him, as I took it from him that was before thee: But I will settle him in mine house and in my kingdom for ever: and his throne shall be established for evermore.

It's the gospel of the kingdom—the great hope, the restitution of all things, about which all the prophets spoke since creation (Acts 3:21).

If you are still having trouble relating to this gospel of 1 Chronicles, turn with me in conclusion to 29:11–15. It's a prayer of thanksgiving and awe-inspiring love by David that foreshadows commonalities found in the Lord's Prayer in Matthew 6:

> Thine, O Lord is the greatness, and the power, and the glory, and the victory, and the majesty: for all that is in the heaven and

in the earth is thine; thine is the kingdom, O LORD, and thou art exalted as head above all. Both riches and honour come of thee, and thou reignest over all; and in thine hand is power and might; and in thine hand it is to make great, and to give strength unto all. Now therefore, our God, we thank thee, and praise thy glorious name. But who am I, and what is my people, that we should be able to offer so willingly after this sort? for all things come of thee, and of thine own have we given thee. For we are strangers before thee, and sojourners, as were all our fathers: our days on the earth are as a shadow, and there is none abiding.

Who in the world today cannot relate to this unmistakable and unambiguous kingdom message? After all, we're all sojourners on this earth. Ultimately, it matters not where we live or from whom we descended. The Lord chose Israel to deliver the oracles of truth and faith in God to the entire world. And they have done so, despite many stumbles. All that remains is for unbelieving Israel to call on the name of the Lord in an hour of great distress, crying, "Blessed is he that cometh in the name of the Lord" (Luke 13:35). Then He will return to deliver the entire world its lasting redemption and restoration.

14

THE GOSPEL IN II CHRONICLES

If my people, which are called by my name, shall humble themselves, and pray, and seek my face, and turn from their wicked ways; then will I hear from heaven, and will forgive their sin, and will heal their land.
—2 CHRONICLES 7:14

READING THE HISTORY OF ISRAEL through its kings is often not very uplifting.

There are exceptions, of course. But to deny there were more ungodly Israeli monarchs than godly ones would be an oversight.

It can also be frustrating because very few consistently sought God, while some of the most promising eventually fell far short of the mark.

None fell further and harder than David's son Solomon—a deep and total story of moral collapse not actually told in this book, whose first nine chapters focuses exclusively on the glorious aspect of his 40-year reign.

Those chapters, representing more than a quarter of the book, offer perhaps the most vivid glimpse of what the future kingdom of God of earth might be like.

As we all know, Solomon got off to a great start.

2 Chronicles 1: "And Solomon the son of David was strengthened in his kingdom, and the Lord his God was with him, and magnified him exceedingly."

God was him. And He was with God. And God spoke to Solomon, as He did with his father David, a man after God's own heart. God invited him to ask for a gift.

Solomon responded in verses 8–10: "Thou hast shewed great mercy unto David my father, and hast made me to reign in his stead. Now, O Lord God, let thy promise unto David my father be established: for thou hast made me king over a people like the dust of the earth in multitude.

Give me now wisdom and knowledge, that I may go out and come in before this people: for who can judge this thy people, that is so great?"

And God responded: "Because this was in thine heart, and thou hast not asked riches, wealth, or honour, nor the life of thine enemies, neither yet hast asked long life; but hast asked wisdom and knowledge for thyself, that thou mayest judge my people, over whom I have made thee king: Wisdom and knowledge is granted unto thee; and I will give thee riches, and wealth, and honour, such as none of the kings have had that have been before thee, neither shall there any after thee have the like."

Solomon uses his wisdom, his wealth and his honor to build the magnificent Temple as a place worthy of God's spirit to reside with His people. He assembles all of the people for the dedication, offering a stirring invocation. The entirety, found in 2 Chronicles 6–7 represents something of a model prayer of humility, supplication and petition for us even today. Here are some key excerpts with added emphasis:

The Lord hath said that he would dwell in the thick darkness.

But I have built an house of habitation for thee, and a place for thy dwelling for ever.

And the king turned his face, and blessed the whole congregation of Israel: and all the congregation of Israel stood.

And he said, **Blessed be the Lord God of Israel**, who hath with his hands fulfilled that which he spake with his mouth to my father David, saying,

Since the day that I brought forth my people out of the land of Egypt I chose no city among all the tribes of Israel to build an house in, that my name might be there; **neither chose I any man to be a ruler over my people Israel**:

But I have chosen Jerusalem, that my name might be there; and have chosen David to be over my people Israel.

Now it was in the heart of David my father to build an house for the name of the Lord God of Israel.

But the Lord said to David my father, Forasmuch as it was in thine heart to build an house for my name, thou didst well in that it was in thine heart:

Notwithstanding thou shalt not build the house; but thy son which shall come forth out of thy loins, he shall build the house for my name.

The Lord therefore hath performed his word that he hath spoken: for I am risen up in the room of David my father, and am set on the throne of Israel, as the Lord promised, and have built the house for the name of the Lord God of Israel.

And in it have I put the ark, wherein is the covenant of the Lord, that he made with the children of Israel.

And he stood before the altar of the Lord in the presence of all the congregation of Israel, and spread forth his hands:

For Solomon had made a brasen scaffold of five cubits long, and five cubits broad, and three cubits high, and had set it in the midst of the court: and upon it he stood, and kneeled down upon his knees before all the congregation of Israel, and spread forth his hands toward heaven.

O Lord God of Israel, there is no God like thee in the heaven, nor in the earth; which keepest covenant, and shewest mercy unto thy servants, that walk before thee with all their hearts: Thou which hast kept with thy servant David my father that which thou hast promised him; and spakest with thy mouth, and hast fulfilled it with thine hand, as it is this day.

Now therefore, O LORD God of Israel, keep with thy servant David my father that which thou hast promised him, saying, There shall not fail thee a man in my sight to sit upon the throne of Israel; yet so that thy children take heed to their way to walk in my law, as thou hast walked before me.

Now then, O LORD God of Israel, let thy word be verified, which thou hast spoken unto thy servant David.

But will God in very deed dwell with men on the earth? behold, heaven and the heaven of heavens cannot contain thee; how much less this house which I have built!

Have respect therefore to the prayer of thy servant, and to his supplication, O LORD my God, to hearken unto the cry and the prayer which thy servant prayeth before thee: that thine eyes may be open upon this house day and night, upon the place whereof thou hast said that thou wouldest put thy name there; to hearken unto the prayer which thy servant prayeth toward this place.

Hearken therefore unto the supplications of thy servant, and of thy people Israel, which they shall make toward this place: hear thou from thy dwelling place, even from heaven; and when thou hearest, forgive.

If a man sin against his neighbour, and an oath be laid upon him to make him swear, and the oath come before thine altar in this house; then hear thou from heaven, and do, and judge thy servants, by requiting the wicked, by recompensing his way upon his own head; and by justifying the righteous, by giving him according to his righteousness.

And if thy people Israel be put to the worse before the enemy, because they have sinned against thee; and shall return and confess thy name and pray and make supplication before thee in this house; then hear thou from the heavens, and forgive the sin of thy people Israel, and bring them again unto the land which thou gavest to them and to their fathers.

When the heaven is shut up, and there is no rain, because they have sinned against thee; yet if they pray toward this place, and confess thy name, and turn from their sin, when thou dost afflict them; then hear thou from heaven, and forgive the sin of thy servants, and of thy people Israel, when thou hast taught them the good way, wherein they should walk; and send rain upon thy land, which thou hast given unto thy people for an inheritance.

If there be dearth in the land, if there be pestilence, if there be blasting, or mildew, locusts, or caterpillers; if their enemies besiege them in the cities of their land; whatsoever sore or what-soever sickness there be: then what prayer or what supplication soever shall be made of any man, or of all thy people Israel, when every one shall know his own sore and his own grief, and shall spread forth his hands in this house: then hear thou from heaven thy dwelling place, and forgive, and render unto every man according unto all his ways, whose heart thou knowest; (for thou only knowest the hearts of the children of men:) that they may fear thee, to walk in thy ways, so long as they live in the land which thou gavest unto our fathers.

Moreover concerning the stranger, which is not of thy people Israel, but is come from a far country for thy great name's sake, and thy mighty hand, and thy stretched out arm; if they come and pray in this house; then hear thou from the heavens, even from thy dwelling place, and do according to all that the stranger calleth to thee for; that all people of the earth may know thy name, and fear thee, as doth thy people Israel, and may know that this house which I have built is called by thy name.

If thy people go out to war against their enemies by the way that thou shalt send them, and they pray unto thee toward this city which thou hast chosen, and the house which I have built for thy name; then hear thou from the heavens their prayer and their supplication, and maintain their cause.

If they sin against thee, (for there is no man which sinneth not,) and thou be angry with them, and deliver them over before their enemies, and they carry them away captives unto a land far off or near; yet if they bethink themselves in the land whither they are carried captive, and turn and pray unto thee in the land of their captivity, saying, We have sinned, we have done amiss, and have dealt wickedly; if they return to thee with all their heart and with all their soul in the land of their captivity, whither they have carried them captives, and pray toward their land, which thou gavest unto their fathers, and toward the city which thou hast chosen, and toward the house which I have built for thy name: then hear thou from the heavens, even from thy dwelling place, their prayer and their supplications, and maintain their cause, and forgive thy people which have sinned against thee.

Now, my God, let, I beseech thee, thine eyes be open, and let thine ears be attent unto the prayer that is made in this place.

Now therefore arise, O LORD God, into thy resting place, thou, and the ark of thy strength: let thy priests, O LORD God, be clothed with salvation, and let thy saints rejoice in goodness.

O LORD God, turn not away the face of thine anointed: remember the mercies of David thy servant. (2 Chronicles 6:1–42)

It's a mighty prayer, one clearly uttered by a man familiar with the Torah and its warnings. It's also one that demonstrates a knowledge of what God requires: complete obedience. It also reveals a knowledge of God's mercy and His willingness—even eagerness—to accept repentance and bestow grace upon His children when they stumble.

In other words, it's a message with overtures of the good news. Such is the book of 2 Chronicles.

And how did God respond? At the conclusion of Solomon's heartfelt and inspired prayer, God sent down fire to consume the offering, and His presence filled the temple.

Later, following the spectacular service, God appeared to Solomon again, offering a blessing and words of caution:

I have heard thy prayer, and have chosen this place to myself for an house of sacrifice.

If I shut up heaven that there be no rain, or if I command the locusts to devour the land, or if I send pestilence among my people; if my people, which are called by my name, shall humble themselves, and pray, and seek my face, and turn from their wicked ways; then will I hear from heaven, and will forgive their sin, and will heal their land.

Now mine eyes shall be open, and mine ears attent unto the prayer that is made in this place.

For now have I chosen and sanctified this house, that my name may be there for ever: and mine eyes and mine heart shall be there perpetually.

And as for thee, if thou wilt walk before me, as David thy father walked, and do according to all that I have commanded thee, and shalt observe my statutes and my judgments; then will I stablish the throne of thy kingdom, according as I have covenanted with David thy father, saying, There shall not fail thee a man to be ruler in Israel.

But if ye turn away, and forsake my statutes and my commandments, which I have set before you, and shall go and serve other gods, and worship them; then will I pluck them up by the roots out of my land which I have given them; and this house, which I have sanctified for my name, will I cast out of my sight, and will make it to be a proverb and a byword among all nations.

And this house, which is high, shall be an astonishment to

every one that passeth by it; so that he shall say, Why hath the Lord done thus unto this land, and unto this house?

And it shall be answered, Because they forsook the LORD God of their fathers, which brought them forth out of the land of Egypt, and laid hold on other gods, and worshipped them, and served them: therefore hath he brought all this evil upon them. (7:12–22)

Of course, we know what happened. Not only did Israel turn away from God, break His commandments, and even worship other gods; so did Solomon, despite all his wisdom and other blessings. He reigned for forty years as king and was succeeded by his son Rehoboam. Then the kingdom was divided.

Judah had a succession of good kings and bad kings, as did Israel. It seems that something was lacking. And we know that *something* was the Redeemer and the outpouring of the Holy Spirit that He brought—the very essence of the long-awaited good news.

But study this prayer by Solomon and the Lord's response. It reveals to us what God had shown about Himself all along:

- that He required obedience as a demonstration of our love for Him—as He does today. (John 14:15)

- that He alone offers perfect justice, forgiveness for the truly repentant, and blessings for the righteous (Matthew 9:13)

- that He intends for all the nations to know His name and to provide a light to the Gentiles and glory to Israel

There's good news and mercy aplenty here in the book of 2 Chronicles. It brings to mind Romans 3:23–26: "For all have sinned, and come short of the glory of God; being justified freely by his grace through the redemption that is in Christ Jesus: whom God hath set forth to be a propitiation through faith in his blood, to declare his righteousness for the remission of sins that are past, through the forbearance of God; to declare, I say, at this time his righteousness: that he might be just, and the justifier of him which believeth in Jesus."

15

THE GOSPEL IN EZRA

*For Ezra had prepared his heart to seek the law of the L*ORD*, and to do it, and to teach in Israel statutes and judgments.* —EZRA 7:10

*And they sang together by course in praising and giving thanks unto the L*ORD*; because he is good, for his mercy endureth for ever toward Israel. And all the people shouted with a great shout, when they praised the L*ORD*, because the foundation of the house of the L*ORD *was laid.* —EZRA 3:11

THE BOOK OF EZRA is historical, written about four and a half centuries before the birth of Messiah Jesus, chronicling events in Persia and Israel during the return of the Jews to the Holy Land from their seventy years of captivity in Babylon.

Captivity. It's a state of existence the children of Israel uniquely knew from the beginning. Have you ever considered that? The nation itself was born in captivity in Egypt. Before Jacob's extended family moved to Egypt to escape a famine in the land, they were hardly yet a nation—just a family of seventy people. Was it a punishment for the sins of Joseph's brothers for casting him into slavery? Or was it by God's design to bring His chosen people to reconciliation? Was it an opportunity to incubate the birth of the nation, according to God's plan from the beginning?

Perhaps it was all three. Certainly, it was an egregious sin for Joseph's brothers to consider killing him and then determine to sell him into slavery. Yet, it also resulted in the complete reconciliation of the brothers, not to mention peace and blessing for Jacob in his elderly years. And after all, in Genesis 15:13, God told Abraham: "Know of a surety that thy seed shall be a stranger in a land that is not theirs, and shall serve them; and they shall afflict them four hundred years;"

Has any other nation in the history of the world been born this way?

Later, as prophesied by Moses, the children of Israel would face exile and captivity again and again—and they did. First the northern kingdom of Israel was conquered by the Assyrians and removed from the land, and later the Babylonians would conquer Judah, again as specifically prophesied, remaining in captivity for precisely seventy years. Again, beginning in AD 70, with the destruction of the temple, the Jews, once again, were conquered and mostly scattered, with the exception of a small remnant, throughout the world.

It was a fate no other nation in history has endured or survived. Yet, miraculously, and again as prophesied, after nearly two thousand years, the children of Israel were back in the land in numbers greater than ever before.

I don't believe today's Christians and Jews fully appreciate the uniqueness of this history. It should be considered proof, not just evidence, of the divine hand that has been on the children of Israel from the time before Jacob—later renamed Israel—was himself born. And this Israel would serve as the set-apart nation through which the Messiah, the Redeemer of the world, would come forth.

The book of Ezra begins with a lengthy recitation of the booty captured by the Babylonian and stored by Nebuchadnezzar during the Jewish captivity, but also a census of the people returning to their land at the order of Cyrus the Great, with the specific goal of rebuilding their temple. In other words, not only were their needs for the future provided by God, but the heritage of Jacob was protected while in exile. And what is the heritage of Jacob, referenced in Isaiah 58:14? It was the Torah, the teachings of the law.

So, who was Ezra? He was the scholar of the law whom God provided to ensure that the children of Israel would follow the law when they got back to the Holy Land.

The entire history is too neat to consider simply a matter of "coincidence." The most common definition of the English word "coincidence" is "a striking occurrence of two or more events at one time apparently by mere chance."[1] Sometimes, though, we rightly determine that mere chance cannot explain such striking occurrences. And the entirety of the history of Israel, more than any other nation the world has ever known, is literally "against all odds."

Think about it.

In Egypt, too, the exodus and reentry by the children of Israel to the promised land was financed by the captors. Exodus 12:36 tells us: "And the LORD gave the people favour in the sight of the Egyptians, so that they lent unto them such things as they required. And they spoiled the Egyptians."

What possessed Cyrus and, later, Darius—two Persian kings—to instigate and support another unlikely plan not only to resettle the children of Israel in their homeland but to finance the rebuilding of the temple?

In Ezra 1:1–2, we're told, "Now in the first year of Cyrus king of Persia, that the word of the LORD by the mouth of Jeremiah might be fulfilled, the LORD stirred up the spirit of Cyrus king of Persia, that he made a proclamation throughout all his kingdom, and put it also in writing, saying, Thus saith Cyrus king of Persia, The LORD God of heaven hath given me all the kingdoms of the earth; and he hath charged me to build him an house at Jerusalem, which is in Judah."

There's the answer: that prophecy might be fulfilled, "the LORD stirred up the spirit of Cyrus."

In the book of Ezra, we see a continuation of the biblical theme of "the remnant." Whenever disaster or judgment falls, God always preserves a remnant for His purposes. And that's part of the gospel message, is it not? Paul preached in Romans 11:1–5:

> I say then, Hath God cast away his people? God forbid. For I also am an Israelite, of the seed of Abraham, of the tribe of Benjamin. God hath not cast away his people which he foreknew. Wot ye not what the scripture saith of Elias? how he maketh intercession to God against Israel saying, Lord, they have killed thy prophets, and digged down thine altars; and I am left alone, and they seek my life. But what saith the answer of God unto him? I have reserved to myself seven thousand men, who have not bowed the knee to the image of Baal. Even so then at this present time also there is a remnant according to the election of grace.

And even so today.

Secondly, the book of Ezra is a chronicle of hope and restoration—the very heart of the gospel message. For though we are all scarred by sin and rebellion against God, He always holds out His hand to us with the gift of mercy and forgiveness.

In Ezra 10:1, the author weeps and casts himself down before the house of God, very much as Jesus wept over the city when He beheld it in Luke 19:41. Then Ezra, a teacher of the law, called the people to account for marrying foreigners who practiced pagan idolatry after their return to the land. Why? To preserve the seed of Jacob that would eventually lead, several centuries later, to the birth of the Messiah, whose genealogy is meticulously laid out in the gospels of Matthew and Luke. When Ezra realized how God's people had been faithless in matters of worship and marriage, he tore his clothes, pulled out his hair, and sat in mourning for an entire day. Later, he bowed down before God and offered a prayer of intercession and repentance, in which he humbly numbered himself among the transgressors:

> O my God, I am ashamed and blush to lift up my face to thee, my God: for our iniquities are increased over our head, and our trespass is grown up unto the heavens.
>
> Since the days of our fathers have we been in a great trespass unto this day; and for our iniquities have we, our kings, and our priests, been delivered into the hand of the kings of the lands, to the sword, to captivity, and to a spoil, and to confusion of face, as it is this day.
>
> And now for a little space grace hath been shewed from the LORD our God, to leave us a remnant to escape, and to give us a nail in his holy place, that our God may lighten our eyes, and give us a little reviving in our bondage.
>
> For we were bondmen; yet our God hath not forsaken us in our bondage, but hath extended mercy unto us in the sight of the kings of Persia, to give us a reviving, to set up the house of our God, and to repair the desolations thereof, and to give us a wall in Judah and in Jerusalem.
>
> And now, O our God, what shall we say after this? for we have forsaken thy commandments, which thou hast commanded by thy servants the prophets, saying, The land, unto which ye go to possess it, is an unclean land with the filthiness of the people of the lands, with their abominations, which have filled it from one end to another with their uncleanness.
>
> Now therefore give not your daughters unto their sons, neither take their daughters unto your sons, nor seek their peace or their wealth for ever: that ye may be strong, and eat the good of the land, and leave it for an inheritance to your children for ever.
>
> And after all that is come upon us for our evil deeds, and for our great trespass, seeing that thou our God hast punished us less than our iniquities deserve, and hast given us such deliverance as this; should we again break thy commandments,

and join in affinity with the people of these abominations? wouldest not thou be angry with us till thou hadst consumed us, so that there should be no remnant nor escaping?

O LORD God of Israel, thou art righteous: for we remain yet escaped, as it is this day: behold, we are before thee in our trespasses: for we cannot stand before thee because of this.

How did the people respond? They recognized Ezra's heart for holiness and responded with contrition in Ezra 10:1: "Now when Ezra had prayed, and when he had confessed, weeping and casting himself down before the house of God, there assembled unto him out of Israel a very great congregation of men and women and children: for the people wept very sore."

Why was Ezra so effective, both among the people and in finding favor with the king? Because the hand of the Lord his God was upon him (Ezra 7:6). How was he able to complete the long journey from Persia with the precious goods he carried? Again, the good hand of His God was upon him (Ezra 7:9). And what did he seek to accomplish? "Ezra had prepared his heart to seek the law of the LORD, and to do it, and to teach in Israel statutes and judgments" (Ezra 7:10). Ezra studied the law, taught the law, and obeyed the law, calling others to do so as well. Why? Because the law and the prophets all pointed to the gospel—the coming of the Messiah and the restoration of all things.

What emboldened Ezra? The conviction that God had not given up on His people and His plan of redemption.

Like Jesus, Ezra interceded for his people. He stood in the gap for them, just as Jesus does for us today. And Jesus cries, just as Ezra did, "Come home, O sinner, come home."

16

THE GOSPEL OF NEHEMIAH

The God of heaven, he will prosper us; therefore we his servants will arise and build . . . —NEHEMIAH 2:20

But thou art a God ready to pardon, gracious and merciful, slow to anger, and of great kindness. —NEHEMIAH 9:17

I CONFESS that I have read the book of Nehemiah many times, but somehow never really saw the gospel in it until I searched for it in my research for this book. Now I can't believe I had missed it for so long. It's so obvious.

Nehemiah had a comfortable life as the cupbearer for the king of Persia. Apparently, he was very happy with his position and his life. How do we know this? In Nehemiah 2:1, we read: "And it came to pass in the month Nisan, in the twentieth year of Artaxerxes the king, that wine was before him: and I took up the wine, and gave it unto the king. *Now I had not been beforetime sad in his presence"* (emphasis added). In other words, he enjoyed his life, his relationship with the good king; he'd never had a bad day—until this one. The king then asked him, "Why is thy countenance sad, seeing thou art not sick? this is nothing else but sorrow of heart" (v. 2). What had happened to make him so sorrowful?

Shortly before, Nehemiah had met with Hanani and other men of Judah about the status of those brethren who remained in the Holy Land or who had returned from captivity. He also asked about the state of Jerusalem, the Holy City. "And they said unto me, The remnant that are left of the captivity there in the province are in great affliction and reproach: the wall of Jerusalem also is broken down, and the gates thereof are burned with fire. And it came to pass, when I heard these words, that I sat down and wept, and mourned certain days, and fasted, and prayed before the God of heaven" (1:3–4).

He prayed indeed. He prayed fervently for the children of Israel. He prayed for forgiveness of their sins—including his own: "Now these are thy servants and thy people, whom thou hast redeemed by thy great power, and by thy strong hand. O LORD, I beseech thee, let now thine ear be attentive to the prayer of thy servant, and to the prayer of thy servants, who desire to fear thy name: and prosper, I pray thee, thy servant this day, and grant him mercy in the sight of this man. For I was the king's cupbearer."

Just hearing about the state of judgment still in evidence in Judah and Jerusalem broke Nehemiah's heart, reminding him of who he was—a follower of the God of Israel, one who had found comfort in captivity and, temporarily, perhaps, forgotten his identity.

As we recall from the previous book, Ezra had rebuilt the temple. Now, his co-laborer, Nehemiah, would rebuild the walls of Jerusalem.

It would be another of those restorations we read about throughout the Old Testament, each and every one of them pointing to the ultimate restoration that all the prophets pointed to from creation onward, as Peter tells us in Acts 3:18–26.

With the blessing of the king, Nehemiah set out to fulfill his destiny.

He was immediately met with opposition, very similar to the kind facing the modern state of Israel today. He was opposed by Sanballat and Tobiah, two foreigners living among the children of Israel, who were perfectly content with the depressing state of affairs in Jerusalem. In fact, it grieved the pair that a man had come seeking the welfare of the Jews. Oftentimes the biblical names of characters reveal much about them. The name "Sanballat" translates as "enemy in secret." And Tobiah may mean "the Lord is good," but the man in Nehemiah did not live up to the name, so he, too, was a kind of "enemy in secret." The third prominent member of the opposition Nehemiah encountered was Geshem the Arabian. Geshem translates to "heavy rains," like those that fall menacingly though necessarily and mercifully in Israel in the autumn and winter.

After three days in Jerusalem, Nehemiah announced his intentions to the rulers and the people:

> Then said I unto them, Ye see the distress that we are in, how Jerusalem lieth waste, and the gates thereof are burned with fire: come, and let us build up the wall of Jerusalem, that we be no more a reproach. Then I told them of the hand of my God which was good upon me; as also the king's words that he had spoken unto me. And they said, Let us rise up and build. So they strengthened their hands for this good work. But when Sanballat the Horonite, and Tobiah the servant, the Ammonite, and Geshem the Arabian, heard it, they laughed us to scorn, and despised us, and said, What is this thing that ye do? will ye rebel against the king? Then answered I them, and said unto them, The God of heaven, he will prosper us; therefore we his servants will arise and build: but ye have no portion, nor right, nor memorial, in Jerusalem (Nehemiah 2:17–20).

Nehemiah not only inspired the entire congregation of the children of Israel throughout this book to rebuild the walls of Jerusalem; he did so in spite of scorn, threats, and ridicule from the enemy. As Ezra taught the law and rebuilt the temple, Nehemiah reorganized and revived the nation.

Interestingly, the name Ezra means "help" or "saving help." Nehemiah means "comfort." While both Nehemiah and Ezra are types of the Messiah, Nehemiah in particular hints at the empowering Holy Spirit, or Comforter (see John 14:16, 26).

The book of Nehemiah covers about eleven years of Israel's history and a period of return, repair, repentance, revival, resettlement, and being set apart in holiness—all elements of the gospel. More specifically, a careful reading of the book reveals commonality with two kingdom events: the restoration of civil government and Israel's national supremacy in the millennial age.

Why did God bless the labors of Nehemiah and the children of Israel during this period?

- The people "had a mind to work" (Nehemiah 4:6).

- Nehemiah and the people watched and prayed. "We made our prayer . . . and set a watch" (Nehemiah 4:9).

- Not only did they work with their hands in rebuilding the wall, but they came to work armed for warfare, so no enemy could derail their efforts. "Everyone with one of his hands wrought in the work, and with the other hand held a weapon" (Nehemiah 4:17).

There are glaring similarities between the characteristics and actions of Nehemiah and those of Jesus:

- Both worked for the king/King and were dispatched to save Israel by the king/King.

- Both wept over the state of Jerusalem.

- Both dealt with trials and opposition over their faith in God.

- Both were mocked for doing the will of God.

- Both restored the covenant.

- Both lived a pure life.

- Both judged the children of Israel.

- Both prayed frequently and often alone.

And what was the ultimate goal of both?

Restoration.

In Nehemiah's case, it meant restoration of Israel spiritually and physically as a set-apart congregation secured by the building of walls that would both shelter them from the temptations of the outside world and keep them safe from attack. In the case of Jesus the Messiah, the ultimate outcome is the fulfillment of His kingdom on earth, centered in Israel and Jerusalem—the message of the gospel.

17

THE GOSPEL IN ESTHER

*For if thou altogether holdest thy peace at this time, then shall there enlarge-
ment and deliverance arise to the Jews from another place; but thou and thy
father's house shall be destroyed: and who knoweth whether thou art come to
the kingdom for such a time as this?* —ESTHER 4:14

THE BOOK OF ESTHER is seemingly unlike any other in Scripture.

On the surface, it's a thrilling page-turner about a secretly Jewish young woman living in Persia during the captivity, who auditions to become the queen to a pagan king, thus saving her people from annihilation.

The God of Israel is never specifically mentioned. The words *pray* and *prayer* are never used.

The historicity of the book has been questioned by skeptics, although that is not unusual.

Martin Luther, the father of the Reformation, suggested the

book didn't even belong in the Bible.[1]

The book of Esther has been adapted in movies, plays, books, TV miniseries, musicals, music videos, cartoons, and even an episode of *Veggie Tales*, thus making the story line as familiar to nonbelievers as almost any in the Bible.

So, what are we to make of the book of Esther and its relationship to the gospel of the kingdom of heaven?

Let's start with the obvious.

Satan has, on many occasions, attempted to foil God's redemptive plan by killing His chosen people. He did it in Egypt by persuading Pharaoh to slay the newborn baby boys in the time of Moses. He did it again when the children of Israel left Egypt, at the Red Sea. And he did again, using a variety of attackers—including Amalek—during the Israelites' forty-year trek through the wilderness after the exodus.

He even tried to kill the Redeemer-Messiah Himself through Herod's slaughter of the innocents in Bethlehem.

Clearly, what we see in Esther is another important telling of a similarly unsuccessful genocidal bid against the Jews by a man named Haman, an Agagite—which is synonymous with Amalekite, by the way—during the Persian diaspora.

Yet, there's clearly much more in this thoroughly engaging story. In fact, the entire book can easily be viewed as an allegorical retelling of the gospel message, as my good friend and colleague Joe Kovacs explains in his book *Shocked by the Bible 2*.[2] Think about it:

- King Ahasuerus (or Xerxes in some translations) symbolizes God the Father.

- Queen Vashti symbolizes the physical nation of Israel, who rejected the commandments of her King and suffered divorce as a result (Jeremiah 3:8).

- Esther represents spiritual Israel, all faithful followers of God.

- Mordecai symbolizes Jesus.

- Haman represents Satan.

It's hard to miss it when reading Esther with this possibility in mind. In other words, despite the fact that God does not explicitly enter the picture in Esther, it's hard to miss the story of redemption, the good news that still causes Jews, and some Christians, even today to observe the feast of Purim, which celebrates the foiling of Haman's plot to eradicate the Jews by Esther.

It's also hard to miss the fact that Esther plays a dual role as Gentile and Jew—and part of the good news is that the way of redemption was opened wide to non-Jews (Galatians 3:28).

Furthermore, aren't we told in Luke 24 of the way Jesus, on the road to Emmaus, opened up the Hebrew Scriptures and explained how they all pointed to His coming? And the book of Esther was a part of those Hebrew Scriptures at the time of Jesus—as they are to this day. In fact, a pretty good case can be made for Jesus having observed Purim during His life on earth. Why would that be significant? Because it would affirm the book of Esther.

In John 5:1 there is mention of an unnamed feast "of the Jews; and Jesus," we are told, "went up to Jerusalem." In John 6:3–4, we learn a little bit about the timing of the observance: "And Jesus went up into a mountain, and there he sat with his disciples. And the passover, a feast of the Jews, was nigh." In John 5:16, we learn that this feast fell on a weekly sabbath day, yet, that was not true of any spring feasts in the years from AD 25 through AD 35 except Purim in AD 28. So clearly, Jesus was in Jerusalem in John 5:1 for Purim.

One last thought about Esther.

Without question, the most famous verse in the book is Esther 4:14: "For if thou altogether holdest thy peace at this time, then shall there enlargement and deliverance arise to the Jews from another place; but thou and thy father's house shall be destroyed: and who knoweth whether thou art come to the kingdom for such a time as this?" While there is no explicit mention of God in the book, it is certainly implied in this key verse. Here, Mordecai was warning Esther that if she did not act, she and her household may perish, but deliverance for the Jews would arise from another place. What does that suggest? It suggests that Mordecai believed that "deliverance" was inevitable, because it had been promised by God. I also note the use of the term "kingdom" somewhat ambiguously and possibly purposefully. Which kingdom was Mordecai referring to—the kingdom of Persia or the kingdom of God?

Perhaps both.

18

THE GOSPEL IN JOB

For I know that my redeemer liveth, and that he shall stand at the latter day upon the earth. —JOB 19:25

He also shall be my salvation: for an hypocrite shall not come before him. —JOB 13:16

WHEN I EMBARKED on the daunting study that would culminate in *The Gospel in Every Book of the Old Testament*, I sensed it could be problematic for several reasons.

Did I have the time to do such a comprehensive study?

Was I up to the job? Certainly, there were others more experienced, better trained, with more impressive credentials, more highly respected, more learned, more insightful, more gifted in their writing ability, and more articulate.

Was I being pretentious in tackling such an assignment?

Would it seem contrived? At the end of the day, would I be stretching the case that the gospel could really be found in every book of the Old Testament? Would I merely be reading the Greek Scriptures back into the Hebrew Scriptures?

Yes, I had many inward struggles about that. I was not up to the job. Who was I—someone who never attended seminary—attempting to write a non-scholarly, popular book about a subject so vast and so important?

Looking back, however, it was while reading the book of Job that such self-doubts were conquered. The idea became a passion for me. I felt the call of the Holy Spirit to take on this project. I knew that if I finished it and found it was not worthy to share with the general public, I would be no worse off for trying. In fact, in simply embarking on this study, it would give me new purpose to review the entire Tanakh with fresh eyes and a galvanized spirit. And what could be wrong with that? If it was worth sharing, it might inspire others to take their own, similar journey through the Old Testament.

Like many others, the book of Job was not a book I gravitated toward except, like others perhaps, in times of despondency and depression. Yet, it was in one of my efforts to read through every book of the Bible systematically that some of the words in Job seemed to jump off the pages at me as if seeing them for the first time.

Nineteen of those words, as powerful as any found in the Hebrew Scriptures, were in chapter 19: "For I know that my redeemer liveth, and that he shall stand at the latter day upon the earth." That *is* to me the very essence of the gospel: "I know that my redeemer liveth, and . . . he shall stand" at the end of the age. It's a simple, yet profound proclamation—straightforward, unambiguous, and sure.

Yet, it's not just a random verse in the book of Job. It's the big story of the entire book. It's the summation. It's the bottom line. It's the inevitable conclusion. It's the main idea. It's the substance.

Most everyone is familiar with the ancient story of Job. It begins: "There was a man in the land of Uz, whose name was Job;

and that man was perfect and upright, and one that feared God, and eschewed evil" (1:1).

Was this Job's self-description? No, this was the way God, the all-powerful, omnipotent Creator of the universe, looked upon him. How do we know that? Because God Himself repeated the description, underlined it for us, a few verses later, in Job 1:8: "And the LORD said unto Satan, Hast thou considered my servant Job, that there is none like him in the earth, a perfect and an upright man, one that feareth God, and escheweth evil?" Does this mean, then, that Job had never fallen short of God's perfect law? No. What it means in context is that when he fell short, he was penitent. He recognized a Redeemer was promised who would atone for those confessed transgressions from which he had already turned away.

Job was not living in the perfected kingdom of God. He was, instead, living in a fallen world under the spell of Satan, the tempter, the deceiver, the murderer, the liar, the adversary of God. As such, Job did not have an expectation that he would escape suffering and death in his mortal life, but rather that through his Redeemer, he would be resurrected and restored to a state of perfection and immortality.

And of course, we see a foreshadowing of that ultimate resurrection in Job's story.

Reading Job reminds me of the very purpose of our mortal lives on earth. God created human beings as His children. When Adam and Eve fell, they needed to be redeemed, or God's children—not just the first two, but all of their descendants—would die. The good news was that God already had the plan of redemption in the person of the "Lamb slain from the foundation of the world" (Revelation 13:8). It is His Son who speaks to us as God throughout the Scriptures—both Old Testament and New. Remember: Jesus is the Creator of all things (John 1:3). When we see God speaking, issuing His commandments, giving us His teachings, even talking to Satan in the book of Job, it is Jesus' words we are hearing.

Naturally, when human beings read of the conversation between

God and Satan in Job 1:7–12, it can be very disturbing to us. To us, it sounds like a bet, a wager, a challenge:

> And the LORD said unto Satan, Whence comest thou? Then Satan answered the LORD, and said, From going to and fro in the earth, and from walking up and down in it. And the LORD said unto Satan, Hast thou considered my servant Job, that there is none like him in the earth, a perfect and an upright man, one that feareth God, and escheweth evil? Then Satan answered the LORD, and said, Doth Job fear God for nought? Hast not thou made an hedge about him, and about his house, and about all that he hath on every side? thou hast blessed the work of his hands, and his substance is increased in the land. But put forth thine hand now, and touch all that he hath, and he will curse thee to thy face. And the LORD said unto Satan, Behold, all that he hath is in thy power; only upon himself put not forth thine hand. So Satan went forth from the presence of the LORD."

What we need to keep in mind here is the assurance that "all things work together for good to them that love God, to them who are the called according to his purpose" (Romans 8:28). What is God's purpose? To save His children, those who love Him, from death—and to ensure that they will be His children forever. In my opinion, and from my experience, we don't think about this and talk about it enough. Whatever fate befalls us during our relatively brief lives on earth, the important thing is how we spend eternity—with God or without.

Satan's fate is written. It was written before the time of Job. He had rebelled. Sin was found in him. Jesus said in John 8:44 that the devil "was a murderer from the beginning, and abode not in the truth, because there is no truth in him. When he speaketh a lie, he speaketh of his own: for he is a liar, and the father of it." He has already been judged (John 6:11). He will not escape the second death (Revelation 20:10, 14). He is not one of God's children.

Because of Satan's pride and evil personality, he is determined to take as many human beings with him into death. Yet, God has a purpose for him until the Redeemer casts him into the lake of fire. That purpose is to separate—to set apart—the children of God from the children of the devil.

One of the most provocative questions we hear asked about the nature of God is: "Why do bad things happen to good people?" The answer is found so clearly in the book of Job.

From our human vantage point, when we see suffering and death, we can't imagine anything worse. Yet there is something worse in God's economy. It's the possibility of spending eternity apart from God in the bowels of the earth, instead of in paradise.

Even so, trials are what *this* life is all about—challenges that test our belief and commitment to God and His ways. Because, in eternity, we're not just going to be strumming harps in the clouds; we're going to be ruling and reigning with God on earth as it is in heaven. Job's mettle was tested, indeed. That's why I'm sure that his position in the kingdom of God is assured.

"Well, what about his family?" you may ask. We don't know. But God does. All or some of them could be in the kingdom too. But we are all judged individually. Note that in Job 1:4–5, he is found making sacrifices for his family members: "And his sons went and feasted in their houses, every one his day; and sent and called for their three sisters to eat and to drink with them. And it was so, when the days of their feasting were gone about, that Job sent and sanctified them, and rose up early in the morning, and offered burnt offerings according to the number of them all: for Job said, It may be that my sons have sinned, and cursed God in their hearts. Thus did Job continually."

Job's model is an example to us today to intervene in prayer for our families and others whom we love.

That brings us back to why Job was "perfect" in God's eyes. Read again Job 1:9–12:

Then Satan answered the LORD, and said, Doth Job fear God for nought? Hast not thou made an hedge about him, and about his house, and about all that he hath on every side? thou hast blessed the work of his hands, and his substance is increased in the land. But put forth thine hand now, and touch all that he hath, and he will curse thee to thy face. And the LORD said unto Satan, Behold, all that he hath is in thy power; only upon himself put not forth thine hand. So Satan went forth from the presence of the LORD.

Satan was inferring that Job walked with God because he was blessed with much and because he had a hedge of protection around him. Take it away, Satan said, and he would curse God to His face. God, thus, gave permission to Satan to take away everything from Job that was in his power—meaning all earthly blessing, from wealth to family members. Remember that Satan is the prince of this world (John 12:31; 14:30; 16:11; 1 Corinthians 2:6, 8; Ephesians 2:2). He can kill, main, and torture any of us, but he has no power to take away our eternal life.

What did Jesus say in Matthew 10:28? "And fear not them which kill the body, but are not able to kill the soul: but rather fear him which is able to destroy both soul and body in hell." He instructed us not to fear the devil, but—like Job —to fear God.

After Satan was unleashed to torment God's faithful servant, Job was struck with a series of calamities in rapid succession. His cattle were wiped out. His flocks were destroyed, and his herds were captured. His sons and daughters were killed when wind knocked down the house where they were gathered.

Job's response? "Then Job arose, and rent his mantle, and shaved his head, and fell down upon the ground, and worshipped, and said, Naked came I out of my mother's womb, and naked shall I return thither: the LORD gave, and the LORD hath taken away; blessed be the name of the LORD. In all this Job sinned not, nor charged God foolishly" (Job 1:20–22).

Then came the next test. In chapter 2, after God pointed out how Job had responded to test number 1, Satan said that Job would turn against God if his own flesh was cursed. God gave Satan permission to torment Job in his flesh, but to spare his life. "So went Satan forth from the presence of the LORD, and smote Job with sore boils from the sole of his foot unto his crown" (v. 7).

Then Job's wife came to him in his misery and said: "Dost thou still retain thine integrity? curse God, and die."

"Thou speakest as one of the foolish women speaketh," Job responded. "What? shall we receive good at the hand of God, and shall we not receive evil? And Job did not sin with his lips," we're told (vv. 9–10).

The longest section of the book of Job follows. It's a running dialogue between Job and some misguided friends who assumed that because of tragedies he had endured, he must be guilty of sin. They didn't pray as intercessors on behalf of their righteous friend. Instead they condemned him ansd his children. Like Job's wife, they had no compassion for him. They didn't uplift the man they knew. Job needed a true friend—a mediator. But he found none.

In Job 4:7, a man named Eliphaz disputed Job's righteousness, asking this remarkable question: "Who ever perished, being innocent? or where were the righteous cut off?" Of course, it's a dumb question on one level. Has not every righteous person in the history of humankind died? But there's something much more conspicuous and revealing here. It should remind every reader of when Jesus Himself was "cut off." It was even prophesied that He would be in Daniel 9:26: "And after threescore and two weeks shall Messiah be cut off, but not for himself." Likewise, Job was not being tormented for his own behavior.

Likewise, in Isaiah 53:8, we read of the coming Redeemer, "for he was cut off out of the land of the living: for the transgression of my people was he stricken."

And what about Bildad, another of Job's "comforters"? He asked, "Doth God pervert judgment? or doth the Almighty pervert justice?" Well, no. And if he'd stopped there, he would have been just fine. But instead, Bildad went on to say, "If thy children have sinned against him, and he have cast them away for their transgression; If thou wouldest seek unto God betimes, and make thy supplication to the Almighty; If thou wert pure and upright; surely now he would awake for thee, and make the habitation of thy righteousness prosperous" (Job 8:3–6). Bildad, it seems, was preaching an early version of the prosperity gospel—not the gospel of the kingdom.

Still despite the condemnation from his self-proclaimed judges, Job continued to be faithful to God—even in his misery.

- Job 14:14: "If a man die, shall he live again? all the days of my appointed time will I wait, till my change come."

- He even sounds like Jesus on the cross in Job 16:10–11: "They have gaped upon me with their mouth; they have smitten me upon the cheek reproachfully; they have gathered themselves together against me. God hath delivered me to the ungodly, and turned me over into the hands of the wicked." This sounds like it is right out of Psalm 22, often seen as a prophecy about Jesus' future suffering.

- He asked for a Redeemer in Job 16:21: "O that one might plead for a man with God, as a man pleadeth for his neighbour!"

To all this humiliation from the wisdom of men, Job responded confidently: "Oh that my words were now written! oh that they were printed in a book! That they were graven with an iron pen and lead in the rock for ever! For I know that my redeemer liveth, and that he shall stand at the latter day upon the earth: And though after my skin worms destroy this body, yet in my flesh shall I see God" (19:23–26).

In the end, of course, Job is fully restored, just as all God's children will be restored in the kingdom. But until that time, he suffered pain, humiliation, and loss.

We all fear losing what Job lost and experiencing the pain and humiliation he endured. Yet, clearly the lesson we take away from the book of Job is that we are to live like the main character, running the race to the very end in spite of the slings and arrows launched our way. If we do, we, too, will see our Redeemer "at the latter day upon the earth (19:25).

That's the gospel of the kingdom from the beginning to the end!

19

THE GOSPEL IN PSALMS

Kiss the Son, lest he be angry, and ye perish from the way, when his wrath is kindled but a little. Blessed are all they that put their trust in him.
—PSALM 2:12

IT'S OFTEN REFERRED TO as a poetic book, and, while it is stunningly beautiful poetry, the book of Psalms is so much more.

It is believed to be the most-read book in the Bible. It's the one Jesus quoted most frequently.

Of the collection of 150 songs, poems, and prayers that make up the book of Psalms, David wrote about half; the rest were written by temple worship leaders.

Jesus quoted the Psalms on eleven different occasions in the Gospels:

- He challenged the Pharisees with references to Psalm 8:2 and Psalm 110:1 in Matthew 21:16, Matthew 22:44, Mark 12:36, and Luke 20:42–43.

- He quoted Psalm 22:1 while dying on the cross ("My God, my God, why hast thou forsaken me?") in Matthew 27:46 and Mark 15:34 before fulfilling Psalm 31:5 by committing his spirit to the Father in Luke 23:46.

- Jesus was hated without cause, which He said in John 15:25 that the Psalms foretold (Psalm 35:19; 69:4).

- He quoted Psalm 41:9 in John 13:18 when talking about his betrayal.

- He recalled Psalm 78:24 regarding the manna in the wilderness after feeding the multitude in John 6:31.

- When He was threatened with stoning for claiming to be God in John 10:34, He responded with a quote from Psalm 82:6.

- In Matthew 26:64, He made reference to Psalm 110:1 when Pilate asked if he was the Son of God.

- He quoted Psalm 118:22–23 to the chief priests and elders in Matthew 21:42, Mark 12:10, and Luke 20:17, calling Himself the "head of the corner," or, the chief cornerstone.

- Jesus referenced Psalm 118:26 when foretelling Jerusalem's destruction in Matthew 23:39 and Luke 13:35.

- In Matthew 5:5, Jesus proclaims: "Blessed are the meek: for they shall inherit the earth," a variation on Psalm 37:11, a reference to the kingdom of God on earth.

- In Psalm 31:5, we read Jesus' last words on the cross, fourteen generations before He was born in Bethlehem: "Into thine hand I commit my spirit" (Luke 23:46).

Even His mother, Mary, alluded to Psalms 103:17 and 111:9 in her memorable prophecy about Jesus' role as Messiah, Redeemer, and King in Luke 1:49–50.

There are dozens of other references to the Psalms in the Gospels, for example, when Psalm 118:25–26 is repeated in Matthew 21:9: "And the multitudes that went before, and that followed, cried, saying, Hosanna to the son of David: Blessed is he that cometh in the name of the Lord; Hosanna in the highest."

It's not surprising that tens of millions of copies of abbreviated editions of the Scriptures, containing only the four Gospels and the Psalms, have been published and distributed in nearly all languages.

But let's take a walk through some of the most striking examples of how the Psalms prophesied and foreshadowed the good news of Jesus' ministry and His role as the coming Redeemer.

It starts in rather spectacular fashion in Psalm 2:

Why do the heathen rage, and the people imagine a vain thing?

The kings of the earth set themselves, and the rulers take counsel together, against the LORD, and against his anointed, saying, Let us break their bands asunder, and cast away their cords from us.

He that sitteth in the heavens shall laugh: the LORD shall have them in derision. Then shall he speak unto them in his wrath, and vex them in his sore displeasure. Yet have I set my king upon my holy hill of Zion.

I will declare the decree: the LORD hath said unto me, Thou art my Son; this day have I begotten thee.

Ask of me, and I shall give thee the heathen for thine inheritance, and the uttermost parts of the earth for thy possession.

Thou shalt break them with a rod of iron; thou shalt dash

them in pieces like a potter's vessel. Be wise now therefore, O ye kings: be instructed, ye judges of the earth.

Serve the LORD with fear, and rejoice with trembling. Kiss the Son, lest he be angry, and ye perish from the way, when his wrath is kindled but a little. Blessed are all they that put their trust in him.

A "begotten" Son who will judge the earth and rule it? Here is a dramatic reference in the Hebrew Scriptures to God's Son—the future King reigning in Jerusalem. It's hard to miss, yet there are those who still deny any mention of God's Son in the Old Testament. And it's hardly the only one, as we will see. The apostles didn't miss it, bringing attention to it in Acts 13:33. Further, it seems clear they interpreted their own persecution in the light of the raging of the heathen (Acts 4:25–28).

I suspect one of the reasons even many Christians don't connect the dots between the Old Testament prophecies and the Gospels is because of the former's heavy focus on the kingdom of God on earth, ruled by Messiah—a key component of the good news common to all the Hebrew prophecies, as brought home by Peter in Acts 3:18–25. The gospel, for them, was not limited to the atonement of sin. It clearly included a fully restored earth under the reign of God, an element of the gospel sometimes overlooked in sermons, books, and Bible studies today, as I wrote in my previous book, *The Restitution of All Things*,

Psalm 8 also focuses prophetically on this future kingdom on earth, also introducing another term familiar in the Gospels to refer to the person of Jesus—the "son of Man" (v. 4). It continues, "For thou hast made him a little lower than the angels, and hast crowned him with glory and honour. Thou madest him to have dominion over the works of thy hands; thou hast put all things under his feet" (vv, 5–6). The writer of Hebrews 2, quoting Psalms 8, makes clear that this reference is, without doubt, about Jesus.

Psalm 9, likewise, is substantively a sure prophecy about the future kingdom of the gospel, especially verses 7–14:

But the LORD shall endure for ever: he hath prepared his throne for judgment.

And he shall judge the world in righteousness, he shall minister judgment to the people in uprightness.

The LORD also will be a refuge for the oppressed, a refuge in times of trouble.

And they that know thy name will put their trust in thee: for thou, LORD, hast not forsaken them that seek thee.

Sing praises to the LORD, which dwelleth in Zion: declare among the people his doings.

When he maketh inquisition for blood, he remembereth them: he forgetteth not the cry of the humble.

Have mercy upon me, O LORD; consider my trouble which I suffer of them that hate me, thou that liftest me up from the gates of death: that I may shew forth all thy praise in the gates of the daughter of Zion: I will rejoice in thy salvation.

Psalm 10:16 hints again on the perfection of the earth under the rulership of God: "The LORD is King for ever and ever: the heathen are perished out of his land."

Psalm 14:7 reminds us that the Lord will bring Israel peace and joy everlasting with the advent of the messianic age.

Psalm 16:10 hints at the resurrection of "thine Holy One." If that wasn't clear from a straight reading of the text, it is confirmed by Peter, under the inspiration of the Holy Spirit on Pentecost and quoting David, in Acts 2:25–31.

But those are just glimpses of the gospel compared to Psalm 22, 23, and 24, which form a trilogy all about the three major personae of Jesus—the Suffering Servant, the Good Shepherd, and the sovereign King.

Already mentioned is that Jesus Himself quoted Psalm 22 before dying on the cross, but there's so much more in this chapter:

My God, my God, why hast thou forsaken me? why art thou so far from helping me, and from the words of my roaring?

O my God, I cry in the day time, but thou hearest not; and in the night season, and am not silent.

But thou art holy, O thou that inhabitest the praises of Israel.

Our fathers trusted in thee: they trusted, and thou didst deliver them.

They cried unto thee, and were delivered: they trusted in thee, and were not confounded. But I am a worm, and no man; a reproach of men, and despised of the people.

All they that see me laugh me to scorn: they shoot out the lip, they shake the head, saying, He trusted on the LORD that he would deliver him: let him deliver him, seeing he delighted in him.

But thou art he that took me out of the womb: thou didst make me hope when I was upon my mother's breasts.

I was cast upon thee from the womb: thou art my God from my mother's belly. Be not far from me; for trouble is near; for there is none to help.

Many bulls have compassed me: strong bulls of Bashan have beset me round. They gaped upon me with their mouths, as a ravening and a roaring lion.

I am poured out like water, and all my bones are out of joint: my heart is like wax; it is melted in the midst of my bowels.

My strength is dried up like a potsherd; and my tongue cleaveth to my jaws; and thou hast brought me into the dust of death.

For dogs have compassed me: the assembly of the wicked have inclosed me: they pierced my hands and my feet.

I may tell all my bones: they look and stare upon me.

They part my garments among them, and cast lots upon my vesture.

But be not thou far from me, O LORD: O my strength, haste thee to help me. Deliver my soul from the sword; my darling from the power of the dog.

Save me from the lion's mouth: for thou hast heard me from the horns of the unicorns.

I will declare thy name unto my brethren: in the midst of the congregation will I praise thee.

Ye that fear the LORD, praise him; all ye the seed of Jacob, glorify him; and fear him, all ye the seed of Israel.

For he hath not despised nor abhorred the affliction of the afflicted; neither hath he hid his face from him; but when he cried unto him, he heard.

My praise shall be of thee in the great congregation: I will pay my vows before them that fear him.

The meek shall eat and be satisfied: they shall praise the LORD that seek him: your heart shall live for ever.

All the ends of the world shall remember and turn unto the LORD: and all the kindreds of the nations shall worship before thee.

For the kingdom is the LORD's: and he is the governor among the nations.

All they that be fat upon earth shall eat and worship: all they that go down to the dust shall bow before him: and none can keep alive his own soul.

A seed shall serve him; it shall be accounted to the Lord for a generation.

They shall come, and shall declare his righteousness unto a people that shall be born, that he hath done this.

It's clearly part prophecy about Jesus' actual experience of suffering—written by David, yet reflecting what the Messiah would encounter in His mortal form. Much of it is a vivid word picture of what Jesus must have felt as He hung from the cross, but ends victoriously further into the future when He returns to redeem and restore the earth under His Kingship.

Psalm 23, so familiar to even those not immersed in the Bible, emphasizes in majestically poetic form what it means to have the Lord as our Shepherd, as well as what a gift it will be to dwell with God forever.

Then, Psalm 24 reminds the reader that God is the Creator of all things, the Restorer of all things and our future King. It points to a coming generation that recognize Him, welcome Him, and invite Him to redeem the earth from its fallen state and assume His rightful throne: "This is the generation of them that seek him, that seek thy face, O Jacob. Selah. Lift up your heads, O ye gates; and be ye lift up, ye everlasting doors; and the King of glory shall come in. Who is this King of glory? The LORD strong and mighty, the LORD mighty in battle. Lift up your heads, O ye gates; even lift them up, ye everlasting doors; and the King of glory shall come in. Who is this King of glory? The LORD of hosts, he is the King of glory. Selah" (vv. 6–10).

Psalm 37:10–18 encourages righteous behavior by pointing to the ultimate justice God will bring in His future kingdom for those who are obedient:

> For yet a little while, and the wicked shall not be: yea, thou shalt diligently consider his place, and it shall not be. But the meek shall inherit the earth; and shall delight themselves in the abundance of peace. The wicked plotteth against the just, and gnasheth upon him with his teeth. The LORD shall laugh at him: for he seeth that his day is coming. The wicked have drawn out the sword, and have bent their bow, to cast down the poor and needy, and to slay such as be of upright conversation. Their sword shall enter into their own heart, and their bows shall be broken. A little that a righteous man hath is better than the riches of many wicked. For the arms of the wicked shall be broken: but the LORD upholdeth the righteous. The LORD knoweth the days of the upright: and their inheritance shall be for ever.

Notice the inspiration for Jesus' words in the Sermon on the Mount: "Blessed are the meek: for they shall inherit the earth" (Matthew 5:5).

As mentioned earlier, the gospel is not just about Jesus' suffering, death, and resurrection. It's also about the complete restoration of the kingdom of Israel as the centerpiece of a perfected earth—a return to the way things were intended by God before the fall of man.

And that's what comes forth in the entirety of Psalm 47. It's one big happy praise for the Coming kingdom:

> O clap your hands, all ye people; shout unto God with the voice of triumph.
>
> For the LORD most high is terrible; he is a great King over all the earth.
>
> He shall subdue the people under us, and the nations under our feet.
>
> He shall choose our inheritance for us, the excellency of Jacob whom he loved. Selah.
>
> God is gone up with a shout, the Lord with the sound of a trumpet.
>
> Sing praises to God, sing praises: sing praises unto our King, sing praises. For God is the King of all the earth: sing ye praises with understanding.
>
> God reigneth over the heathen: God sitteth upon the throne of his holiness.
>
> The princes of the people are gathered together, even the people of the God of Abraham: for the shields of the earth belong unto God: he is greatly exalted.

Psalm 51 is pure gospel. If you read this entire Psalm to one hundred random people on the street and ask them whether it is from the Old Testament or the New Testament, I suspect nine of ten will guess New Testament. It's the language of total forgiveness, something that, for some reason, we don't expect to see in the Scriptures before the advent of Jesus, even though, as we should know, the Bible is one integrated, systematic message that is unchanging, and our God is the same yesterday, today and tomorrow.

Psalm 67 is the kind of praise for God that we love to share in our churches because of His abundant mercy and blessings. But there's more here again—the other neglected part of the gospel about our collective destiny with Him when He governs the nations of the earth.

Psalm 68 is a portrait of the conquering King to come.

In Psalm 69, we read the words of David, yet under the inspiration of the Holy Spirit, he provides insight into what Jesus experienced as the Suffering Servant.

Psalm 72 is a paean to the kingdom:

- **VERSE 7** "In his days shall the righteous flourish; and abundance of peace so long as the moon endureth."

- **VERSE 11** "Yea, all kings shall fall down before him: all nations shall serve him."

- **VERSE 17** "His name shall endure for ever: his name shall be continued as long as the sun: and men shall be blessed in him: all nations shall call him blessed."

- **VERSE 19** "And blessed be his glorious name for ever: and let the whole earth be filled with his glory; Amen, and Amen."

Why was David said to be a man after God's own heart? I strongly suspect it was because David understood, appreciated, and sought forgiveness so eagerly. He was quick and certain in his repentance when he fell. And I believe it is that central characteristic that established His own throne as the everlasting one of Israel—the one upon which Jesus Himself will sit and judge all nations. Reading Psalm 86 reminds me of this component of David's character. It demonstrates from beginning to end David's humility and contrition. Sometimes believers act as if God's forgiveness was something new and unprecedented in the

Greek Scriptures. It was not. It was, for instance, why God saw Job as "perfect" in his ways. We know David sinned grievously in his life. Yet, God loved him so much because of his ability and willingness to turn back to his beloved Creator in penitence.

In Psalm 91, the Lord explains why He offers forgiveness and blessing to those with the spirit of David: "Because he hath set his love upon me, therefore will I deliver him: I will set him on high, because he hath known my name. He shall call upon me, and I will answer him: I will be with him in trouble; I will deliver him, and honour him. With long life will I satisfy him, and shew him my salvation" (vv. 14–16).

On a side note, Satan quoted Psalm 91:11–12 in his testing of Jesus in the wilderness as recorded in Matthew 4:6: "If thou be the Son of God, cast thyself down: for it is written, He shall give his angels charge concerning thee: and in their hands they shall bear thee up, lest at any time thou dash thy foot against a stone." Jesus' response was: "It is written again, Thou shalt not tempt the Lord thy God.

Once again, Psalm 110 is all about Jesus:

The LORD said unto my Lord, Sit thou at my right hand, until I make thine enemies thy footstool.

The LORD shall send the rod of thy strength out of Zion: rule thou in the midst of thine enemies.

Thy people shall be willing in the day of thy power, in the beauties of holiness from the womb of the morning: thou hast the dew of thy youth.

The LORD hath sworn, and will not repent, Thou art a priest for ever after the order of Melchizedek.

The Lord at thy right hand shall strike through kings in the day of his wrath.

He shall judge among the heathen, he shall fill the places with the dead bodies; he shall wound the heads over many countries.

He shall drink of the brook in the way: therefore shall he lift up the head.

Jesus would have some fun with the Pharisees using the first line from Psalm 110: In Matthew 22:42–46, he quizzed them, saying, "What think ye of Christ? whose son is he? They say unto him, The son of David. He saith unto them, How then doth David in spirit call him Lord, saying, The Lord said unto my Lord, Sit thou on my right hand, till I make thine enemies thy footstool? If

David then call him Lord, how is he his son? And no man was able to answer him a word, neither durst any man from that day forth ask him any more questions."

Further, in Psalm 110 we see the future Messiah portrayed as not only conquering King but High Priest, though He is not a Levite. Instead, the psalmist explains that He will be a priest "after the order of Melchizedek" (v. 4), and this is affirmed in Hebrews 7.

Psalm 112 offers another glimpse of the kingdom of God for those who fear the Lord (His seed) and delight in His commandments: In verses 2–3, we see: "His seed shall be mighty upon earth: the generation of the upright shall be blessed. Wealth and riches shall be in his house: and his righteousness endureth for ever."

Psalm 117, short and sweet though it is, was used by the apostles in Romans 15:11 as proof the gospel would be preached to and believed by the Gentiles: "O praise the LORD, all ye nations: praise him, all ye people. For his merciful kindness is great toward us: and the truth of the LORD endureth for ever. Praise ye the LORD."

Many of the psalms spoke about Jesus, but maybe none as clearly and unequivocally as Psalm 118 and especially verse 22: "The stone which the builders refused is become the head stone of the corner." It is referenced in Matthew 21:42, Mark 12:10, Acts 4:11 and 1 Peter 2:7. So there is no ambiguity about what it means. Jesus is that stone.

You not only find Psalms all over the Gospels; you also find the gospel all over the Psalms.

After all, what did Jesus say to Cleopas and his companion on the road to Emmaus?

These are the words which I spake unto you, while I was yet with you, that all things must be fulfilled, *which were written in the law of Moses, and in the prophets, and in the psalms, concerning me.*

Then opened he their understanding, that they might understand the scriptures, And said unto them, Thus it is written, and thus it behooved Christ to suffer, and to rise from the dead the third day: and that repentance and remission of sins should be preached in his name among all nations, beginning at Jerusalem. And ye are witnesses of these things. (Luke 24:44–48, emphasis added)

20

THE GOSPEL IN PROVERBS

Who hath ascended up into heaven, or descended? who hath gathered the wind in his fists? who hath bound the waters in a garment? who hath established all the ends of the earth? what is his name, and what is his son's name, if thou canst tell? —PROVERBS 30:4

By mercy and truth iniquity is purged: and by the fear of the LORD men depart from evil. —PROVERBS 16:6

EVERYONE LOVES TO READ PROVERBS. We call it a "wisdom book," and with good reason. The words *wise* and *wisdom* are found more than a hundred times in its thirty-one chapters, conveniently one for each day of the longest months. I think of it as reaffirmation of Torah principles in poetic form.

There's plenty of wisdom here. But is there gospel?

Incredibly, many have actually read it, presumably studied it, and *inexplicably* missed it. I don't even know how that's possible. Maybe they just weren't looking.

Let's take something really basic and obvious. One of the great controversies that Jesus faced in the Gospels was the notion that He was the Son of God. The Pharisees and the Sanhedrin found this to be a blasphemous claim, much as Muslims do today by claiming a different Jesus (Issa) as their own, but denying He was the Son of God. They call the notion that God has a Son, as do many non-messianic Jews today, non-monotheistic, or polytheistic.

Here in Proverbs 30, we see something stunning. Here's how it begins:

> The words of Agur the son of Jakeh, even the prophecy: the man spake unto Ithiel, even unto Ithiel and Ucal,
>
> Surely I am more brutish than any man, and have not the understanding of a man. I neither learned wisdom, nor have the knowledge of the holy.
>
> *Who hath ascended up into heaven, or descended? who hath gathered the wind in his fists? who hath bound the waters in a garment? who hath established all the ends of the earth? what is his name, and what is his son's name, if thou canst tell?* (vv. 1–4, emphasis added)

Notice that this wisdom book, this poetic book, begins by labeling the proverb as a "prophecy." Indeed, it is, for it explicitly and unambiguously foreshadows the revelation of God's holy Son, the Savior, the Redeemer, the Messiah, the King of kings. It's a gospel bombshell!

I have actually read commentaries on the Proverbs and other Old Testament books that say one can't find the gospel explicitly. It was statements like that, as much as the challenge by Jesus on the road to Emmaus, that compelled me to undertake this study. After all, even as a casual reader of the Hebrew Scriptures, I ran smack-dab into verses like this that blew my mind. I wondered, "How did the sages miss this? How could they deny God had a Son?"

Yet, they did and they do. How did they miss the plain words on the pages? How do people still miss them today? Maybe they don't *want* to see.

In Proverbs 1:7, we read, "The fear of the LORD is the beginning of knowledge: but fools despise wisdom and instruction." Wisdom is not much in fashion in the church today. Yet, for King Solomon, it was his utmost desire and his endless pursuit. Sadly, our world's neglect of this pursuit will have dire consequences. Jesus Himself said, "The queen of the south shall rise up in the judgment with this generation, and shall condemn it: for she came from the uttermost parts of the earth to hear the wisdom of Solomon; and, behold, a greater than Solomon is here" (Matthew 12:42, emphasis added). Unfortunately, this generation has abandoned not just the pursuit of wisdom, but Wisdom Himself.

And what about what He said in Luke 21:15? "For I will give you a mouth and wisdom, which all your adversaries shall not be able to gainsay nor resist." Jesus didn't just speak wisdom, He is wisdom. Remember: He is the Word of God. And He encourages us to be as "wise as serpents, and harmless as doves" (Matthew 10:15). We are to be wise men and women who build our houses on a rock of wisdom from God's Word (see Matthew 7:23-25).

I can't speak for others, but when I read the words of Proverbs 1:23–33, I hear the clear voice of Jesus:

> Turn you at my reproof: behold, I will pour out my spirit unto you, I will make known my words unto you. Because I have called, and ye refused; I have stretched out my hand, and no man regarded; But ye have set at nought all my counsel, and would none of my reproof: I also will laugh at your calamity; I will mock when your fear cometh; When your fear cometh as desolation, and your destruction cometh as a whirlwind; when distress and anguish cometh upon you. Then shall they call upon me, but I will not answer; they shall seek me early,

but they shall not find me: For that they hated knowledge, and did not choose the fear of the LORD: They would none of my counsel: they despised all my reproof. Therefore shall they eat of the fruit of their own way, and be filled with their own devices. For the turning away of the simple shall slay them, and the prosperity of fools shall destroy them. But whoso hearkeneth unto me shall dwell safely, and shall be quiet from fear of evil.

It's not a coincidence that Jesus is called "the wisdom of God" in 1 Corinthians 1:24. Likewise, He's called in Colossians 2:3 the one "in whom are hid all the treasures of wisdom and knowledge." So, the entire book of Proverbs could, and perhaps should, be viewed as a tribute to Him—along with all the Hebrew Scriptures, which, "beginning at Moses and all the prophets" were "things concerning *himself*" (Luke 24:27, emphasis added).

Meditate, for instance, on Proverbs 8—not just the following passages, but in its entirety. Could these be the very words of Jesus, who is the personification of Wisdom, with a capital *W*? I strongly expect these are His very words, at least in the sense of dictation to a human scribe:

VERSES 5–10: "O ye simple, understand wisdom: and, ye fools, be ye of an understanding heart. Hear; for I will speak of excellent things; and the opening of my lips shall be right things. For my mouth shall speak truth; and wickedness is an abomination to my lips. All the words of my mouth are in righteousness; there is nothing froward or perverse in them. They are all plain to him that understandeth, and right to them that find knowledge. Receive my instruction, and not silver; and knowledge rather than choice gold."

No mere mortal, of course, could make such assertions. But there's more. Read the following and ask yourself who else but Jesus could speak these words.

VERSES 12–36 "I wisdom dwell with prudence, and find out knowledge of witty inventions. The fear of the Lord is to hate evil: pride, and arrogancy, and the evil way, and the froward mouth, do I hate. Counsel is mine, and sound wisdom: I am understanding; I have strength. By me kings reign, and princes decree justice. By me princes rule, and nobles, even all the judges of the earth. I love them that love me; and those that seek me early shall find me. Riches and honour are with me; yea, durable riches and righteousness. My fruit is better than gold, yea, than fine gold; and my revenue than choice silver. I lead in the way of righteousness, in the midst of the paths of judgment: That I may cause those that love me to inherit substance; and I will fill their treasures. The Lord possessed me in the beginning of his way, before his works of old. I was set up from everlasting, from the beginning, or ever the earth was. When there were no depths, I was brought forth; when there were no fountains abounding with water. Before the mountains were settled, before the hills was I brought forth: While as yet he had not made the earth, nor the fields, nor the highest part of the dust of the world. When he prepared the heavens, I was there: when he set a compass upon the face of the depth: When he established the clouds above: when he strengthened the fountains of the deep: When he gave to the sea his decree, that the waters should not pass his commandment: when he appointed the foundations of the earth: Then I was by him, as one brought up with him: and I was daily his delight, rejoicing always before him; Rejoicing in the habitable part of his earth; and my delights were with the sons of men. Now therefore hearken unto me, O ye children: for blessed are they that keep my ways. Hear instruction, and be wise, and refuse it not. Blessed is the man that heareth me, watching daily at my gates, waiting at the posts of my doors. For whoso findeth me findeth life, and shall obtain favour of the Lord. But he that sinneth against me wrongeth his own soul: all they that hate me love death.

In John 1, Jesus is revealed as the Creator of all things. Who but He could utter these words of good news? He is the only Mediator between God and man. He was there at Creation, we're reminded in John 1, making everything that was made. It's Him in whom we find life. Those who hate Him hate life.

Indeed, the entirety of the Proverbs is poetic encouragement to righteousness and discouragement to sin. All the words found within this book affirm all the instructions of the Bible, including the words of Jesus in the Gospels. That's why they are so valuable to read regularly, systematically, even daily. They are not just beautiful and inspirational; they are true reminders about our behavior and our state of mind. They are also a reminder that God seeks for us our best interests, as seen in Proverbs 18:24, where we are reminded that "there is a friend that sticketh closer than a brother," a friend that preachers and Bible scholars consistently identify as Jesus Himself. In Proverbs 22:11, we are reminded that that friend who is closer than a brother is our King: "He that loveth pureness of heart, for the grace of his lips the king shall be his friend." And in Proverbs 29:14, we're told: "The king that faithfully judgeth the poor, his throne shall be established for ever."

Proverbs 20:9 obseres, simply and poignantly, that, while we are to seek the path of righteousness, we need help in atoning for our transgressions of the law: "Who can say, I have made my heart clean, I am pure from my sin? And in Proverbs 21:2 we find out why we so desperately need that help: "Every way of a man is right in his own eyes: but the LORD pondereth the hearts."

What does the gospel itself tell us?

- **MATTHEW 6:21** "For where your treasure is, there will your heart be also."

- **MATTHEW 5:8** "Blessed are the pure in heart: for they shall see God."

- MATTHEW 22:37 "Thou shalt love the Lord thy God with all thy heart, and with all thy soul, and with all thy mind."

Summing it all up, the book of Proverbs is a study in the biblical principle of actions and consequences. In the economy of the kingdom of God, behavior always predicts outcome. We hear the same warning from Paul in Galatians 6:7: "Be not deceived; God is not mocked: for whatsoever a man soweth, that shall he also reap." It's one thing to hear it once. It's another when a book like Proverbs gives the message over and over, repeatedly, using different words with the same meaning. It's more than encouragement, it's also *dis*couragement of behavior that can deprive us of entering the kingdom. Think of it as a training manual for the kingdom of God that instructs us on what to do and what not to do.

In a nutshell, Proverbs is about righteous behavior versus unrighteous behavior, a clean heart versus an unclean heart.

Paul tells us in Romans 1: "For I am not ashamed of the gospel of Christ: for it is the power of God unto salvation to every one that believeth; to the Jew first, and also to the Greek. For therein is the righteousness of God revealed from faith to faith: as it is written, The just shall live by faith." He then warns, "For the wrath of God is revealed from heaven against all ungodliness and unrighteousness of men, who hold the truth in unrighteousness" (vv. 16–18).

It was true before Jesus came to earth to minister in human form. It remained true after He ascended. And it will still be true when He returns in power and might to set up His kingdom on earth.

One more thing: As you know, the word *gospel* translates to "good news." Do you know there's only one place in the Bible where that common expression is actually translated as "good news"? It's in Proverbs 25:25: "As cold waters to a thirsty soul, so is good news from a far country." Well, the *real* good news is the *gospel*. So were we to say instead, "As cold waters to a thirsty soul, so is the *gospel* from a far country," is it still true? Does it still make sense? Indeed, it makes *more* sense than ever.

21

THE GOSPEL IN ECCLESIASTES

Vanity of vanities, saith the Preacher, vanity of vanities; all is vanity.
—ECCLESIASTES 1:2

I OFTEN WONDER, when I read the book of Ecclesiastes, which Solomon wrote it.

Was it the Solomon who walked with God and talked with God at the time the temple was built and dedicated? Or was it the young king who loved the Lord and walked in the statutes of David his father, but sacrificed and burned incense in high places?

Was it the Solomon who loved many strange women, together with the daughter of Pharaoh, women of the Moabites, Ammonites, Edomites, Zidonians, and Hittites who turned his heart after their gods—Ashteroth, the goddess of the Zidonians, and Milcom, the abomination of the Ammonites —so that it was not perfect with the Lord his God?

Was it the Solomon who did evil in the sight of the Lord and who built a high place for Chemosh, the abomination of Moab, and for Molech, the abomination of Ammon?

Or was it the Solomon who was the wisest man in the world? It's hard to know.

Some have even wondered whether this book belongs in Holy Scripture. But I don't. I believe if the one true God of Israel didn't purpose it to be there, it would not be found today in the Bible.

But some disagree. Why? What is Ecclesiastes' purpose? How does this book lead people to Truth with a capital *T*—meaning, Jesus and the salvation message of the gospel?

Whichever Solomon wrote this book, whether the author of the Proverbs or the one whose kingdom would be divided after his death because of his sinfulness, it was written under the inspiration of the Holy Spirit and has the power to lead people to God.

After all, when are people most inclined to search for meaning in life? Is it when they are at the top of the world, prosperous, seemingly in command of their own destiny, when they are looked upon by the world as having all the answers? Or is it when they fall into despair and are on the verge of losing everything?

The answer to that question is *yes*. People are most apt to search for God at *both* those times.

Ecclesiastes is for all of us, because every human being faces temptations and challenges in life that raise doubts about God, even Solomon who had relationship with Him. Like Adam and Eve, Solomon had real, tangible, multiple encounters with God. Yet all three fell. Whether they ultimately repented we know not with certainty.

Yet, the questions raised by Solomon in Ecclesiastes, at whatever stage of life he recorded them, are valuable to all of us. As Paul wrote in Romans 3:23: "For all have sinned, and come short of the glory of God;"

I believe Ecclesiastes is for those who have doubts about God but can't stop thinking about Him. Yet, how could Solomon, the son of David, the wisest man on earth, a man who had met with Him and spoken with Him, cease from musing about God?

Think of Ecclesiastes as an intellectual and spiritual challenge— perhaps, not unlike the parables of Jesus, about which He spoke "because it is given unto you [His disciples] to know the mysteries of the kingdom of heaven, but to them [the world] it is not given" (Matthew 13:11). Consider that gospel message.

Vanity? What did Paul say in Romans 8:20–21? "For the creature was made subject to vanity, not willingly, but by reason of him who hath subjected the same in hope, Because the creature itself also shall be delivered from the bondage of corruption into the glorious liberty of the children of God."

Isaiah 41 speaks of vanity too. It's the vanity of men's works, we see in verses 28–29: "For I beheld, and there was no man; even among them, and there was no counsellor, that, when I asked of them, could answer a word. Behold, they are all vanity; their works are nothing: their molten images are wind and confusion." It will all be undone, if you will, by the work of God's Redeemer when the earth is restored.

As Solomon wrote in Ecclesiastes 7:29: "Lo, this only have I found, that God hath made man upright; but they have sought out many inventions." We know from his own history in Scripture that Solomon found this out through personal experience—experience he has shared with us in this book.

And what do the gospels say about Solomon?

- MATTHEW 6:28–29 "And why take ye thought for raiment? Consider the lilies of the field, how they grow; they toil not, neither do they spin: And yet I say unto you, That even Solomon in all his glory was not arrayed like one of these."

- MATTHEW 12:42 "The queen of the south shall rise up in the judgment with this generation, and shall condemn it: for she came from the uttermost parts of the earth to hear the wisdom of Solomon; and, behold, a greater than Solomon is here."

Jesus affirmed the historical reality of what we know about Solomon from the Hebrew Scriptures. Solomon was born into prosperity and power and gifted by God with unparalleled wisdom. Yet, without his example, Jesus would not be able to point out the simple fact that One "greater than Solomon is here."

If not in God, what do people think would give them lasting fulfillment and happiness? Solomon had it all: wealth, power, wisdom, respect, a thousand wives, and even more servants to do his bidding. He also got to talk with God, to hear from Him directly. I think most of us believe that if we had all that—worldly treasures and direct proof of God— there would be no temptation in our lives, no reason for despair, no reason for doubt. Ecclesiastes is there to dispel any such notion. It demonstrates for us the true nature of human beings, just as we recognize how Adam and Eve, living in an idyllic paradise in the garden of Eden, fell hard and fast.

Is it not worth a reminder in the Bible of how this works?

As negative as many of the passages of Ecclesiastes tend to be, consider the other side: think of what Solomon unequivocally proclaimed in this book:

- What we do in this world will have eternal consequences. (3:1–15)

- God will judge the entire world. (3:16–17)

- Only those who fear God and trust in Him will experience eternal happiness. (7:18; 8:12–13; 9:7)

- Fearing God is the key to mercy and His acceptance of us as His children. (5:1–6)

- One should live prudently and in moderation. (7:1–27 et al.)

- Riches and worldly pleasures are vanities that can rob us of eternal life. (5:10–14)

- Standing in our own righteousness is a vanity that leads to destruction. (7:16–18)

- This life is not vanity, for it's man's only chance to impact his eternal destiny. (9:1–6)

So, what do we have here in the book of Ecclesiastes? We have the gospel, albeit in a perhaps unexpected and surprising form of expression. Should we expect anything else from an all- knowing and all-powerful Creator God who has seen it all?

If you doubt what I am saying, I will conclude by quoting the last six verses of chapter 9, which I consider to be a simple foreshadowing of the coming of the Messiah:

> This wisdom have I seen also under the sun, and it seemed great unto me: There was a little city, and few men within it; and there came a great king against it, and besieged it, and built great bulwarks against it: Now there was found in it a poor wise man, and he by his wisdom delivered the city; yet no man remembered that same poor man. Then said I, Wisdom is better than strength: nevertheless the poor man's wisdom is despised, and his words are not heard. The words of wise men are heard in quiet more than the cry of him that ruleth among fools. Wisdom is better than weapons of war: but one sinner destroyeth much good (vv. 13–18).

Jesus delivered all humanity from the curse of the law and will one day deliver the entire world from the presence of evil, and the Bible tells us that He, like the wise man in this passage, had no place to lay His head (Matthew 8:20), and He was rejected of men. Note how similarly in this passage "no man remembered that same poor man." Solomon, blessed with wisdom, considered the insight he shared here "great." At the end of the day, I guess it matters not at which point in his life Solomon wrote Ecclesiastes. As he wrote, there's a time to every purpose under the sun. Perhaps he wrote it throughout his tumultuous and remarkable time on earth.

What matters, for the purpose of this book, is that the gospel is found In Ecclesiastes, as it is in every book of the Old Testament.

22

THE GOSPEL IN SONG OF SOLOMON

A fountain of gardens, a well of living waters, and streams from Lebanon.
—SONG OF SOLOMON 4:15

IF ECCLESIASTES WAS FOUND by some to be questionable material for scripture, what of the Song of Solomon?

"Let him kiss me with the kisses of his mouth: for thy love is better than wine," it begins. "Because of the savour of thy good ointments thy name is as ointment poured forth, therefore do the virgins love thee. Draw me, we will run after thee: the king hath brought me into his chambers: we will be glad and rejoice in thee, we will remember thy love more than wine: the upright love thee."

But is this the writing of Solomon about one of his racy love affairs? Or, is it the allegorical story of God's relationship with "His bride"—otherwise known as His remnant, His assembly, His elect.

While most of Scripture is to be viewed literally as history or prophecy of future events. One cannot forget that there is allegory found in the Bible. When Jesus speaks in parables, He is telling stories that require interpretation. Those stories are intended to be understood in context. They are intended to be understood by those with discernment under the anointing of the Holy Spirit. Thus, the Song of Solomon is written in a similar vein.

So, whom is God's bride? That's how scripture refers to God's relationship with His elect—akin to a marriage covenant first made with Abraham and Sarah through their son, Isaac, and his son Jacob or Israel.

- ISAIAH 61:10 "I will greatly rejoice in the Lord, my soul shall be joyful in my God; for he hath clothed me with the garments of salvation, he hath covered me with the robe of righteousness, as a bridegroom decketh himself with ornaments, and as a bride adorneth herself with her jewels."

- ISAIAH 62:5 "For as a young man marrieth a virgin, so shall thy sons marry thee: and as the bridegroom rejoiceth over the bride, so shall thy God rejoice over thee."

- JEREMIAH 2:32 "Can a maid forget her ornaments, or a bride her attire? yet my people have forgotten me days without number."

- JEREMIAH 33:11 "The voice of joy, and the voice of gladness, the voice of the bridegroom, and the voice of the bride, the voice of them that shall say, Praise the Lord of hosts: for the Lord is good; for his mercy endureth for ever: and of them that shall bring the sacrifice of praise into the house of the Lord. For I will cause to return the captivity of the land, as at the first, saith the Lord."

- **JOEL 2:16** "Gather the people, sanctify the congregation, assemble the elders, gather the children, and those that suck the breasts: let the bridegroom go forth of his chamber, and the bride out of her closet."

Of course, Jesus Himself used similar allusions in the gospels:

- **MATTHEW 9:15** "And Jesus said unto them, Can the children of the bridechamber mourn, as long as the bridegroom is with them? but the days will come, when the bridegroom shall be taken from them, and then shall they fast."

- **MATTHEW 25:1** "Then shall the kingdom of heaven be likened unto ten virgins, which took their lamps, and went forth to meet the bridegroom."

That's the way the ancient rabbis interpreted the Song of Solomon—as a metaphor for the relationship between God and His elect. Christians, too, from the earliest times, have similarly seen the bride as the elect through faith and the Bridegroom as Jesus. Indeed, throughout the Hebrew scriptures, God is pictured as pursuing Israel as His bride. On the other side of the coin, Israel's unfaithfulness to God, is called adultery.

- **JEREMIAH 3:8** "And I saw, when for all the causes whereby backsliding Israel committed adultery I had put her away, and given her a bill of divorce; yet her treacherous sister Judah feared not, but went and played the harlot also."

- **EZEKIEL 23:37** "That they have committed adultery, and blood is in their hands, and with their idols have they committed adultery, and have also caused their sons, whom they bare unto me, to pass for them through the fire, to devour them."

The Exodus from Egypt, in fact, took 40 years in the wilderness because God saw Israel chasing after other gods and called those actions "whoredoms." (Numbers 14:33)

So, what we see in the Song of Solomon is God's relentless pursuit of his bride, Israel and, and later, the gentiles. And the Bridegroom is none other than Jesus. In fact, this was affirmed by John the Baptist who explained His role in the gospels: "He that hath the bride is the bridegroom: but the friend of the bridegroom, which standeth and heareth him, rejoiceth greatly because of the bridegroom's voice: this my joy therefore is fulfilled. He must increase, but I must decrease." (John 3:29-30)

Likewise, there is much to be learned about the relationship between bride and Bridegroom in the Song of Solomon that may be instructive to us today, when the Bridegroom's return may be imminent.

- In Song of Solomon 3:1-2, the bride looks for her lover and finds Him not. "I will rise now, and go about the city in the streets, and in the broad ways I will seek him whom my soul loveth: I sought him, but I found him not." Why did she find Him not? Because she was looking in the "broad ways." But it's the narrow gate that followers of Jesus are to seek because the broad paths lead to destruction, as we learn in the Gospel of Matthew 7:13.

- In Song of Solomon 5, the Bridegroom knocks on the door of His bride, but she is sleeping. By the time she gets up out of bed, He is gone. In Mark 13:32-36, Jesus warns His Bride not to be caught in that condition when He returns. "But of that day and that hour knoweth no man, no, not the angels which are in heaven, neither the Son, but the Father. Take ye heed, watch and pray: for ye know not when the time is. For the Son of Man is as a man taking a far journey, who left his house, and gave authority to his servants, and to every man his work, and commanded the porter to watch. Watch ye therefore: for ye know not when the master of the house cometh, at even, or at midnight, or at the cockcrowing, or in the morning: Lest coming suddenly he find you sleeping."

- In chapter the final chapter, the two are still beckoning to each other—seemingly in love with being in love—yet somehow missing one another. There's much love and passion expressed in this book, but it seems the bride and the Bridegroom are somehow not always communicating effectively.

Again in chapter 5:5-9, the bride looks for her "beloved" who has "had withdrawn himself, and was gone," just as Jesus withdrew Himself and was "gone" after His ascension. "[M] soul failed when he spake: I sought him, but I could not find him; I called him, but he gave me no answer," she says. And this is where it gets interesting. "The watchmen that went about the city found me, they smote me, they wounded me; the keepers of the walls took away my veil from me." If this bride is indeed a representation of the bride of the Messiah, could this be a prophetic allusion to the kind of persecution witnessed by the messianic believers in Jerusalem in the first century? If you think that's a stretch, consider what follows: "I charge you," the bride continues, "O daughters of Jerusalem, if ye find my beloved, that ye tell him, that I am sick of love." Thus, the "daughters of Jerusalem" are those who are as yet unmarried—metaphorically, those who have not committed themselves to Jesus the Messiah. Their response to the bride is thus: "What is thy beloved more than another beloved, O thou fairest among women? what is thy beloved more than another beloved, that thou dost so charge us?" This is confirmation that these maidens do not recognize anything special about this particular bridegroom, who may represent the Bridegroom.

I recognize that some might not see Song of Solomon as an analogy for the pursuit of the Bridegroom of all bridegrooms—the

Messiah, despite how often that allegory is made throughout Scripture. However, the very phrase found in Song of Solomon "Daughters of Jerusalem" is found in the words of Jesus as He carried His cross to Calvary. He was speaking to women who were "bewailing and lamenting Him," we see in Luke 23:27. Now that Jesus has been tortured and is heading to His execution, they are mourning for Him. He then addresses them thusly in verses 28-31: "Daughters of Jerusalem, weep not for me, but weep for yourselves, and for your children. For, behold, the days are coming, in the which they shall say, Blessed are the barren, and the wombs that never bare, and the paps which never gave suck. Then shall they begin to say to the mountains, Fall on us; and to the hills, Cover us. For if they do these things in a green tree, what shall be done in the dry?" Jesus is obviously referring to the judgment that will soon fall of Jerusalem.

There's one more important gospel element found in Song of Solomon, but most people miss it. There is a fleeting mention—the very first in scripture—of "living waters." The next time we'll hear about these living waters, which accompany Jesus' return in the Kingdom of Heaven on Earth, is in Jeremiah. It's only a hint here—without explanation. But you'll learn more about why it's important in future chapters.

And to whom is Jesus, who personifies "Living Waters" as He Himself explains to the Samaritan woman at the well, comparing to "living waters"? His bride—the faithful believers in Him. And there it is, the first mention of "living waters" in the Bible—in an allegorical reference in which Jesus compares His bride to Himself.

23

THE GOSPEL IN ISAIAH

Come now, and let us reason together, saith the LORD: *though your sins be as scarlet, they shall be as white as snow; though they be red like crimson, they shall be as wool.* —ISAIAH 1:18

But he was wounded for our transgressions, he was bruised for our iniquities: the chastisement of our peace was upon him; and with his stripes we are healed. —ISAIAH 53:5

ADMITTEDLY, you might have to search for the gospel in the Song of Solomon, which we looked at in the last chapter. You might even think it's a stretch *connecting* it to the gospel. Not so with Isaiah.

While some books of the Tanakh allude to the gospel message, the coming of Messiah and the coming kingdom of Jesus, Isaiah is bursting with it. In fact, friends of mine who spend a lot of their time evangelizing unsaved Jews have told me that when they quote passages of Isaiah as part of their witness, they are often challenged that they are quoting the New Testament, not the Old.

I believe it. I have no doubts. The gospel is so apparent, so obvious, so conspicuous in Isaiah that one would need no other book to make the persuasive intellectual case for Jesus as Messiah. Understandably, Isaiah is the most quoted prophet in the New Testament.

Yet, it's more than that. For the gospel message is spelled out in Isaiah in its entirety:

- God is holy: "I am the LORD, your Holy One, the creator of Israel, your King" (43:15).

- Everyone has fallen short: "For our transgressions are multiplied before thee, and our sins testify against us: for our transgressions are with us; and as for our iniquities, we know them" (59:12).

- Sin separates us from God: "But your iniquities have separated between you and your God, and your sins have hid his face from you, that he will not hear" (59:2).

- Messiah has taken our sin upon Himself: "All we like sheep have gone astray; we have turned every one to his own way; and the LORD hath laid on him the iniquity of us all" (53:6).

- We must seek Him and call on Him for salvation: "Seek ye the LORD while he may be found, call ye upon him while he is near" (55:6).

- The fallen nature of man will be redeemed in the future kingdom of God on earth: "Thy Redeemer [is] the Holy One of Israel; the God of the whole earth shall he be called" (54:5); cf. Mark 1:24; Luke 4:34

Even Isaiah's very name, like Jesus', is meaningful in this context: "YHWH is salvation." Yet, Isaiah, one of four major prophets, lived about eight centuries before the coming of Jesus, at a time when Assyria was threatening the southern kingdom of Judah. Some readers have observed that there are sixty-six chapters in Isaiah and sixty-six books in the Bible and that the second half of Isaiah is more messianic in nature, just as the second half of the Bible is.

Before we walk through Isaiah systematically and chronologically for the in-depth study this unique book deserves, let me point out that I began with more than fifty thousand words in notes for this chapter before I began writing. Obviously, one could easily write an entire book or even a multi-book series on the gospel in Isaiah, for you can find it in every chapter. For that reason, however, I will only mention the most remarkable gospel verses. If I don't mention some of your favorites, forgive me in advance.

CHAPTER 1

Isaiah opens with a strong condemnation of his generation. God speaks through him in deploring even the prayers, sacrifices, and oblations of the people. Yet, hope is offered in Isaiah 1:16–18 in these familiar and comforting words: "Wash you, make you clean; put away the evil of your doings from before mine eyes; cease to do evil; learn to do well; seek judgment, relieve the oppressed, judge the fatherless, plead for the widow. Come now, and let us reason together, saith the LORD: though your sins be as scarlet, they shall be as white as snow; though they be red like crimson, they shall be as wool."

Isaiah returns to indictment of his generation, then shifting to a picture of the coming kingdom, the component of the gospel Peter explained in Acts 3, to which all the prophets pointed with hope and expectation: "Therefore saith the LORD, the LORD of hosts, the mighty One of Israel, Ah, I will ease me of mine adversaries, and avenge me of mine enemies: And I will turn my hand upon thee, and purely purge away thy dross, and take away all thy tin: And I will restore thy judges as at the first, and thy counsellors as at the beginning: afterward thou shalt be called, The city of righteousness, the faithful city. Zion shall be redeemed with judgment, and her converts with righteousness" (1:24–27).

CHAPTER 2

Having written a book on this kingdom, I can attest that in Isaiah there are more glimpses into this future paradise on earth, presided over by Messiah Jesus, than in any other single book in the Bible. And it resumes immediately in Isaiah 2:2–4:

> And it shall come to pass in the last days, that the mountain of the LORD's house shall be established in the top of the mountains, and shall be exalted above the hills; and all nations shall flow unto it. And many people shall go and say, Come ye, and let us go up to the mountain of the LORD, to the house of the God of Jacob; and he will teach us of his ways, and we will walk in his paths: for out of Zion shall go forth the law, and the word of the LORD from Jerusalem. And he shall judge among the nations, and shall rebuke many people: and they shall beat their swords into plowshares, and their spears into pruninghooks: nation shall not lift up sword against nation, neither shall they learn war any more.

More unmistakable flashes of the kingdom continue in Isaiah 2:10–12: "Enter into the rock, and hide thee in the dust, for fear of the LORD, and for the glory of his majesty. The lofty looks of man shall be humbled, and the haughtiness of men shall be bowed down, and the LORD alone shall be exalted in that day. For the day of the LORD of hosts shall be upon every one that is proud and lofty, and upon every one that is lifted up; and he shall be brought low:"

CHAPTER 4

Contrasting with the evildoing of Isaiah's time, he points to the future of Jesus' everlasting kingdom on earth in Isaiah 4:2–3: "In that day shall the branch of the LORD be beautiful and glorious, and the fruit of the earth shall be excellent and comely for them that are escaped of Israel. And it shall come to pass, that he that is left in Zion, and he that remaineth in Jerusalem, shall be called holy, even every one that is written among the living in Jerusalem." He further prophesied for that kingdom that there will be a giant canopy of protection over Jerusalem: "And the LORD will create upon every dwelling place of mount Zion, and upon her assemblies, a cloud and smoke by day, and the shining of a flaming fire by night: for upon all the glory shall be a defence. And there shall be a tabernacle for a shadow in the day time from the heat, and for a place of refuge, and for a covert from storm and from rain" (4:5–6).

CHAPTER 5

Once again, Isaiah 5:15–17 peers into the future, presenting a vivid depiction of what it will be like in the redeemed world ruled over by Messiah Jesus: "And the mean man shall be brought down, and the mighty man shall be humbled, and the eyes of the lofty shall be humbled: But the LORD of hosts shall be exalted in judgment, and God that is holy shall be sanctified in righteousness. Then shall the lambs feed after their manner, and the waste places of the fat ones shall strangers eat."

CHAPTER 6

Much of this chapter is dark, but the hope and light come forth in the last verse 13 as the holy remnant is saved: "But yet in it shall be a tenth, and it shall return, and shall be eaten: as a teil tree, and as an oak, whose substance is in them, when they cast their leaves: so the holy seed shall be the substance thereof" (v. 13).

CHAPTER 7

In Isaiah 7:14, we see this amazing prophecy about the birth of Jesus: "Therefore the LORD himself shall give you a sign; Behold, a virgin shall conceive, and bear a son, and shall call his name Immanuel." This same prophecy is quoted in Matthew 1:23.

CHAPTER 9

One of the most remarkable passages in all the Bible is Isaiah 9:6–8. You can find it on Christmas cards in the twenty-first century. Just reading these words, one cannot think of any other person in history besides Jesus. If you read this passage to the average person, he will swear it's from the New Testament. Stranger still is the context. These three verses are dropped into the middle of an ancient history lesson from Isaiah's time—seemingly without any transition. And for that reason, their impact is dramatic:

> For unto us a child is born, unto us a son is given: and the government shall be upon his shoulder: and his name shall be called Wonderful, Counsellor, The mighty God, The everlasting Father, The Prince of Peace. Of the increase of his government and peace there shall be no end, upon the throne of David, and upon his kingdom, to order it, and to establish it with judgment and with justice from henceforth even for ever. The zeal of the LORD of hosts will perform this. The Lord sent a word into Jacob, and it hath lighted upon Israel.

CHAPTER 10

Again, in Isaiah 10:20–22, the light of hope is briefly shone in the midst of the spiritual darkness of the prophet's day: "And it shall come to pass in that day, that the remnant of Israel, and such as are escaped of the house of Jacob, shall no more again stay upon him that smote them; but shall stay upon the LORD, the Holy One of Israel, in truth. The remnant shall return, even the remnant of Jacob, unto the mighty God. For though thy people Israel be as the sand of the sea, yet a remnant of them shall return: the consumption decreed shall overflow with righteousness."

CHAPTER 11

The entirety of Isaiah 11 is about the coming of the Lord, not when He appeared as the Suffering Servant, who laid down His life for the sins of the world, but when He comes in the future as the conquering King. Verses 1 and 2 read, "And there shall come forth a rod out of the stem of Jesse, and a Branch shall grow out of his roots: And the spirit of the LORD shall rest upon him, the spirit of wisdom and understanding, the spirit of counsel and might, the spirit of knowledge and of the fear of the LORD."

CHAPTER 12

Likewise, Isaiah 12 is entirely about the coming kingdom, ruled and reigned over by Jesus from Jerusalem:

> And in that day thou shalt say, O LORD, I will praise thee: though thou wast angry with me, thine anger is turned away, and thou comfortedst me. Behold, God is my salvation; I will trust, and not be afraid: for the LORD JEHOVAH is my strength and my song; he also is become my salvation. Therefore with joy shall ye draw water out of the wells of salvation. And in that day shall ye say, Praise the LORD, call upon his name, declare his doings among the people, make mention that his name is exalted. Sing unto the LORD; for he hath done excellent things: this is known in all the earth. Cry out and shout, thou inhabitant of Zion: for great is the Holy One of Israel in the midst of thee.

CHAPTER 14

This is a most interesting chapter that deals with the restoration of Israel and the whole earth being at rest, while Satan is being cut down to the ground: Verses 5–7: "The LORD hath broken the staff of the wicked, and the sceptre of the rulers. He who smote the people in wrath with a continual stroke, he that ruled the nations in anger, is persecuted, and none hindereth. The whole earth is at rest, and is quiet: they break forth into singing."

CHAPTER 16

This chapter mostly deals with the judgment of Moab, but one of the most famous prophecies of the coming kingdom is found in Isaiah 16:5: "And in mercy shall the throne be established: and he shall sit upon it in truth in the tabernacle of David, judging, and seeking judgment, and hasting righteousness." That's Jesus, of course, on the throne of David.

CHAPTER 19

Isaiah 19 has always fascinated me, I refer to it as "God's Middle East Peace Plan"—and this one is guaranteed to work. Read the entire, sometimes mystifying chapter, but I'll give away the ending here, with the final four verses, which show what the kingdom will be like when God makes peace in the roughest neighborhood in the world:

> And the LORD shall smite Egypt: he shall smite and heal it: and they shall return even to the LORD, and he shall be intreated of them, and shall heal them. In that day shall there be a highway out of Egypt to Assyria, and the Assyrian shall come into Egypt, and the Egyptian into Assyria, and the Egyptians shall serve with the Assyrians. In that day shall Israel be the third with Egypt and with Assyria, even a blessing in the midst of the land: Whom the LORD of hosts shall bless, saying, Blessed be Egypt my people, and Assyria the work of my hands, and Israel mine inheritance.

CHAPTER 22

See if *you* can tell who Isaiah 22:21–25 is about:

> And I will clothe him with thy robe, and strengthen him with thy girdle, and I will commit thy government into his hand: and he shall be a father to the inhabitants of Jerusalem, and to the house of Judah. And the key of the house of David will I lay upon his shoulder; so he shall open, and none shall shut; and he shall shut, and none shall open. And I will fasten him as a nail in a sure

place; and he shall be for a glorious throne to his father's house. And they shall hang upon him all the glory of his father's house, the offspring and the issue, all vessels of small quantity, from the vessels of cups, even to all the vessels of flagons. In that day, saith the LORD of hosts, shall the nail that is fastened in the sure place be removed, and be cut down, and fall; and the burden that was upon it shall be cut off: for the LORD hath spoken it.

CHAPTER 25

Here's another beautiful kingdom passage: "He will swallow up death in victory; and the Lord GOD will wipe away tears from off all faces; and the rebuke of his people shall he take away from off all the earth: for the LORD hath spoken it. And it shall be said in that day, Lo, this is our God; we have waited for him, and he will save us: this is the LORD; we have waited for him, we will be glad and rejoice in his salvation" (Isaiah 25:8–9).

CHAPTER 26

"In that day shall this song be sung in the land of Judah; We have a strong city; salvation will God appoint for walls and bulwarks," begins chapter 26. "Open ye the gates, that the righteous nation which keepeth the truth may enter in. Thou wilt keep him in perfect peace, whose mind is stayed on thee: because he trusteth in thee. Trust ye in the LORD for ever: for in the LORD JEHOVAH is everlasting strength" (vv. 1–4). It sounds like a gospel song, and it is. The entire chapter describes the return of the Lord and the establishment of His kingdom.

CHAPTER 28

Here's a key verse about Jesus, that is referenced in the New Testament: "Therefore thus saith the Lord GOD, Behold, I lay in Zion for a foundation a stone, a tried stone, a precious corner stone, a sure foundation: he that believeth shall not make haste" (Isaiah 28:16; see Romans 9:33).

CHAPTER 29

While much of Isaiah, as you can see, is prophecy about the second coming of Jesus, at which time He establishes the "perfect peace" mentioned in chapter 26, there are also so many striking predictions of the Messiah's first appearance. In Isaiah 29:13, we actually see words that will later be quoted by Jesus, whose ministry was controversial to the Pharisees, Sadducees, and other religious authorities of that time. What was that great controversy all about? Why was there so much conflict between Jesus and the Pharisees? Jesus explained in Matthew 15:7–9: "Ye hypocrites, well did Esaias [Isaiah] prophesy of you, saying, This people draweth nigh unto me with their mouth, and honoureth me with their lips; but their heart is far from me. But in vain they do worship me, teaching for doctrines the commandments of men." Here's the text from Isaiah, with its accompanying prophecy: "Wherefore the Lord said, Forasmuch as this people draw near me with their mouth, and with their lips do honour me, but have removed their heart far from me, and their fear toward me is taught by the precept of men: Therefore, behold, I will proceed to do a marvellous work among this people, even a marvellous work and a wonder: for the wisdom of their wise men shall perish, and the understanding of their prudent men shall be hid" (29:13–14).

CHAPTER 30

More good news, in Isaiah 30:18–19: "And therefore will the LORD wait, that he may be gracious unto you, and therefore will he be exalted, that he may have mercy upon you: for the LORD is a God of judgment: blessed are all they that wait for him. For the people shall dwell in Zion at Jerusalem: thou shalt weep no more: he will be very gracious unto thee at the voice of thy cry; when he shall hear it, he will answer thee."

CHAPTER 32

"Behold," we're reminded in Isaiah 32:1, "a king shall reign in righteousness, and princes shall rule in judgment." This is not just any king and not just any princes, but the King who will rule over the entire earth from Jerusalem and who will choose His princes to reign with Him. How can we be sure? Because Isaiah 32:3–4 goes on to say: "And the eyes of them that see shall not be dim, and the ears of them that hear shall hearken. The heart also of the rash shall understand knowledge, and the tongue of the stammerers shall be ready to speak plainly." And there's more, in verses 14–18: "The palaces shall be forsaken . . . until the spirit be poured upon us from on high, and the wilderness be a fruitful field, and the fruitful field be counted for a forest. Then judgment shall dwell in the wilderness, and righteousness remain in the fruitful field. And the work of righteousness shall be peace; and the effect of righteousness quietness and assurance for ever. And my people shall dwell in a peaceable habitation, and in sure dwellings, and in quiet resting places."

CHAPTER 33

"The LORD is exalted; for he dwelleth on high: he hath filled Zion with judgment and righteousness," Isaiah 33says, pointing to the coming kingdom. "And wisdom and knowledge shall be the stability of thy times, and strength of salvation: the fear of the LORD is his treasure" (vv. 5–6). The Lord speaks of rising and being exalted—lifting Himself up in verse 10. Then in verses 16 and 17 we read: "He shall dwell on high: his place of defence shall be the munitions of rocks: bread shall be given him; his waters shall be sure. Thine eyes shall see the king in his beauty: they shall behold the land that is very far off." And more hints of the kingdom follow in verses 20–24

> Look upon Zion, the city of our solemnities: thine eyes shall see Jerusalem a quiet habitation, a tabernacle that shall not be taken down; not one of the stakes thereof shall ever be removed, neither shall any of the cords thereof be broken. But there the glorious LORD will be unto us a place of broad rivers and streams; wherein shall go no galley with oars, neither shall gallant ship pass thereby. For the LORD is our judge, the LORD is our lawgiver, the LORD

is our king; he will save us. Thy tacklings are loosed; they could not well strengthen their mast, they could not spread the sail: then is the prey of a great spoil divided; the lame take the prey. And the inhabitant shall not say, I am sick: the people that dwell therein shall be forgiven their iniquity.

CHAPTER 34

There is a time of judgment of all nations and all people for "the controversy of Zion," or Jerusalem (v. 8), a controversy that we can plainly see in our world today, as most of the world denies its special place in God's economy. Isaiah 34:16–17 reminds all: "Seek ye out of the book of the LORD, and read . . . And he hath cast the lot for them, and his hand hath divided it unto them by line: they shall possess it for ever, from generation to generation shall they dwell therein."

CHAPTER 35

This is entirely a chapter describing how the Lord will save Jerusalem, Israel, and the world as God rules and reigns in peace, justice, and truth:

The wilderness and the solitary place shall be glad for them; and the desert shall rejoice, and blossom as the rose. It shall blossom abundantly, and rejoice even with joy and singing: the glory of Lebanon shall be given unto it, the excellency of Carmel and Sharon, they shall see the glory of the LORD, and the excellency of our God. Strengthen ye the weak hands, and confirm the feeble knees. Say to them that are of a fearful heart, Be strong, fear not: behold, your God will come with vengeance, even God with a recompence; he will come and save you. Then the eyes of the blind shall be opened, and the ears of the deaf shall be unstopped. Then shall the lame man leap as an hart, and the tongue of the dumb sing: for in the wilderness shall waters break out, and streams in the desert. And the parched ground shall become a pool, and the thirsty land springs of water: in the habitation of dragons, where each lay, shall be grass with reeds and rushes. And an highway shall be there, and a way, and it shall be called The way of holiness; the unclean shall not pass over it; but it shall be for those: the wayfaring men, though fools, shall not err therein. No lion shall be there, nor any ravenous beast shall go up thereon, it shall not be found there; but the redeemed shall walk there: And the ransomed of the LORD shall return, and come to Zion with songs and everlasting joy upon their heads: they shall obtain joy and gladness, and sorrow and sighing shall flee away.

CHAPTER 40

We read a familiar verse in Isaiah 40:3: "The voice of him that crieth in the wilderness, Prepare ye the way of the LORD, make straight in the desert a highway for our God." It's a prophecy about John the Baptist, we are told in Matthew 3:3. He would introduce the Savior of the world. Then, we're told in Isaiah 40:4–5: "Every valley shall be exalted, and every mountain and hill shall be made low: and the crooked shall be made straight, and the rough places plain: And the glory of the LORD shall be revealed, and all flesh shall see it together: for the mouth of the LORD hath spoken it." In verses 9–14 we see that this Messiah is not just a man, but God, who laid the foundations of the earth and was the Source of all creation:

> O Zion, that bringest good tidings, get thee up into the high mountain; O Jerusalem, that bringest good tidings, lift up thy voice with strength; lift it up, be not afraid; say unto the cities of Judah, Behold your God! Behold, the Lord GOD will come with strong hand, and his arm shall rule for him: behold, his reward is with him, and his work before him. He shall feed his flock like a shepherd: he shall gather the lambs with his arm, and carry them in his bosom, and shall gently lead those that are with young. Who hath measured the waters in the hollow of his hand, and meted out heaven with the span, and comprehended the dust of

the earth in a measure, and weighed the mountains in scales, and the hills in a balance? Who hath directed the Spirit of the LORD, or being his counsellor hath taught him? With whom took he counsel, and who instructed him, and taught him in the path of judgment, and taught him knowledge, and shewed to him the way of understanding?

They who trust in the Lord will be empowered, we see in the last verse of the chapter: "But they that wait upon the LORD shall renew their strength; they shall mount up with wings as eagles; they shall run, and not be weary; and they shall walk, and not faint."

CHAPTER 41

"I have raised up one from the north, and he shall come: from the rising of the sun shall he call upon my name: and he shall come upon princes as upon morter, and as the potter treadeth clay," we're told in this chapter. "Who hath declared from the beginning, that we may know? and beforetime, that we may say, He is righteous? yea, there is none that sheweth, yea, there is none that declareth, yea, there is none that heareth your words. The first shall say to Zion, Behold, behold them: and I will give to Jerusalem one that bringeth good tidings" (vv. 25–27). That "one" is Jesus Christ!

CHAPTER 42

Here we see a picture of Jesus both in His earthly ministry, healing the blind and freeing people of their bondage to sin, and in his kingdom ministry:

Behold my servant, whom I uphold; mine elect, in whom my soul delighteth; I have put my spirit upon him: he shall bring forth judgment to the Gentiles. He shall not cry, nor lift up, nor cause his voice to be heard in the street. A bruised reed shall he not break, and the smoking flax shall he not quench: he shall bring forth judgment unto truth. He shall not fail nor be discouraged, till he have set judgment in the earth: and the isles shall wait for his law. Thus saith God the LORD, he that created the heavens, and stretched them out; he that spread forth the earth, and that which cometh out of it; he that giveth breath unto the people upon it, and spirit to them that walk therein: the LORD have called thee in righteousness, and will hold thine hand, and will keep thee, and give thee for a covenant of the people, for a light of the Gentiles; to open the blind eyes, to bring out the prisoners from the prison, and them that sit in darkness out of the prison house.

When John the Baptist was imprisoned by Herod and sent messengers to Jesus to see if He was the One who was to come, or whether there would be another, Jesus explained in Luke 7:22: "Go your way, and tell John what things ye have seen and heard; how that the blind see, the lame walk, the lepers are cleansed, the deaf hear, the dead are raised, to the poor the gospel is preached." It had *already* been preached in this chapter of Isaiah!

CHAPTER 43
Likewise, in this chapter, we see a picture of the Messiah-Creator assuring Israel He is their One and only Savior. It's pure gospel— once again referring to the healing of the blind and lame, the proof text that Jesus is the One. Consider Isaiah 43:25: "I, even I, am he that blotteth out thy transgressions for mine own sake, and will not remember thy sins." In the Gospels, Jesus made no bones about His authority to forgive sins (Matthew 9:6; Mark 2:10; Luke 5:24).

CHAPTER 44
There are some key gospel verses in this chapter. Verses 1–2 show that God chose Israel, in fact, created it from the womb. Verse 3 says, "For I will pour water upon him that is thirsty, and floods upon the dry ground: I will pour my spirit upon thy seed, and my blessing upon thine offspring." Now read verses 6–8:

Thus saith the LORD the King of Israel, and his redeemer the LORD of hosts; I am the first, and I am the last; and beside me there is no God. And who, as I, shall call, and shall declare it, and set it in order for me, since I appointed the ancient people? and the things that are coming, and shall come, let them shew unto them. Fear ye not, neither be afraid: have not I told thee from that time, and have declared it? ye are even my witnesses. Is there a God beside me? yea, there is no God; I know not any.

And in verses 21–24 we learn that not only has God formed Israel; He formed the nation as His servant. He has "blotted out, as a thick cloud, thy transgressions, and, as a cloud, thy sins: return unto me; for I have redeemed thee."

CHAPTER 45

In Isaiah 45:11–13, the Lord declares Himself the "the Holy One of Israel" and the Creator. "I have made the earth, and created man upon it: I, even my hands, have stretched out the heavens, and all their host have I commanded. [See John 1:1–3.] I have raised him up in righteousness, and I will direct all his ways: he shall build my city, and he shall let go my captives, not for price nor reward, saith the LORD of hosts." Later, in verses 22–25, we see:

Look unto me, and be ye saved, all the ends of the earth: for I am God, and there is none else. I have sworn by myself, the word is gone out of my mouth in righteousness, and shall not return, That unto me every knee shall bow, every tongue shall swear. Surely, shall one say, in the Lord have I righteousness and strength: even to him shall men come; and all that are incensed against him shall be ashamed. In the LORD shall all the seed of Israel be justified, and shall glory." (See Romans 11:26.)

CHAPTER 46

We're reminded in this chapter that there is none like God, who declares "the end from the beginning, and from ancient times the things that are not yet done, saying, My counsel shall stand, and I will do all my pleasure" (v. 10). He will also bring His righteousness to the world. "My salvation," he said, "shall not tarry: and I will place salvation in Zion for Israel my glory" (v. 13).

CHAPTER 47

This chapter promises that there will be judgment of all evil, just as we see in the book of Revelation.

CHAPTER 48

In verse 12 of this chapter, God declares: "Hearken unto me, O Jacob and Israel, my called; I am he; I am the first, I also am the last." Four times in Revelation, the risen Jesus declares that He is the "Alpha and Omega, the beginning and the ending, the first and the last." Thus, this is Jesus speaking in Isaiah when He concludes: "Mine hand also hath laid the foundation of the earth, and my right hand hath spanned the heavens: when I call unto them, they stand up together" (v. 13). There's more here. Again, clearly, we hear the voice of Jesus in verses 16–18:

> Come ye near unto me, hear ye this; I have not spoken in secret from the beginning; from the time that it was, there am I: and now the Lord God, and his Spirit, hath sent me. Thus saith the Lord, thy Redeemer, the Holy One of Israel; I am the Lord thy God which teacheth thee to profit, which leadeth thee by the way that thou shouldest go. O that thou hadst hearkened to my commandments! then had thy peace been as a river, and thy righteousness as the waves of the sea.

Note that the Lord God and His Spirit have sent this messenger. Many see this as an Old Testament reference to the triune nature of God.

CHAPTER 49

Would you like to read a long passage spoken by Jesus—perhaps one you have never really seen or fully digested before? That would be quite a treat. That's the way I see Isaiah 49. Read it in its entirety and see if you don't agree. Many Bibles put the words of Jesus in red letters. It would seem obvious to me that this entire chapter could be in red. It includes some amazing insights and clues that it is Jesus speaking to us through eternity:

- **VERSE 1** "The Lord hath called me from the womb; from the bowels of my mother hath he made mention of my name." If it's not Jesus, born of a woman, who?

- **VERSE 2** "And he hath made my mouth like a sharp sword; in the shadow of his hand hath he hid me, and made me a polished shaft; in his quiver hath he hid me." Jesus is the Word, it is established in the gospel of John, and we are told in Hebrews 4:12: "For the word of God is quick, and powerful, and sharper than any twoedged sword, piercing even to the dividing asunder of soul and spirit, and of the joints and marrow, and is a discerner of the thoughts and intents of the heart."

- **VERSE 3** "And said unto me, Thou art my servant, O Israel, in whom I will be glorified." It is Jesus who will be glorified when He rules and reigns over Israel and the world.

- **VERSE 5** "And now, saith the Lord that formed me from the womb to be his servant, to bring Jacob again to him, Though Israel be not gathered, yet shall I be glorious in the eyes of the Lord, and my God shall be my strength." Can it be any other who will be glorified by regathering Israel through the strength of God?

- **VERSE 6** "And he said, It is a light thing that thou shouldest be my servant to raise up the tribes of Jacob, and to restore the preserved of Israel: I will also give thee for a light to the Gentiles, that thou mayest be my salvation unto the end of the earth." Who else gives light to the Gentiles?

- **VERSE 16** "Behold, I have graven thee upon the palms of my hands; thy walls are continually before me." That's what Jesus did by submitting to the cross. He took our sins upon His hands and covered them in His blood.

- **VERSE 22** "Thus saith the Lord GOD, Behold, I will lift up mine hand to the Gentiles, and set up my standard to the people: and they shall bring thy sons in their arms, and thy daughters shall be carried upon their shoulders."

- **VERSE 26** ". . . and all flesh shall know that I the Lord am thy Saviour and thy Redeemer, the mighty One of Jacob." Shouldn't these words be in red letters? Not only is this the gospel in the Old Testament; these are the actual words of Jesus, the light to the Gentiles. And there's more to come in this amazing book of Isaiah.

CHAPTER 51

If Isaiah 49 could be published in red letter, so, too, could all of Isaiah 51. "Hearken to me, ye that follow after righteousness, ye that seek the LORD: look unto the rock whence ye are hewn, and to the hole of the pit whence ye are digged," it says.

> Look unto Abraham your father, and unto Sarah that bare you: for I called him alone, and blessed him, and increased him. For the LORD shall comfort Zion: he will comfort all her waste places; and he will make her wilderness like Eden, and her desert like the garden of the LORD; joy and gladness shall be found therein,

thanksgiving, and the voice of melody. Hearken unto me, my people; and give ear unto me, O my nation: for a law shall proceed from me, and I will make my judgment to rest for a light of the people. My righteousness is near; my salvation is gone forth, and mine arms shall judge the people; the isles shall wait upon me, and on mine arm shall they trust (vv. 1–5).

CHAPTER 52

This passage contains two striking prophecies about Jesus: one regarding His sacrificial atonement and another about His Kingship over the earth: "Behold, my servant shall deal prudently, he shall be exalted and extolled, and be very high. As many were astonied at thee; his visage was so marred more than any man, and his form more than the sons of men: So shall he sprinkle many nations; the kings shall shut their mouths at him: for that which had not been told them shall they see; and that which they had not heard shall they consider" (vv. 13–15).

CHAPTER 53

This could well be one of those passages that if read to people with only limited knowledge of the Scriptures, they might easily and understandably conclude it's an excerpt from the New Testament—even the Gospels. Verses 3–12 read:

He is despised and rejected of men; a man of sorrows, and acquainted with grief: and we hid as it were our faces from him; he was despised, and we esteemed him not. Surely he hath borne our griefs, and carried our sorrows: yet we did esteem him stricken, smitten of God, and afflicted. But he was wounded for our transgressions, he was bruised for our iniquities: the chastisement of our peace was upon him; and with his stripes we are healed. All we like sheep have gone astray; we have turned every one to his own way; and the LORD hath laid on him the iniquity of us all. He was oppressed, and he was afflicted, yet he opened not his mouth: he is brought as a lamb to the slaughter, and as a sheep before her shearers is dumb, so he openeth not his mouth. He was taken from prison and from judgment: and who shall declare his generation? for he was cut off out of the land of the living: for the transgression of my people was he stricken. And he made his grave with the wicked, and with the rich in his death; because he had done no violence, neither was any deceit in his mouth. Yet it pleased the LORD to bruise him; he hath put him to grief: when thou shalt make his soul an offering for sin, he shall see his seed, he shall prolong his days, and the pleasure of the LORD shall prosper in his hand. He shall see of the travail of his soul, and shall be satisfied: by his knowledge shall my righteous servant justify many; for he shall bear their iniquities. Therefore will I divide him a portion with the great, and he shall divide the spoil with the strong; because he hath poured out his soul unto death: and he was numbered with the transgressors; and he bare the sin of many, and made intercession for the transgressors.

Who else could this be describing but Jesus?

CHAPTER 54

There's a great promise to the servants of the Lord in Isaiah 54:17: "No weapon that is formed against thee shall prosper; and every tongue that shall rise against thee in judgment thou shalt condemn. This is the heritage of the servants of the LORD, and their righteousness is of me, saith the LORD." Compare that promise with this verse from Revelation: "The accuser of our brothers has been thrown down, who accuses [God's people] day and night before our God" (12:10) and Jesus' promise that "the gates of hell" would not "prevail" against the church (Matthew 16:18).

CHAPTER 55

This passage could also be published entirely in red, for it seems no one else could speak these words but Jesus: Pay special attention to verses 4–9:

> Behold, I have given him for a witness to the people, a leader and commander to the people. Behold, thou shalt call a nation that thou knowest not, and nations that knew not thee shall run unto thee because of the LORD thy God, and for the Holy One of Israel; for he hath glorified thee. Seek ye the LORD while he may be found, call ye upon him while he is near: Let the wicked forsake his way, and the unrighteous man his thoughts: and let him return unto the LORD, and he will have mercy upon him; and to our God, for he will abundantly pardon. For my thoughts are not your thoughts, neither are your ways my ways, saith the LORD. For as the heavens are higher than the earth, so are my ways higher than your ways, and my thoughts than your thoughts.

CHAPTER 56

I haven't counted, but it is entirely possible that there are more words of Jesus in Isaiah than in the book of Matthew—maybe all four Gospels combined. It doesn't really matter, I suppose. But it makes the point. How often do Christians read the prophets and the Torah and the poetry books of the Bible for Jesus and the gospel message? Not often enough. Isaiah 56 is another one of those remarkable chapters that reveal the actual words of Jesus, apparently as dictated to Isaiah through the Holy Spirit, in the Old Testament. Here is an excerpt of some of the most memorable of those words:

> Even unto them will I give in mine house and within my walls a place and a name better than of sons and of daughters: I will give them an everlasting name, that shall not be cut off. Also the sons of the stranger, that join themselves to the LORD, to serve him, and to love the name of the LORD, to be his servants, every one

that keepeth the sabbath from polluting it, and taketh hold of my covenant; Even them will I bring to my holy mountain, and make them joyful in my house of prayer: their burnt offerings and their sacrifices shall be accepted upon mine altar; for mine house shall be called an house of prayer for all people (vv. 5–7).

CHAPTER 57

There's another message from Jesus in Isaiah 57:15–21:

> For thus saith the high and lofty One that inhabiteth eternity, whose name is Holy; I dwell in the high and holy place, with him also that is of a contrite and humble spirit, to revive the spirit of the humble, and to revive the heart of the contrite ones. For I will not contend for ever, neither will I be always wroth: for the spirit should fail before me, and the souls which I have made. For the iniquity of his covetousness was I wroth, and smote him: I hid me, and was wroth, and he went on frowardly in the way of his heart. I have seen his ways, and will heal him: I will lead him also, and restore comforts unto him and to his mourners. I create the fruit of the lips; Peace, peace to him that is far off, and to him that is near, saith the LORD; and I will heal him. But the wicked are like the troubled sea, when it cannot rest, whose waters cast up mire and dirt. There is no peace, saith my God, to the wicked.

CHAPTER 58

Just as Jesus criticized the Pharisees for following their own customs and traditions rather than the commandments of God, likewise we see similar criticism of religious rituals and practices that are not conducted in the right spirit in Isaiah 58:2–8:

> Yet they seek me daily, and delight to know my ways, as a nation that did righteousness, and forsook not the ordinance of their God: they ask of me the ordinances of justice; they take delight in approaching to God. Wherefore have we fasted, say they, and

thou seest not? wherefore have we afflicted our soul, and thou takest no knowledge? Behold, in the day of your fast ye find pleasure, and exact all your labours. Behold, ye fast for strife and debate, and to smite with the fist of wickedness: ye shall not fast as ye do this day, to make your voice to be heard on high. Is it such a fast that I have chosen? a day for a man to afflict his soul? is it to bow down his head as a bulrush, and to spread sackcloth and ashes under him? wilt thou call this a fast, and an acceptable day to the LORD? Is not this the fast that I have chosen? to loose the bands of wickedness, to undo the heavy burdens, and to let the oppressed go free, and that ye break every yoke? Is it not to deal thy bread to the hungry, and that thou bring the poor that are cast out to thy house? when thou seest the naked, that thou cover him; and that thou hide not thyself from thine own flesh? Then shall thy light break forth as the morning, and thine health shall spring forth speedily: and thy righteousness shall go before thee; the glory of the LORD shall be thy reward.

This chapter should be studied by today's believers as a reality check on our own spirits. Are we following the commandments of God or the traditions of men—especially in light of Matthew 25:31–40, which represents a re-expression of much of this Isaiah passage?

CHAPTER 59

This entire chapter is the gospel. It could be used to evangelize the lost today, just as it was before the New Testament was written and published. Verses 20–21 stand out: "And the Redeemer shall come to Zion, and unto them that turn from transgression in Jacob, saith the LORD. As for me, this is my covenant with them, saith the LORD; My spirit that is upon thee, and my words which I have put in thy mouth, shall not depart out of thy mouth, nor out of the mouth of thy seed, nor out of the mouth of thy seed's seed, saith the LORD, from henceforth and for ever." Read this entire chapter. Embrace it. Study it. Share it.

CHAPTER 60

Chapter 60 is the good news for the Gentiles. And what did Jesus say? "And other sheep I have, which are not of this [Jewish] fold: them also I must bring, and they shall hear my voice; and there shall be one fold, and one shepherd." Romans 3:29 echoes this good news. "Is he the God of the Jews only? is he not also of the Gentiles? Yes, of the Gentiles also."

CHAPTER 61

This chapter might seem very familiar to you—even if you have never read it before. That's because Jesus spoke the opening words of Isaiah 61 in Luke 4:18–19. Then He closed the Torah scroll. If you don't know why, let's look at the complete passage in Isaiah:

The Spirit of the Lord GOD is upon me; because the LORD hath anointed me to preach good tidings unto the meek; he hath sent me to bind up the brokenhearted, to proclaim liberty to the captives, and the opening of the prison to them that are bound; To proclaim the acceptable year of the LORD, and the day of vengeance of our God; to comfort all that mourn; To appoint unto them that mourn in Zion, to give unto them beauty for ashes, the oil of joy for mourning, the garment of praise for the spirit of heaviness; that they might be called trees of righteousness, the planting of the LORD, that he might be glorified. And they shall build the old wastes, they shall raise up the former desolations, and they shall repair the waste cities, the desolations of many generations. And strangers shall stand and feed your flocks, and the sons of the alien shall be your plowmen and your vinedressers. But ye shall be named the Priests of the LORD: men shall call you the Ministers of our God: ye shall eat the riches of the Gentiles, and in their glory shall ye boast yourselves. For your shame ye shall have double; and for confusion they shall rejoice in their portion: therefore in their land they shall possess the double: everlasting joy shall be unto them. For

I the LORD love judgment, I hate robbery for burnt offering; and I will direct their work in truth, and I will make an everlasting covenant with them. And their seed shall be known among the Gentiles, and their offspring among the people: all that see them shall acknowledge them, that they are the seed which the LORD hath blessed. I will greatly rejoice in the LORD, my soul shall be joyful in my God; for he hath clothed me with the garments of salvation, he hath covered me with the robe of righteousness, as a bridegroom decketh himself with ornaments, and as a bride adorneth herself with her jewels. For as the earth bringeth forth her bud, and as the garden causeth the things that are sown in it to spring forth; so the Lord GOD will cause righteousness and praise to spring forth before all the nations.

So, why did Jesus close the book after the words "to proclaim the acceptable year of the Lord"? And why did He say, "This day is this scripture fulfilled in your ears" (Luke 4:21)? Very simple.

At that time, Jesus' mission was to preach good tidings, bind up the brokenhearted, offer a pardon to those captive by sin. It was not yet the time for the day of vengeance or the ushering in of His kingdom on earth. He came as the Lamb of God, the Suffering Servant. When He comes again, He will come as the conquering King, the Lion of Judah.

CHAPTER 62

We get another glimpse into the future kingdom in Isaiah 62:10–12: "Go through, go through the gates; prepare ye the way of the people; cast up, cast up the highway; gather out the stones; lift up a standard for the people. Behold, the LORD hath proclaimed unto the end of the world, Say ye to the daughter of Zion, Behold, thy salvation cometh; behold, his reward is with him, and his work before him. And they shall call them, The holy people, The redeemed of the LORD: and thou shalt be called, Sought out, A city not forsaken."

CHAPTER 63

This chapter provides a powerful look into the day of judgment, when Jesus finishes His mission to restore the earth and reign over Israel from Jerusalem. If you don't believe that you can see Jesus in this chapter, I dare you to read even the first three verses alongside Revelation 14:20 and 19:13.

CHAPTER 64

This passage describes a time following the judgment of the earth and demonstrates the recognition by His people of their Savior and Redeemer.

CHAPTER 65

This chapter begins with the recognition of the Messiah by the Gentiles, and so there can be no mistake that Israel is forsaken, we read in Isaiah 65:9, "And I will bring forth a seed out of Jacob, and out of Judah an inheritor of my mountains: and mine elect shall inherit it, and my servants shall dwell there."

CHAPTER 66

The chapter begins with Jesus proclaiming in verses 1–2: "The heaven is my throne, and the earth is my footstool: where is the house that ye build unto me? and where is the place of my rest? For all those things hath mine hand made, and all those things have been, saith the LORD: but to this man will I look, even to him that is poor and of a contrite spirit, and trembleth at my word." There's good news for believers—both Gentile and the children of Israel in Isaiah 66:10–14:

> Rejoice ye with Jerusalem, and be glad with her, all ye that love her: rejoice for joy with her, all ye that mourn for her: That ye may suck, and be satisfied with the breasts of her consolations; that ye may milk out, and be delighted with the abundance of her glory. For thus saith the LORD, Behold, I will extend peace to her

like a river, and the glory of the Gentiles like a flowing stream: then shall ye suck, ye shall be borne upon her sides, and be dandled upon her knees. As one whom his mother comforteth, so will I comfort you; and ye shall be comforted in Jerusalem. And when ye see this, your heart shall rejoice, and your bones shall flourish like an herb: and the hand of the LORD shall be known toward his servants, and his indignation toward his enemies.

Of this there can be no doubt. The book of Isaiah is full of the gospel message—from beginning to end. So many of Isaiah's prophecies focus on humankind's sinfulness and a coming, divine Redeemer. There's no wonder Isaiah is often referred to as "the book of salvation."

Now, let's work in reverse—looking at Isaiah references found in the Gospels:

- **MATTHEW 1:23** "Behold, a virgin shall be with child, and shall bring forth a son, and they shall call his name Emmanuel, which being interpreted is, God with us." (See Isaiah 7:14)

- **MATTHEW 3:3** "For this is he that was spoken of by the prophet Esaias, saying, The voice of one crying in the wilderness, Prepare ye the way of the Lord, make his paths straight." (See Isaiah 40:3)

- **MATTHEW 4:15–16** "The land of Zabulon, and the land of Nephthalim, by the way of the sea, beyond Jordan, Galilee of the Gentiles; The people which sat in darkness saw great light; and to them which sat in the region and shadow of death light is sprung up." (See Isaiah 8:23)

- **MATTHEW 5:34** "But I say unto you, Swear not at all; neither by heaven; for it is God's throne:" (See Isaiah 66:1)

- MATTHEW 8:17 "That it might be fulfilled which was spoken by Esaias the prophet, saying, Himself took our infirmities, and bare our sicknesses." (See Isaiah 53:4)

- MATTHEW 11:5 "The blind receive their sight, and the lame walk, the lepers are cleansed, and the deaf hear, the dead are raised up, and the poor have the gospel preached to them." (See Isaiah 26:19; 35:5; 61:1)

- MATTHEW 12:18–21 "Behold my servant, whom I have chosen; my beloved, in whom my soul is well pleased: I will put my spirit upon him, and he shall shew judgment to the Gentiles. He shall not strive, nor cry; neither shall any man hear his voice in the streets. A bruised reed shall he not break, and smoking flax shall he not quench, till he send forth judgment unto victory. And in his name shall the Gentiles trust." (See Isaiah 42:1–4)

- MATTHEW 13:14–15 "And in them is fulfilled the prophecy of Esaias, which saith, By hearing ye shall hear, and shall not understand; and seeing ye shall see, and shall not perceive: For this people's heart is waxed gross, and their ears are dull of hearing, and their eyes they have closed; lest at any time they should see with their eyes and hear with their ears, and should understand with their heart, and should be converted, and I should heal them." (See Isaiah 6:9–10)

- MATTHEW 15:9 "But in vain they do worship me, teaching for doctrines the commandments of men." (See Isaiah 29:13)

- MATHEW 21:13 "And said unto them, It is written, My house shall be called the house of prayer; but ye have made it a den of thieves." (See Isaiah 56:7)

- MATTHEW 24:29 "Then shall they deliver you up to be afflicted, and shall kill you: and ye shall be hated of all nations for my name's sake." (See Isaiah 13:10)

- MATTHEW 24:31 "And he shall send his angels with a great sound of a trumpet, and they shall gather together his elect from the four winds, from one end of heaven to the other." (See Isaiah 27:13)

- MARK 1:3 "The voice of one crying in the wilderness, Prepare ye the way of the Lord, make his paths straight." (See Isaiah 40:3)

- MARK 4:12 "That seeing they may see, and not perceive; and hearing they may hear, and not understand; lest at any time they should be converted, and their sins should be forgiven them. (See Isaiah 6:9–10)

- MARK 7:7 "Howbeit in vain do they worship me, teaching for doctrines the commandments of men." (See Isaiah 29:13)

- MARK 9:48 ". . . where their worm dieth not, and the fire is not quenched." (See Isaiah 66:24)

- MARK 10:32 "And they were in the way going up to Jerusalem; and Jesus went before them: and they were amazed; and as they followed, they were afraid. And he took again the twelve, and began to tell them what things should happen unto him." (See Isaiah 50:6)

- LUKE 1:79 ". . . to give light to them that sit in darkness and in the shadow of death, to guide our feet into the way of peace." (See Isaiah 9:1)

- LUKE 3:5-6 "Every valley shall be filled, and every mountain and hill shall be brought low; and the crooked shall be made straight, and the rough ways shall be made smooth; And all flesh shall see the salvation of God." (See Isaiah 40:3–5)

- LUKE 4:18-19 "The Spirit of the Lord is upon me, because he hath anointed me to preach the gospel to the poor; he hath sent me to heal the brokenhearted, to preach deliverance to the captives, and recovering of sight to the blind, to set at liberty them that are bruised, to preach the acceptable year of the Lord." (See Isaiah 61:1–2)

- LUKE 22:32 "But I have prayed for thee, that thy faith fail not: and when thou art converted, strengthen thy brethren." (See Isaiah 53:12)

- JOHN 6:45 "It is written in the prophets, And they shall be all taught of God. Every man therefore that hath heard, and hath learned of the Father, cometh unto me." (See Isaiah 54:13)

- JOHN 12:38 "That the saying of Esaias the prophet might be fulfilled, which he spake, Lord, who hath believed our report? and to whom hath the arm of the Lord been revealed?" (See Isaiah 53:1)

- JOHN 12:40 "He hath blinded their eyes, and hardened their heart; that they should not see with their eyes, nor understand with their heart, and be converted, and I should heal them." (See Isaiah 6:10)

These, of course, are just references from the Gospels. There are at least a dozen more references to Isaiah in Acts, Romans, 1 Corinthians, Ephesians, and Philippians. And with good reason: Isaiah is rich with the gospel—abundantly rich, as is the entire Old Testament.

24

THE GOSPEL IN JEREMIAH

Before I formed thee in the belly I knew thee; and before thou camest forth out of the womb I sanctified thee, and I ordained thee a prophet unto the nations.
—JEREMIAH 1:5

HAVE YOU WONDERED how the prophets became prophets?

One the many neat things about Jeremiah is that he provides the answer to that question.

Along with Isaiah, Ezekiel, and Daniel, Jeremiah is categorized as one of the four major prophets. Does that mean they were more important than the minor prophets, like Hosea, Joel, Amos, Obadiah, Jonah, Micah, Nahum, Habakkuk, Zephaniah, Haggai, Zechariah, and Malachi? Not at all. It just means the major prophets wrote more. The main distinction was quantity, not quality. By the way, there were other prophets, too. Moses was one. Samuel was another. And, of course David prophesied too.

But Jeremiah gives us some insight into how the prophet is called by God.

First, we're told by God that Jeremiah was "sanctified" and "ordained" by God. Apparently, there was no school for prophets—only a direct pipeline to the Almighty. He must have heard from God at a very early age, because in the first chapter of Jeremiah, we learn about what his response was to God's call: "Then said I, Ah, Lord GOD! behold, I cannot speak: for I am a child" (1:6).

God's response to the young man, was: "Say not, I am a child: for thou shalt go to all that I shall send thee, and whatsoever I command thee thou shalt speak. Be not afraid of their faces: for I am with thee to deliver thee. Then," Jeremiah tells us, "the LORD put forth his hand, and touched my mouth. And the LORD said unto me, Behold, I have put my words in thy mouth" (vv. 6–9).

Apparently, that's how it works—at least with Jeremiah, who lived roughly a hundred years after Isaiah. It's also worth noting that God ordained him to be a prophet to the nations—meaning the Gentiles—not just Judah.

God also tells Jeremiah in chapter 1 that He has set Jeremiah "over the nations and over the kingdoms, to root out, and to pull down, and to destroy, and to throw down, to build, and to plant" (v. 10). One particular nation God had his eye on was Assyria, which had already conquered the northern kingdom of Israel and had similar designs on Judah in the south. Assyria would not capture Judah, but its successor in the history of Middle East empires would—Babylon.

God told Jeremiah:

Out of the north an evil shall break forth upon all the inhabitants of the land. For, lo, I will call all the families of the kingdoms of the north, saith the LORD; and they shall come, and they shall set every one his throne at the entering of the gates of Jerusalem, and against all the walls thereof round about, and against all the cities of Judah. And I will utter my judgments against them touching all their wickedness, who have forsaken me, and have burned incense unto other gods, and worshipped the works of their own hands. Thou therefore gird up thy loins, and arise, and speak unto them all that I command thee: be not dismayed at their faces, lest I confound thee before them. For, behold, I have made thee this day a defenced city, and an iron pillar, and brasen walls against the whole land, against the kings of Judah, against the princes thereof, against the priests thereof, and against the people of the land. And they shall fight against thee; but they shall not prevail against thee; for I am with thee (vv. 14–19).

That's the context of Jeremiah's ministry as a prophet. It was no picnic being a prophet. Judah, like Israel, had turned to idolatry, but had a young king named Josiah, who was a strong believer. Nevertheless, Jeremiah endured a tough life of persecution, disgrace, imprisonment, and eventually, exile to Egypt. And Judah fell—hard.

Let's walk through the book and see what we can find that reveals the gospel message.

God instructed Jeremiah to "cry in the ears of Jerusalem" about His disappointment in the people. The Lord then spoke through Jeremiah to the people, saying:

I remember thee, the kindness of thy youth, the love of thine espousals, when thou wentest after me in the wilderness, in a land that was not sown. Israel was holiness unto the LORD, and the firstfruits of his increase: all that devour him shall offend; evil shall come upon them. . . .

What iniquity have your fathers found in me, that they are gone far from me, and have walked after vanity, and are become vain? Neither said they, Where is the LORD that brought us up out of the land of Egypt, that led us through the wilderness, through a land of deserts and of pits, through a land of drought, and of the shadow of death, through a land that no man passed through, and where no man dwelt? And I brought you into a plentiful country, to eat the fruit thereof and the goodness thereof; but when ye entered, ye defiled my land, and made mine heritage an abomination. The priests said not, Where is the Lord? and they that handle the law knew me not: the pastors also transgressed against me, and the prophets prophesied by Baal, and walked after things that do not profit. Wherefore I will yet plead with you, saith the Lord, and with your children's children will I plead (Jeremiah 2:2–3, 5–9).

Right there is part of the gospel. We serve a loving God, who is patient and relentless in calling us back to Him. We see it so many times throughout the Old Testament. It's one of the most important lessons we need to learn. God doesn't cast His people aside easily. He's a God not just of second chances, but third, fourth, fifth, six and seventh chances. He always has His arm outstretched to His children.

But God offered a stern warning to Judah through Jeremiah.

"Hath a nation changed their gods, which are yet no gods? but my people have changed their glory for that which doth not profit," he said. "Be astonished, O ye heavens, at this, and be horribly afraid, be ye very desolate, saith the Lord" (2:11–12)

The next gospel foreshadowing comes in Jeremiah 2:13: "For my people have committed two evils; they have forsaken me the fountain of living waters, and hewed them out cisterns, broken cisterns, that can hold no water." God was angry because His people had access to living waters that He provided. They had special healing properties. Yet they turned away from them, apparently to drink ordinary river water: "And now what hast thou to do in the way of Egypt, to drink the waters of Sihor? or what hast thou to do in the way of Assyria, to drink the waters of the river?" (v. 18).

As I've already shown in previous chapters, "living waters" point to Jesus. They play a significant part in His return. We will discuss this more in future chapters. But the good news is that we will once again have access to abundant living waters in God's kingdom on earth—real living waters that Jesus will use to restore Israel and, I suspect, the rest of the world. See Revelation 22:1: "And he shewed me a pure river of water of life, clear as crystal, proceeding out of the throne of God and of the Lamb."

But the rejection of "living waters" is not the only thing angering God, who continued His prophetic download to Jeremiah:

> Thine own wickedness shall correct thee, and thy backslidings shall reprove thee: know therefore and see that it is an evil thing and bitter, that thou hast forsaken the LORD thy God, and that my fear is not in thee, saith the Lord GOD of hosts. For of old time I have broken thy yoke, and burst thy bands; and thou saidst, I will not transgress; when upon every high hill and under every green tree thou wanderest, playing the harlot. Yet I had planted thee a noble vine, wholly a right seed: how then art thou turned into the degenerate plant of a strange vine unto me? . . . How canst thou say, I am not polluted, I have not gone after Baalim? see thy way in the valley, know what thou hast done: thou art a swift dromedary traversing her ways. . . . But where are thy gods that thou hast made thee? let them arise, if they can save thee in the time of thy trouble: for according to the number of thy cities are thy gods, O Judah. Wherefore will ye plead with me? ye all have transgressed against me, saith the LORD (2:19–22, 89–29).

As you can see, Jeremiah has his hands full. You get the picture. Judah had strayed, just like Israel. And God was not pleased.

Why was he so angry? Judah was chasing after other gods, which are no gods at all. They're demons, symbolized by rocks and trees and graven images. In chapter 3, you get a picture of why this so troubled the Lord: "They say, If a man put away his wife, and she go from him, and become another man's, shall he return unto her again? shall not that land be greatly polluted? but thou hast played the harlot with many lovers; yet return again to me, saith the LORD" (v. 1).

You see, God sees His relationship with His people as a marriage, as we noted in chapter 22. He seeks a loyal and faithful bride, not one that flirts with other gods.

And here's another place we get a glimpse of the gospel. Why? Because Jesus is the bridegroom and His elect are His collective bride. Jesus referenced this relationship many times in the Gospels (Matthew 9:15; 25:1–10; Mark 2:19–20, Luke 5:34–35; John 3:29), not to mention Revelation.

So, God poured out His heart to Judah and even outcast Israel through Jeremiah:

> And it came to pass through the lightness of her whoredom, that she defiled the land, and committed adultery with stones and with stocks. And yet for all this her treacherous sister Judah hath not turned unto me with her whole heart, but feignedly, saith the LORD.
>
> And the LORD said unto me, The backsliding Israel hath justified herself more than treacherous Judah. Go and proclaim these words toward the north, and say, Return, thou backsliding Israel, saith the LORD; and I will not cause mine anger to fall upon you: for I am merciful, saith the LORD, and I will not keep anger for ever. Only acknowledge thine iniquity, that thou hast transgressed against the LORD thy God, and hast scattered thy ways to the strangers under every green tree, and ye have not obeyed my voice, saith the LORD. Turn, O backsliding children, saith the LORD; for I am married unto you: and I will take you one of a city, and two of a family, and I will bring you to Zion: And I will give you pastors according to mine heart, which shall feed you with knowledge and understanding. And it shall come to pass, when ye be multiplied and increased in the land, in those days, saith the LORD, they shall say no more, The ark of the covenant of the LORD: neither shall it come to mind: neither shall they remember it; neither shall they visit it; neither shall that be done any more. At that time they shall call Jerusalem the throne of the LORD; and all the nations shall be gathered unto it,

to the name of the LORD, to Jerusalem: neither shall they walk any more after the imagination of their evil heart. In those days the house of Judah shall walk with the house of Israel, and they shall come together out of the land of the north to the land that I have given for an inheritance unto your fathers. But I said, How shall I put thee among the children, and give thee a pleasant land, a goodly heritage of the hosts of nations? and I said, Thou shalt call me, My father; and shalt not turn away from me. Surely as a wife treacherously departeth from her husband, so have ye dealt treacherously with me, O house of Israel, saith the LORD. A voice was heard upon the high places, weeping and supplications of the children of Israel: for they have perverted their way, and they have forgotten the LORD their God. Return, ye backsliding children, and I will heal your backslidings. Behold, we come unto thee; for thou art the LORD our God. Truly in vain is salvation hoped for from the hills, and from the multitude of mountains: truly in the LORD our God is the salvation of Israel. For shame hath devoured the labour of our fathers from our youth; their flocks and their herds, their sons and their daughters. We lie down in our shame, and our confusion covereth us: for we have sinned against the LORD our God, we and our fathers, from our youth even unto this day, and have not obeyed the voice of the LORD our God (3:9–25).

This is the heart of the gospel message, and it was preached in Jeremiah: Repent. Turn back to God. All will be forgiven. And you will inherit the kingdom of God. You can hear Jesus' heart breaking in this plea.

In Jeremiah 4, the beseeching continues.

If thou wilt return, O Israel, saith the LORD, return unto me: and if thou wilt put away thine abominations out of my sight, then shalt thou not remove. And thou shalt swear, The LORD liveth, in truth, in judgment, and in righteousness; and the nations shall bless themselves in him, and in him shall they glory. For thus saith the LORD to the men of Judah and Jerusalem, Break up your fallow ground, and sow not among thorns. Circumcise yourselves to the LORD, and take away the foreskins of your heart, ye men of Judah and inhabitants of Jerusalem: lest my fury come forth like fire, and burn that none can quench it, because of the evil of your doings (vv. 1–4).

God was looking for a change of heart from His once-holy nation. "That's all it will take," He says. "It's not the circumcision of the flesh that is important. It's the circumcision of the foreskin of your hearts." That's not the first time God has said this, but it will be mentioned frequently in the Gospels and the New Testament writings.

I want you to consider how far gone this generation in Judah was. They had resorted to sacrificing their own children to false gods. Still, God was calling them to repentance. Still His arm was outstretched. This is clearly the same merciful God who reaches out not just to Gentiles, but to Jews and Gentiles alike, all over the world today with the message of grace and salvation and redemption.

Again, listen to the heart of God in chapter 9: "Oh that my head were waters, and mine eyes a fountain of tears, that I might weep day and night for the slain of the daughter of my people!" (v. 1).

In Jeremiah 12, God's pleadings with His people are not bearing fruit. So, He decides to turn His back on His people, allowing them to be taken captive. But even then, listen to what He says: "And it shall come to pass, after that I have plucked them out I will return, and have compassion on them, and will bring them again, every man to his heritage, and every man to his land, And it shall come to pass, if they will diligently learn the ways of my people, to swear by my name, The LORD liveth; as they taught my people to swear by Baal; then shall they be built in the midst of my people. But if they will not obey, I will utterly pluck up and destroy that nation, saith the LORD" (vv. 15–17).

I want to take you to Jeremiah 16 for a rather remarkable picture of the coming kingdom, which I believe is not far-off.

In the midst of God's pleading with His people through Jeremiah to return to Him, He finally concludes it's not going to happen. He's content with letting them go into captivity. Yet, He will still call them back in the greatest miracle in history. Here's what He says in verses 14–16:

> Therefore, behold, the days come, saith the LORD, that it shall no more be said, The LORD liveth, that brought up the children of Israel out of the land of Egypt; But, The LORD liveth, that brought up the children of Israel from the land of the north, and from all the lands whither he had driven them: and I will bring them again into their land that I gave unto their fathers. Behold, I will send for many fishers, saith the LORD, and they shall fish them; and after will I send for many hunters, and they shall hunt them from every mountain, and from every hill, and out of the holes of the rocks.

Throughout much of the Old Testament, one of God's descriptives is the God who bought up the children of Israel out of the land of Egypt. It was indeed a mighty miracle. Think about it. The children of Israel were about 2.5 or 2.6 million strong. That nation traversed through the wilderness for forty years on its way to the promised land. It was a miracle getting them out.

There was the miracle of the Red Sea parting. There were miracles involved in feeding the people, getting them drink, and so on. But here, God said, it would be an even bigger miracle bringing them back from captivity. We have witnessed that miracle with our own eyes in our own generation.

Have you ever thought about that? In fact, only very recently has the Jewish population of Israel exceeded the Jewish population in the rest of the world combined. While the miracle is not entirely complete, we can certainly see it under way. It is another prophecy fulfilled—and we are eyewitnesses.

Perhaps the single most remarkable revelation in the book of Jeremiah is the detailed way it describes the new covenant and explains how it will be fully realized in the future kingdom, with Jesus reigning in Jerusalem as King of kings. How many believers today recognize that the most complete and thorough explanation of the new covenant—Old Testament or New—is found here in this prophetic book?

It's found in Jeremiah 31:31–37:

> Behold, the days come, saith the LORD, that I will make a new covenant with the house of Israel, and with the house of Judah: Not according to the covenant that I made with their fathers in the day that I took them by the hand to bring them out of the land of Egypt; which my covenant they brake, although I was an husband unto them, saith the LORD: But this shall be the covenant that I will make with the house of Israel; After those days, saith the LORD, I will put my law in their inward parts, and write it in their hearts; and will be their God, and they shall be my people. And they shall teach no more every man his neighbour, and every man his brother, saying, Know the LORD: for they shall all know me, from the least of them unto the greatest of them, saith the LORD: for I will forgive their iniquity, and I will remember their sin no more. Thus saith the LORD, which giveth the sun for a light by day, and the ordinances of the moon and of the stars for a light by night, which divideth the sea when the waves thereof roar; The LORD of hosts is his name: If those ordinances depart from before me, saith the LORD, then the seed of Israel also shall cease from being a nation before me for ever. Thus saith the Lord; If heaven above can be measured, and the foundations of the earth searched out beneath, I will also cast off all the seed of Israel for all that they have done, saith the LORD.

God made this covenant with whom? With the house of Israel and the house of Judah. But don't worry if you are not ethnically a member of one of those houses, for you can be grafted in to that promise through your relationship with the Jewish Messiah. The words written in Jeremiah about the new covenant are quoted extensively in Hebrews 8 for that very reason.

Here's where the new covenant is first introduced—not in the Gospels, but in the "gospel" of Jeremiah. Perhaps no passages in the Old or New Testament discredit more completely the notion that Israel has been abandoned by God because of its sins of the past or will ever do so. This covenant is still in effect, not with a people who have replaced Israel, but with Israel itself, along with a people who have joined the congregation of the houses of Israel and Judah. And that includes every Gentile who confesses his or her sins and seeks the lordship of Jesus.

Note that this new covenant will not be fully realized until the coming kingdom, for we still need to teach the Word of God today. Truly, in the kingdom, it will be literally written on our hearts, according to this promise.

Chapter 33 is nearly as stunning in the detail it offers us into that kingdom. Verse 6 offers a promise of "health and cure" along with "abundance of peace and truth." Verse 8 addresses the return of Israel and Judah to the land where God will "cleanse them from all their iniquity, whereby they have sinned against me; and I will pardon all their iniquities, whereby they have sinned, and whereby they have transgressed against me." Israel will be, God says in verse 9, "a name of joy, a praise and an honour before all the nations of the earth, which shall hear all the good that I do unto them: and they shall fear and tremble for all the goodness and for all the prosperity that I procure unto it." Israel will be restored from its desolation when, verses 14–17 explain, the Lord will "perform that good thing which I have promised unto the house of Israel and to the house of Judah. In those days, and at that time, will I cause the Branch of righteousness to grow up unto David; and he shall execute judgment and righteousness in the land. In those days shall Judah be saved, and Jerusalem shall dwell safely: and this is the name wherewith she shall be called, The LORD our righteousness. For thus saith the LORD; David shall never want a man to sit upon the throne of the house of Israel."

If not a man, who? The living God in the form of Messiah Jesus, of course.

Ultimately, the good news for Israel is the good news for all. A descendant of David will sit upon His throne and serve as the ultimate and eternal King, who rules with justice, but He will also be the Savior of the whole world.

This is the remarkable gospel of Jeremiah.

26

THE GOSPEL IN LAMENTATIONS

Thy prophets have seen vain and foolish things for thee: and they have not discovered thine iniquity, to turn away thy captivity; but have seen for thee false burdens and causes of banishment. —LAMENTATIONS 2:14

It is of the LORD's mercies that we are not consumed, because his compassions fail not. They are new every morning: great is thy faithfulness.
—LAMENTATIONS 3:22–23

IT'S A SHAME human beings don't appreciate what they have until it's gone. That is the story of Lamentations, a book of sorrow and regret, presumed to have been written by the prophet Jeremiah, though his name appears nowhere in the book.

Jeremiah was indeed the great prophet of the historical period in which the story takes place—the time of the conquest of Judah by the Babylonians. It did not come without warning. Jeremiah did his best to alert Judah of the fate at hand, but other so-called prophets did not. Instead, they told the people what they wanted to hear. They tickled their ears, performing a grave disservice to the Judeans.

God is always true to His Word, though. And as we saw in the book of Jeremiah, He pleaded with His people to turn back to Him, to turn away from their idols and false gods, to forsake the sacrifices of their own children and other abominable practices. But the colder the hearts of people become, the harder it is to hear God's voice. And the more people turn to sin, the less God calls.

Yet, amid the suffering and the anguish portrayed so vividly in Lamentations, the voice of hope can still be heard.

How much so? So much that one of the greatest hymns of all time was inspired by chapter 3 of this book.

"Great is Thy faithfulness," O God my Father,
There is no shadow of turning with Thee;
Thou changest not, Thy compassions, they fail not
As Thou hast been Thou forever wilt be.

"Great is Thy faithfulness!" "Great is Thy faithfulness!"
Morning by morning new mercies I see;
All I have needed Thy hand hath provided—
"Great is Thy faithfulness," Lord, unto me!

Summer and winter, and springtime and harvest,
Sun, moon and stars in their courses above,
Join with all nature in manifold witness
To Thy great faithfulness, mercy and love.

Pardon for sin and a peace that endureth,
Thine own dear presence to cheer and to guide;
Strength for today and bright hope for tomorrow,
Blessings all mine, with ten thousand beside![1]

Lamentations recounts some vivid and grisly scenes in the fall of Jerusalem. But it's with a point. When God gives people over to the lusts of their hearts and walks away, what is left behind is a living hell. It's there for us to take notice because we face such a stark choice in life: follow God's teachings and commandments and live; reject them and suffer and die. It's just that simple. There is no other way. Yes, man is given free will by His Creator, but he's not given the freedom to save himself or to rewrite the rules.

God is merciful and forgiving, but His mercy and forgiveness must be sought. How did Jesus say it in the Gospels? "Ye serpents, ye generation of vipers, how can ye escape the damnation of hell?" (Matthew 23:33).

There is only one Savior, and He is found through genuine, contrite repentance only. That is what was lacking in Jerusalem and Judah during the Babylonian invasion, which was a vehicle of God's own judgment on His land.

So, let's go search for those glimpses of the gospel in Lamentations:

- LAMENTATIONS 1:16 "For these things I weep; mine eye, mine eye runneth down with water, because the comforter that should relieve my soul is far from me: my children are desolate, because the enemy prevailed." Who is the Comforter? We learn in the Gospels from Jesus that it is the Holy Spirit. But the Comforter is present amid the body of believers. He is withdrawn, moved far away, in times of judgment, when the spirit of repentance is nowhere to be found.

- LAMENTATIONS 2:17 "The LORD hath done that which he had devised; he hath fulfilled his word that he had commanded in the days of old: he hath thrown down, and hath not pitied: and he hath caused thine enemy to rejoice over thee, he hath set up the horn of thine adversaries." God warned us throughout the Torah and by all the prophets of how we should live. He is long-suffering in His patience with us, but, ultimately, He will fulfill what He promised when His people turn their backs, reject His pleas, and ignore His warnings. Was it not the same in Jesus' time? Within forty years of His ministry, the gospel was flourishing, but His people and land were ravished.

- **LAMENTATIONS 3:20–26** "My soul hath them still in remembrance, and is humbled in me. This I recall to my mind, therefore have I hope. It is of the LORD's mercies that we are not consumed, because his compassions fail not. They are new every morning: great is thy faithfulness. The LORD is my portion, saith my soul; therefore will I hope in him. The LORD is good unto them that wait for him, to the soul that seeketh him. It is good that a man should both hope and quietly wait for the salvation of the LORD." When did the people remember the Lord? When it was too late for them to avert suffering and captivity. Would they have found hope otherwise, without the torment? God knew they would not. It did not come quickly, as we saw in Jeremiah. It did not come without many missed opportunities to turn back—to repent.

- **LAMENTATIONS 3:31–36** "For the LORD will not cast off for ever: But though he cause grief, yet will he have compassion according to the multitude of his mercies. For he doth not afflict willingly nor grieve the children of men. To crush under his feet all the prisoners of the earth. To turn aside the right of a man before the face of the most High, To subvert a man in his cause, the LORD approveth not." Here, again, we see the character of the Lord. He's still going to find a way to fulfill His promises of a kingdom, a Redeemer, a holy city, a holy nation—all of it. It's simply not in this generation. He is merciful and true to His Word. The judgment is temporary. His plans are eternal.

- **LAMENTATIONS 3:38–42** "Out of the mouth of the most High proceedeth not evil and good? Wherefore doth a living man complain, a man for the punishment of his sins? Let us search and try our ways, and turn again to the LORD. Let us lift up our heart with our hands unto God in the heavens. We have transgressed and have rebelled: thou hast not pardoned." Forgiveness and pardon of sins can only come through repentance. That's the very message of the gospel. It matters not in which generation you live—before Jesus, during Jesus, after Jesus. The same rules apply. God is not a captive of time. He sees the end from the beginning and beginning from the end. What's the message of Lamentations? "Let us search . . . our ways, and turn again to the LORD." It's the same message Jesus shared. It's the same message shared by all the prophets.

- **LAMENTATIONS 3:55–59** "I called upon thy name, O LORD, out of the low dungeon. Thou hast heard my voice: hide not thine ear at my breathing, at my cry. Thou drewest near in the day that I called upon thee: thou saidst, Fear not. O LORD, thou hast pleaded the causes of my soul; thou hast redeemed my life. O LORD, thou hast seen my wrong: judge thou my cause." Were all the people of Jerusalem and Judah fated to be cast aside for eternity because of their rebellion? Absolutely not. Listen to the voices of those in Lamentations who got the message a little late to save their homes and their loved ones and their nation. You can hear them in this book. Some of their lives were redeemed—even while facing death and captivity.

- **LAMENTATIONS 4:17** "As for us, our eyes as yet failed for our vain help: in our watching we have watched for a nation that could not save us." To whom were the people of Judah looking to save them? They were looking to their nation—not the God of that nation. Many share the same myopic view today, putting faith in their country over faith in God. Some did the same during Jesus' time, if you recall.

- LAMENTATIONS 5:19 "Thou, O LORD, remainest for ever; thy throne from generation to generation." And here we are—the essence of the good news of the gospel. The Messiah is going to preside on His throne from generation to generation. That throne will be in Jerusalem—no matter how many times it will be destroyed or captured before Jesus returns. God will never forsake His people forever. Just the opposite, for He will set up His kingdom amid His people, in His land, and they shall live in truth, justice, and peace eternally with Him. What was the gospel Jesus preached? What was it called?

Let me remind you (emphases added):

- MATTHEW 4:23 "And Jesus went about all Galilee, teaching in their synagogues, and preaching *the gospel of the kingdom . . .*"

- MATTHEW 9:35 "And Jesus went about all the cities and villages, teaching in their synagogues, and preaching *the gospel of the kingdom . . .*"

- MATTHEW 24:14 "And *this gospel of the kingdom* shall be preached in all the world for a witness unto all nations; and then shall the end come."

- MARK 1:14 "Now after that John was put in prison, Jesus came into Galilee, *preaching the gospel of the kingdom of God . . .*"

- MARK 1:15 ". . . and saying, The time is fulfilled, and *the kingdom of God is at hand:* repent ye, and *believe the gospel.*"

That's right. Jesus preached the gospel of the kingdom. Remember that. We're seldom reminded of it today. The gospel is more than personal salvation. That's just the beginning, not the end. The fulfillment of the gospel is much more. It's the restoration of all things, the removal of sin not just from individuals, but the curse of sin upon the whole earth.

Great is thy faithfulness, indeed!

27

THE GOSPEL IN EZEKIEL

And I will give them one heart, and I will put a new spirit within you; and I will take the stony heart out of their flesh, and will give them an heart of flesh.
—EZEKIEL 11:19

EZEKIEL IS ONE OF MY FAVORITE BOOKS in the Bible. It makes sense because I was led into the faith by the words of the prophets.

But many are put off by Ezekiel because it can be difficult to understand. Take the first chapter, for instance. What's *that* all about?

It seems like a scene right out of *The X Files*. Was it a spacecraft Ezekiel was describing? Was it a chariot of God? An angelic host?

All I can say is, read it for yourself, and you decide. Many people have tried. Many different conclusions have been drawn. This, I believe, is one of the mysteries we'll learn about in the kingdom of God. For now, all I can suggest is that God wanted to get Ezekiel's attention. And it worked. The vivid description Ezekiel provided doesn't help much. Whatever he witnessed was far beyond the imagination of a man living more than five hundred years before the birth of Jesus—and not in Israel, by the way, but in Babylon during the captivity. Unlike Jeremiah, Ezekiel's life was not one of suffering and persecution. He had a wife and a house. And during his decades of service as a prophet, God revealed to him, and through him to us, some of the most amazing things about the future of our world—and our Messiah.

Maybe chapter 1 was just a great Cecil B. DeMille–style theatrical device that leads into the appearance of Jesus in chapter 2. That's right. Ezekiel meets Jesus in chapter 2.

How do we know? Simple. Here's how chapter 1 ends: "This was the appearance of the likeness of the glory of the LORD. And when I saw it, I fell upon my face, and I heard a voice of one that spake" (v. 28).

First of all, whenever man sees God, he sees Jesus—the Creator of heaven and earth, the one who made all things that were made (John 1). Jesus is man's one and only mediator with the Father (1 Timothy 2:5). To me that means that it was Jesus walking in the garden with Adam and Eve (Genesis 3:8), and Jesus meeting Moses on Mount Sinai (Exodus 19:20). And when other prophets met with God face-to-face, I believe it was Jesus they were seeing. Does that make sense? After all, He's the earth's Creator—and man's.

In Ezekiel 2, God—or Jesus—reveals Himself to Ezekiel, and He has the form of a man. He hands Ezekiel a scroll. In chapter 3, God tells Ezekiel to eat the scroll so he has the words to speak to the children of Israel. When Ezekiel does so, the scroll tastes good, like honey. That's what the Word tastes like to me. I can't get enough of it. But it's an acquired taste, which is why I wrote this book—to help introduce people to the beauty, majesty, and relevance of what we call the Old Testament.

We also learn in chapter 3 that Ezekiel's ministry, unlike Jeremiah's, was exclusively to the children of Israel, not the nations.

Then Ezekiel is swept up in what I will call this "chariot of God" and delivered to his audience in dramatic fashion. I'm sure the prophet's heart was beating fast. We also get some insight into the way this prophet business works.

> Son of man, I have made thee a watchman unto the house of Israel: therefore hear the word at my mouth, and give them warning from me. When I say unto the wicked, Thou shalt surely die; and thou givest him not warning, nor speakest to warn the wicked from his wicked way, to save his life; the same wicked man shall die in his iniquity; but his blood will I require at thine hand. Yet if thou warn the wicked, and he turn not from his wickedness, nor from his wicked way, he shall die in his iniquity; but thou hast delivered thy soul. Again, When a righteous man doth turn from his righteousness, and commit iniquity, and I lay a stumbling-block before him, he shall die: because thou hast not given him warning, he shall die in his sin, and his righteousness which he hath done shall not be remembered; but his blood will I require at thine hand. Nevertheless if thou warn the righteous man, that the righteous sin not, and he doth not sin, he shall surely live, because he is warned; also thou hast delivered thy soul.
>
> And the hand of the LORD was there upon me; and he said unto me, Arise, go forth into the plain, and I will there talk with thee (3:17–22).

That's pretty much all we can do in delivering the gospel, is it not? We can do our best to share the good news, but we can't make people accept it. God is looking for a remnant among us who will be His children forever—part of His family, to rule and reign with Him through eternity. Keep in mind, Ezekiel was a prophet to the children of Israel in Babylon, where they would be captive for seventy years. Yet, God told Ezekiel about another dispersion that was coming throughout the entire world (Ezekiel 6:8). There's another judgment coming. God was not talking to

Ezekiel about a return to the promised land.

In chapters 8–11, God shows Ezekiel why the children of Israel were judged, re-creating scenes from history, and even allowing Ezekiel to participate in them. Ezekiel had begun to fear that God was going to put an end to the His people forever before this gospel reassurance in 11:16–21:

> Therefore say, Thus saith the Lord GOD; Although I have cast them far off among the heathen, and although I have scattered them among the countries, yet will I be to them as a little sanctuary in the countries where they shall come. Therefore say, Thus saith the Lord GOD; I will even gather you from the people, and assemble you out of the countries where ye have been scattered, and I will give you the land of Israel. And they shall come thither, and they shall take away all the detestable things thereof and all the abominations thereof from thence. And I will give them one heart, and I will put a new spirit within you; and I will take the stony heart out of their flesh, and will give them an heart of flesh: that they may walk in my statutes, and keep mine ordinances, and do them: and they shall be my people, and I will be their God. But as for them whose heart walketh after the heart of their detestable things and their abominations, I will recompense their way upon their own heads, saith the Lord GOD. (*See also* Hebrews 8:10 and Revelation 21:3.)

That is the gospel. It's good news for the righteous who walk with God. It's justice for the wicked who don't. It's the same message Jesus gave: "So shall it be at the end of the world: the angels shall come forth, and sever the wicked from among the just" (Matthew 13:49).

There's more gospel still in the midst of Ezekiel—much more.

In chapter 12, the Lord refers to a certain proverb among the children of Israel that gives us insight into their thinking. It's one we should all be familiar with because we talk like this in our own time, in our own communities, in our own countries.

> Son of man, what is that proverb that ye have in the land of Israel, saying, The days are prolonged, and every vision faileth? Tell them therefore, Thus saith the Lord GOD; I will make this proverb to cease, and they shall no more use it as a proverb in Israel; but say unto them, The days are at hand, and the effect of every vision. For there shall be no more any vain vision nor flattering divination within the house of Israel. For I am the LORD: I will speak, and the word that I shall speak shall come to pass; it shall be no more prolonged: for in your days, O rebellious house, will I say the word, and will perform it, saith the Lord GOD (vv. 22–25).

This is why the children of Israel wound up in captivity and judgment. They listened to the false prophets who told them, in effect, "Don't worry; everything's going to work out fine." Meanwhile, they dismissed the warnings of the real prophets, sent by God. But God says there will come a time when He shuts the mouths of the false prophets and He will speak directly. And what He speaks will come to pass quickly, immediately—right before their eyes. That's the way things work in Jesus' future kingdom on earth.

What's the first thing that comes to mind when we think of the gospel? It should be repentance—no question about it. It has been the consistent pleading of God throughout Scripture. And we hear it again in Ezekiel 14:6: "Therefore say unto the house of Israel, Thus saith the Lord GOD; Repent, and turn yourselves from your idols; and turn away your faces from all your abominations."

Sometimes in the contemporary church, we forget that Jesus warned that the gate to the kingdom is narrow (Matthew 7:13–14). We hear the same message in Ezekiel 14:20–23, in different words:

> Though Noah, Daniel, and Job were in it, as I live, saith the Lord GOD, they shall deliver neither son nor daughter; they shall but deliver their own souls by their righteousness. For thus saith the Lord GOD; How much more when I send my four sore judgments upon Jerusalem, the sword, and the famine, and the

noisome beast, and the pestilence, to cut off from it man and beast? Yet, behold, therein shall be left a remnant that shall be brought forth, both sons and daughters: behold, they shall come forth unto you, and ye shall see their way and their doings: and ye shall be comforted concerning the evil that I have brought upon Jerusalem, even concerning all that I have brought upon it. And they shall comfort you, when ye see their ways and their doings: and ye shall know that I have not done without cause all that I have done in it, saith the Lord God.

It's a remnant of faithful that God is cultivating. It's not a remnant heading for destruction. It's a remnant who will live in the glory of the Lord in His kingdom. Remember: the gospel is not about universal salvation. That's just not in the Book. Sometimes we have the perception that the Old Testament is a bit harsh compared to the New Testament. Forget that. The story is one and the same. God is the same yesterday, today, and tomorrow (Hebrews 13:8).

In Ezekiel 16, God remembers why He chose Israel as His bride. Then He recalls her "whoredoms." But He ends the story in familiar gospel fashion in verses 60–63:

Nevertheless I will remember my covenant with thee in the days of thy youth, and I will establish unto thee an everlasting covenant. Then thou shalt remember thy ways, and be ashamed, when thou shalt receive thy sisters, thine elder and thy younger: and I will give them unto thee for daughters, but not by thy covenant. And I will establish my covenant with thee; and thou shalt know that I am the Lord: that thou mayest remember, and be confounded, and never open thy mouth any more because of thy shame, when I am pacified toward thee for all that thou hast done, saith the Lord God.

I call the entirety of chapter 18 of Ezekiel "the Gospel 101, According to God." It's about repentance, personal responsibility, and salvation. It's quite simple in its essence: The soul that sins dies. The righteous soul that does not sin lives. The soul that sins but repents lives. If a righteous man has a son who sins, the father lives and the son dies. "The son shall not bear the iniquity of the father, neither shall the father bear the iniquity of the son: the righteousness of the righteous shall be upon him, and the wickedness of the wicked shall be upon him," the Lord says. "But if the wicked will turn from all his sins that he hath committed, and keep all my statutes, and do that which is lawful and right, he shall surely live, he shall not die" (vv. 20–21).

How important is this concept of repentance? God repeats in verse 27, "Again, when the wicked man turneth away from his wickedness that he hath committed, and doeth that which is lawful and right, he shall save his soul alive." Much of this is repeated for emphasis in chapter 33.

The formula works collectively, too, we see in verses 30–32:

> Therefore I will judge you, O house of Israel, every one according to his ways, saith the Lord GOD. Repent, and turn yourselves from all your transgressions; so iniquity shall not be your ruin. Cast away from you all your transgressions, whereby ye have transgressed; and make you a new heart and a new spirit: for why will ye die, O house of Israel? For I have no pleasure in the death of him that dieth, saith the Lord GOD: wherefore turn yourselves, and live ye.

I call the entirety of chapter 20 "the Gospel of the Kingdom 101." First, there's a brief history of Israel and how God incubated the nation in Egypt, took them out, and led them through the wilderness, giving them His commandments. But they fell short and sinned. He considered destroying them, but for His name's sake and the witness this would give the Gentiles, he did not. Things got no better when He brought them into the promised land. They fell away from His commandments. But there will come a time in the future where things will be different, He says in verses 33–41. It's a picture of the coming kingdom:

As I live, saith the Lord GOD, surely with a mighty hand, and with a stretched out arm, and with fury poured out, will I rule over you: and I will bring you out from the people, and will gather you out of the countries wherein ye are scattered, with a mighty hand, and with a stretched out arm, and with fury poured out. And I will bring you into the wilderness of the people, and there will I plead with you face to face. Like as I pleaded with your fathers in the wilderness of the land of Egypt, so will I plead with you, saith the Lord GOD. And I will cause you to pass under the rod, and I will bring you into the bond of the covenant: And I will purge out from among you the rebels, and them that transgress against me: I will bring them forth out of the country where they sojourn, and they shall not enter into the land of Israel: and ye shall know that I am the LORD. As for you, O house of Israel, thus saith the Lord GOD; Go ye, serve ye every one his idols, and hereafter also, if ye will not hearken unto me: but pollute ye my holy name no more with your gifts, and with your idols. For in mine holy mountain, in the mountain of the height of Israel, saith the Lord GOD, there shall all the house of Israel, all of them in the land, serve me: there will I accept them, and there will I require your offerings, and the firstfruits of your oblations, with all your holy things. I will accept you with your sweet savour, when I bring you out from the people, and gather you out of the countries wherein ye have been scattered; and I will be sanctified in you before the heathen. And ye shall know that I am the LORD, when I shall bring you into the land of Israel, into the country for the which I lifted up mine hand to give it to your fathers. And there shall ye remember your ways, and all your doings, wherein ye have been defiled; and ye shall lothe yourselves in your own sight for all your evils that ye have committed. And ye shall know that I am the LORD when I have wrought with you for my name's sake, not according to your wicked ways, nor according to your corrupt doings, O ye house of Israel, saith the Lord GOD.

Likewise, Ezekiel 28 hints at the future kingdom in verses 25–26:

Thus saith the Lord GOD; When I shall have gathered the house of Israel from the people among whom they are scattered, and shall be sanctified in them in the sight of the heathen, then shall they dwell in their land that I have given to my servant Jacob. And they shall dwell safely therein, and shall build houses, and plant vineyards; yea, they shall dwell with confidence, when I have executed judgments upon all those that despise them round about them; and they shall know that I am the LORD their God.

You've heard of the Good Shepherd, right? Yes, that's Jesus. We learn all about Him and the proper role of the shepherd in Ezekiel 34. There we see that this Good Shepherd will rule and reign over Israel:

And I will set up one shepherd over them, and he shall feed them, even my servant David; he shall feed them, and he shall be their shepherd. And I the LORD will be their God, and my servant David a prince among them; I the LORD have spoken it. And I will make with them a covenant of peace, and will cause the evil beasts to cease out of the land: and they shall dwell safely in the wilderness, and sleep in the woods. And I will make them and the places round about my hill a blessing; and I will cause the shower to come down in his season; there shall be showers of blessing. And the tree of the field shall yield her fruit, and the earth shall yield her increase, and they shall be safe in their land, and shall know that I am the LORD, when I have broken the bands of their yoke, and delivered them out of the hand of those that served themselves of them. And they shall no more be a prey to the heathen, neither shall the beast of the land devour them; but they shall dwell safely, and none shall make them afraid. And I will raise up for them a plant of renown, and they shall be no more consumed with hunger in the land, neither bear the shame of the heathen any more. Thus shall they know that I the LORD their God am with them, and that they, even the house of Israel, are my people, saith the Lord GOD. And ye my flock, the flock of my pasture, are men, and I am your God, saith the Lord GOD (vv. 23–31).

Ezekiel 36 has long been known as a key prophetic passage. Prophecy watchers look at Ezekiel 36–38 to determine what the end of age will look like. But there's gospel here, too, in 36:6–38, which I encourage you to read on your own. But let me call out verses 24–28 for special attention, for insight into the future kingdom, and some of it prophecy that we have witnessed in our own time:

> For I will take you from among the heathen, and gather you out of all countries, and will bring you into your own land. Then will I sprinkle clean water upon you, and ye shall be clean: from all your filthiness, and from all your idols, will I cleanse you. A new heart also will I give you, and a new spirit will I put within you: and I will take away the stony heart out of your flesh, and I will give you an heart of flesh. And I will put my spirit within you, and cause you to walk in my statutes, and ye shall keep my judgments, and do them. And ye shall dwell in the land that I gave to your fathers; and ye shall be my people, and I will be your God.

What will Israel be like in that kingdom of the future? See verse 35: "This land that was desolate is become like the garden of Eden; and the waste and desolate and ruined cities are become fenced, and are inhabited."

Ezekiel 37 references the literal resurrection of the nation of

Israel from the dead—a powerful prophecy that could be applied to no other nation in the world, turning "dry bones" into living souls. This is the happily-ever-after ending of the future kingdom of God. Verses 21–28 read:

> Thus saith the Lord GOD; Behold, I will take the children of Israel from among the heathen, whither they be gone, and will gather them on every side, and bring them into their own land: And I will make them one nation in the land upon the mountains of Israel; and one king shall be king to them all: and they shall be no more two nations, neither shall they be divided into two kingdoms any more at all. Neither shall they defile themselves any more with their idols, nor with their detestable things, nor with any of their transgressions: but I will save them out of all their dwellingplaces, wherein they have sinned, and will cleanse them: so shall they be my people, and I will be their God. And David my servant shall be king over them; and they all shall have one shepherd: they shall also walk in my judgments, and observe my statutes, and do them. And they shall dwell in the land that I have given unto Jacob my servant, wherein your fathers have dwelt; and they shall dwell therein, even they, and their children, and their children's children for ever: and my servant David shall be their prince for ever. Moreover I will make a covenant of peace with them; it shall be an everlasting covenant with them: and I will place them, and multiply them, and will set my sanctuary in the midst of them for evermore. My tabernacle also shall be with them: yea, I will be their God, and they shall be my people. And the heathen shall know that I the Lord do sanctify Israel, when my sanctuary shall be in the midst of them for evermore.

Who is that King? That's King Jesus, the Son of David and the Son of God, sitting on David's throne (Luke 1:32).

Could there possibly be more gospel in Ezekiel? Yes.

You've heard of "living waters." We've discussed this phrase in previous chapters. Read about how they will be manifested in the kingdom ruled over by Jesus in Ezekiel 47.

In Zechariah 14:8, a prophetic book about the Day of the Lord, what Christians believe to be the second coming of Jesus the Messiah, we learn, "And it shall be in that day, that living waters shall go out from Jerusalem; half of them toward the former sea, and half of them toward the hinder sea: in summer and in winter shall it be." There's far more detail on the flow of these living waters provided in Ezekiel 47 as waters rush out from under the threshold of the temple in Jerusalem toward the east. This will not be trickle of water, as we see today in the Jordan River. It will be a river that cannot be passed over. It runs eastward and goes down into the Judean desert and into the Dead Sea. "And it shall come to pass, that every thing that liveth, which moveth, whithersoever the rivers shall come, shall live: and there shall be a very great multitude of fish, because these waters shall come thither: for they shall be healed; and every thing shall live whither the river cometh" (Ezekiel 47:9).

While we know these "living waters" are of God and could be produced entirely supernaturally, we also know that God uses what He has created in the natural world for His own purposes.

Could it be these waters are just waiting to break forth in His timing?

Everyone has heard of the Dead Sea, the shore of which is the lowest point on dry land. It's truly lifeless, with a mind-blowing salinity level of more than 34 percent—nearly ten times saltier than ocean water and about twice as salty as Utah's Great Salt Lake.[1] Tourists from all over the world come to the Dead Sea today to experience the healing properties of its minerals, the very low levels of pollens and other allergens in the atmosphere, the reduced ultraviolet component of solar radiation, and the higher atmospheric pressure. They also come to float haplessly in the water that won't allow you to sink.

There's a historic town near the Dead Sea that served as a refuge for David when he was running from King Saul, who was trying to kill him. It's called En Gedi, as it was then. It's one of my favorite places to visit when I am in Israel. It's a rocky, mountainous oasis in the midst of a wilderness today. But it, too, will take on new life when Jesus returns, becoming an abundant fishing village where today no fish are found.

It seems En Gedi will become lakefront beach property in the kingdom.

Ezekiel 47:10–12 tells us:

> And it shall come to pass, that the fishers shall stand upon it from Engedi even unto Eneglaim; they shall be a place to spread forth nets; their fish shall be according to their kinds, as the fish of the great sea, exceeding many. But the miry places thereof and the marishes thereof shall not be healed; they shall be given to salt. And by the river upon the bank thereof, on this side and on that side, shall grow all trees for meat, whose leaf shall not fade, neither shall the fruit thereof be consumed: it shall bring forth new fruit according to his months, because their waters they issued out of the sanctuary: and the fruit thereof shall be for meat, and the leaf thereof for medicine.

Thus, the Dead Sea will be resurrected like the land of Israel and the nations during Jesus' earthly reign as King.

But that's not all these living waters will bring. Ezekiel 36:9–11 tells us the mountains of Israel will be tilled and sown and will shoot forth branches and yield abundant fruit. But it will also cleanse people of their sins, an illustration of why believers partake in the ritual of baptism today, just as they did in the time of Jesus and John the Baptist. "Then will I sprinkle clean water upon you, and ye shall be clean: from all your filthiness, and from all your idols, will I cleanse you," we're told in Ezekiel 46:25.

God promises to give Israel a new heart and a new spirit that will cause the nation to walk in His statutes and keep His commandments (Ezekiel 36:26–27). And that is the literal fulfillment of what Christians call the new covenant—which was prophesied in Jeremiah 31 long before it was mentioned in the Greek Scriptures. Israel will become what it was always designed by God to be: a light to the nations. These "living waters" will manifest not just spiritually but literally and physically.

All this blessing will cause people to say, "This land that was desolate is become like the garden of Eden; and the waste and desolate and ruined cities are become fenced, and are inhabited" (Ezekiel 36:35).

Are you ready for a brand-new world like the garden of Eden restored? That's what the Bible promises us. It's our destiny. It's where we will be resurrected and judged. It's where we will live for a thousand years if we are saved through repentance and by the precious atoning blood sacrifice of our Messiah Jesus. It's the full story of the gospel seldom, unfortunately, told to nonbelievers. The world is going to be restored. Humanity is going to be restored—made whole again, free of sin, to live with God, in the person of King Jesus ruling and reigning over the whole world from Jerusalem.

And unlike the world today, there will be no shortage of water— there will be healing water, cleansing water, miraculous water, *living water.*

28

THE GOSPEL IN DANIEL

And they that be wise shall shine as the brightness of the firmament; and they that turn many to righteousness as the stars for ever and ever.
—DANIEL 12:3

And at the end of the days I Nebuchadnezzar lifted up mine eyes unto heaven, and mine understanding returned unto me, and I blessed the most High, and I praised and honoured him that liveth for ever, whose dominion is an everlasting dominion, and his kingdom is from generation to generation.
—DANIEL 4:34

DO YOU RECALL what Ezekiel recorded about his contemporary Daniel in the previous chapter?

In Ezekiel 14, the Lord cited three righteous figures from the Scriptures—men we will undoubtedly meet someday if we are blessed to enter the kingdom of God—Noah, Job and Daniel. They were cited as examples of people well-known for their extraordinary faith. Daniel is mentioned again in Ezekiel as a figure of towering wisdom. Notice it's not Solomon who was renowned in his time for wisdom, but Daniel who is acknowledged.

Daniel is an extraordinary figure whose revelations about Bible prophecy and the dual comings of the Messiah set the stage for and inspired John's apocalyptic writing in the final book of the New Testament.

Jesus, too, gives a hat tip to Daniel in the gospels of Matthew and Mark, and the context of the first of these references is most interesting. In Matthew 24, the chapter well-known as Jesus' look into the end of the age, Jesus says,

> And this gospel of the kingdom shall be preached in all the world for a witness unto all nations; and then shall the end come. When ye therefore shall see the abomination of desolation, spoken of by Daniel the prophet, stand in the holy place, (whoso readeth, let him understand:) then let them which be in Judaea flee into the mountains: let him which is on the housetop not come down to take any thing out of his house: neither let him which is in the field return back to take his clothes. And woe unto them that are with child, and to them that give suck in those days! But pray ye that your flight be not in the winter, neither on the sabbath day: for then shall be great tribulation, such as was not since the beginning of the world to this time, no, nor ever shall be. And except those days should be shortened, there should no flesh be saved: but for the elect's sake those days shall be shortened (vv. 14–22).

Daniel was just a child when Jerusalem fell and he was taken into Babylonian captivity along with three other eunuch prodigies schooled in the knowledge of science, diplomacy, and languages, Shadrach, Meshach and Abednego. All four would take on Babylonian names: Daniel became Belteshazzar; Shadrach became Hananiah; Meshach became Mishael, and Abednego became Azariah. The four found favor with the prince of eunuchs in captivity who facilitated their effort to eat clean and remain undefiled.

Daniel 1 concludes:

> As for these four children, God gave them knowledge and skill in all learning and wisdom: and Daniel had understanding in all visions and dreams. Now at the end of the days that the king had said he should bring them in, then the prince of the eunuchs brought them in before Nebuchadnezzar. And the king communed with them; and among them all was found none like Daniel, Hananiah, Mishael, and Azariah: therefore stood they before the king. And in all matters of wisdom and understanding, that the king enquired of them, he found them ten times better than all the magicians and astrologers that were in all his realm. And Daniel continued even unto the first year of king Cyrus (vv. 17–21).

In chapter 2, Daniel famously interprets a disturbing dream for Nebuchadnezzar, not unlike Joseph, when he did the same for Pharaoh in Genesis. So impressed with Daniel's interpretation was the king that we are told:

> Then the king Nebuchadnezzar fell upon his face, and worshipped Daniel, and commanded that they should offer an oblation and sweet odours unto him. The king answered unto Daniel, and said, Of a truth it is, that your God is a God of gods, and a Lord of kings, and a revealer of secrets, seeing thou couldest reveal this secret.
>
> Then the king made Daniel a great man, and gave him many great gifts, and made him ruler over the whole province of Babylon, and chief of the governors over all the wise men of Babylon. Then Daniel requested of the king, and he set Shadrach, Meshach, and Abednego, over the affairs of the province of Babylon: but Daniel sat in the gate of the king (vv. 46–49).

Despite Nebuchadnezzar's seeming acknowledgment of the God of Israel, in chapter 3 he builds a statue of himself that is to be worshipped by everyone in the kingdom. Because of their sudden rise to power in the Babylonian Empire, Daniel and his three pals are targeted by jealous conspirators who tell the king that Shadrach, Meshach and Abednego won't worship the golden icon. He summons the trio and demands to know if this is true, threatening them with being cast into a fiery furnace.

"O Nebuchadnezzar, we are not careful to answer thee in this matter," they responded. "If it be so, our God whom we serve is able to deliver us from the burning fiery furnace, and he will deliver us out of thine hand, O king. But if not, be it known unto thee, O king, that we will not serve thy gods, nor worship the golden image which thou hast set up" (3:16–18)

Enraged, Nebuchadnezzar ordered the furnace to be heated seven times hotter and had the three young men cast inside.

Then Nebuchadnezzar the king was astonished, and rose up in haste, and spake, and said unto his counsellors, Did not we cast three men bound into the midst of the fire? They answered and said unto the king, True, O king. He answered and said, Lo, I see four men loose, walking in the midst of the fire, and they have no hurt; and the form of the fourth is like the Son of God. Then Nebuchadnezzar came near to the mouth of the burning fiery furnace, and spake, and said, Shadrach, Meshach, and Abednego, ye servants of the most high God, come forth, and come hither. Then Shadrach, Meshach, and Abednego, came forth of the midst of the fire. And the princes, governors, and captains, and the king's counsellors, being gathered together, saw these men, upon whose bodies the fire had no power, nor was an hair of their head singed, neither were their coats changed, nor the smell of fire had passed on them. Then Nebuchadnezzar spake, and said, Blessed be the God of Shadrach, Meshach, and Abednego, who hath sent his angel, and delivered his servants that trusted in him, and have changed the king's word, and yielded their bodies, that they might not serve nor worship any god, except their own God. Therefore I make a decree, That every people, nation, and language, which speak any thing amiss against the God of Shadrach, Meshach, and Abednego, shall be cut in pieces, and their houses shall be made a dunghill: because there is no other God that can deliver after this sort. Then the king promoted Shadrach, Meshach, and Abednego, in the province of Babylon (vv. 24–30).

Who was this Savior like "the Son of God" seen in the midst of the fiery furnace with the young children of Israel? Clearly this was Jesus making a visual appearance in the Old Testament, one of those cameo roles we know as "theophanies."

In chapter 4, Nebuchadnezzar has another dream that perplexes him. Daniel gives the interpretation in verse 25 under the inspiration of the Holy Spirit: "They shall drive thee from men, and thy dwelling shall be with the beasts of the field, and they shall make thee to eat grass as oxen, and they shall wet thee with the dew of heaven, and seven times shall pass over thee, till thou know that the most High ruleth in the kingdom of men, and giveth it to whomsoever he will."

This response caused the king to despair for twelve months, but then, in a moment of great arrogance, he asks, "Is not this great Babylon, that I have built for the house of the kingdom by the might of my power, and for the honour of my majesty?" (v. 30).

What follows is one of the most remarkable developments in the Bible, leading to the salvation of the tyrant of Babylon.

While the word was in the king's mouth, there fell a voice from heaven, saying, O king Nebuchadnezzar, to thee it is spoken; The kingdom is departed from thee. And they shall drive thee from men, and thy dwelling shall be with the beasts of the field: they shall make thee to eat grass as oxen, and seven times shall pass over thee, until thou know that the most High ruleth in the kingdom of men, and giveth it to whomsoever he will. The same hour was the thing fulfilled upon Nebuchadnezzar: and he was driven from men, and did eat grass as oxen, and his body was wet with the dew of heaven, till his hairs were grown like eagles' feathers, and his nails like birds' claws. And at the end of the days I Nebuchadnezzar lifted up mine eyes unto heaven, and mine understanding returned unto me, and I blessed the most High, and I praised and honoured him that liveth for ever, whose dominion is an everlasting dominion, and his kingdom is from generation to generation: And all the inhabitants of the earth are reputed as nothing: and he doeth according to his will in the army of heaven, and among the inhabitants of the earth: and none can stay his hand, or say unto him, What doest thou? At the same time my reason returned unto me; and for the glory of my kingdom, mine honour and brightness returned unto me; and my counsellors and my lords sought unto me; and I was established in my kingdom, and excellent majesty was added unto me. Now I Nebuchadnezzar praise and extol and honour the King of heaven, all whose works are truth, and his ways judgment: and those that walk in pride he is able to abase (vv. 31–37).

Notice that Nebuchadnezzar actually authored these words himself in the book of Daniel. So, here is yet another sanctified one we may someday meet in the kingdom of God.

In Ezekiel 5, we get to read about the "handwriting on the wall" from which we get the popular phrase still in use today. There's a new king in command—Nebuchadnezzar's son, Belshazzar, not to be confused with Daniel's Babylonian name, Belteshazzar.

The new king threw a party and decided to break out the golden vessels that had been taken out of the Jerusalem temple when Babylon conquered God's people, drinking from them and praising "the gods of gold, and of silver, of brass, of iron, of wood, and of stone" (v. 4).

Big mistake.

"In the same hour came forth fingers of a man's hand, and wrote over against the candlestick upon the plaister of the wall of the king's palace: and the king saw the part of the hand that wrote," we read. "Then the king's countenance was changed, and his thoughts troubled him, so that the joints of his loins were loosed, and his knees smote one against another" (vv. 5–6). The king's soothsayers could not even read the message. Daniel was thus summoned.

The chapter concludes:

> [Daniel said,] this is the writing that was written, MENE, MENE, TEKEL, UPHARSIN. This is the interpretation of the thing: MENE; God hath numbered thy kingdom, and finished it. TEKEL; Thou art weighed in the balances, and art found wanting. PERES; Thy kingdom is divided, and given to the Medes and Persians. Then commanded Belshazzar, and they clothed Daniel with scarlet, and put a chain of gold about his neck, and made a proclamation concerning him, that he should be the third ruler in the kingdom. In that night was Belshazzar the king of the Chaldeans slain. And Darius the Median took the kingdom, being about threescore and two years old (vv. 25–31).

In chapter 6, Darius gives Daniel another promotion, making him second in command in the kingdom. Immediately, the princes of lower rank begin conspiring against him. You know the rest of the story. The princes persuade Darius to sign a decree that anyone petitioning a god other than the king be thrown into the lion's den. Daniel is spied praying to God. The decree cannot be changed. Darius is despondent over having been tricked, but as a matter of honor to the law, casts Daniel into the den overnight, saying, "Thy God whom thou servest continually, he will deliver thee" (v. 16).

In the morning, the king rushes to the lion's den to find Daniel alive and unhurt. The chapter concludes:

Then king Darius wrote unto all people, nations, and languages, that dwell in all the earth; Peace be multiplied unto you. I make a decree, That in every dominion of my kingdom men tremble and fear before the God of Daniel: for he is the living God, and stedfast for ever, and his kingdom that which shall not be destroyed, and his dominion shall be even unto the end. He delivereth and rescueth, and he worketh signs and wonders in heaven and in earth, who hath delivered Daniel from the power of the lions. So this Daniel prospered in the reign of Darius, and in the reign of Cyrus the Persian (vv. 25–28).

Chapter 7 revisits the reign of Belshazzar, the son of Nebuchadnezzar. Like his father, he had a dream needing interpretation by Daniel. Daniel saw the dream as an explanation of future history, kingdoms, and empires—ending climactically with the establishment of the kingdom of God of the gospel on earth in verse 27: "And the kingdom and dominion, and the greatness of the kingdom under the whole heaven, shall be given to the people of the saints of the most High, whose kingdom is an everlasting kingdom, and all dominions shall serve and obey him."

Daniel was a learned man, as we have seen. In chapter 9, we see that he determined, from reading the prophecy scrolls of the prophet Jeremiah, that the captivity of Israel was drawing to a close after seventy years. This prompted Daniel to pray a forthright gospel prayer. As a result, he was visited by the angel Gabriel, who revealed the prophecy of the seventy weeks, which starts the countdown for the Messiah to come, to be cut off (killed), but to return again to establish His everlasting kingdom—the fulfillment of the gospel:

Seventy weeks are determined upon thy people and upon thy holy city, to finish the transgression, and to make an end of sins, and to make reconciliation for iniquity, and to bring in everlasting righteousness, and to seal up the vision and prophecy, and to anoint the most Holy. Know therefore and understand, that from the going forth of the commandment to restore and to build Jerusalem unto the Messiah the Prince shall be seven weeks, and threescore and two weeks: the street shall be built again, and the wall, even in troublous times. And after threescore and two weeks shall Messiah be cut off, but not for himself: and the people of the prince that shall come shall destroy the city and the sanctuary; and the end thereof shall be with a flood, and unto the end of the war desolations are determined. And he shall confirm the covenant with many for one week: and in the midst of the week he shall cause the sacrifice and the oblation to cease, and for the overspreading of abominations he shall make it desolate, even until the consummation, and that determined shall be poured upon the desolate (vv. 24–27).

In chapter 12, we learn more about the way the kingdom will be established:

And at that time shall Michael stand up, the great prince which standeth for the children of thy people: and there shall be a time of trouble, such as never was since there was a nation even to that same time: and at that time thy people shall be delivered, every one that shall be found written in the book. And many of them that sleep in the dust of the earth shall awake, some to everlasting life, and some to shame and everlasting contempt. And they that be wise shall shine as the brightness of the firmament; and they that turn many to righteousness as the stars for ever and ever. But thou, O Daniel, shut up the words, and seal the book, even to the time of the end: many shall run to and fro, and knowledge shall be increased (vv. 1–4).

Daniel is an amazing gospel book, isn't it? It's a virtual historical timeline to the fulfillment of the gospel. First, atonement must be made for wickedness. That is accomplished by the Messiah being cut off. Then comes the resurrection of the Messiah, and finally, His return as King of kings—to bring in everlasting righteousness. What a day that will be . . . and I want you to see it.

28

THE GOSPEL IN HOSEA

Therefore turn thou to thy God: keep mercy and judgment and wait on thy God continually. —HOSEA 12:6

Yet I am the LORD thy God from the land of Egypt, and thou shalt know no god but me: for there is no saviour beside me. —HOSEA 13:4

IF YOU'VE READ THROUGH all the Hebrew Scriptures discussed in this study, you've seen a pattern emerge. We've addressed this pattern before, and it is pretty simple, obvious, and relevant to believers today.

First God lifts up the children of Israel, blesses them, gives them promise and hope—as long as they follow His commandments and stay true to Him and His Word.

But after a time, Israel strays. The God of Israel is no longer number 1 in their lives. It can happen as quickly as one generation or two. In God's eyes, it's harlotry. The Israelites betray their marriage with the one true God, their Creator, their Provider, their unique Blessing, to play the role of an adulteress. Because God is long-suffering and has such great patience, He gives them space to repent . . . but they don't. And so, the consequences of their own behavior are manifested—God's blessings are removed and the promised curses begin.

The removal of blessings and the substitution of curses are intended to be correctional. Sometimes they work; sometimes they don't. Let's review some examples.

We first see the pattern in the exodus. Remember the miracles God performed in Egypt to persuade Pharaoh to let His people go? All of God's children saw those mighty works, the plagues that befell Egypt but did not affect the Hebrews. How long after their departure was it before they forgot what they had seen and lost their faith? As soon as they saw the Egyptians pursuing them, what did they say to Moses? "Because there were no graves in Egypt, hast thou taken us away to die in the wilderness? wherefore hast thou dealt thus with us, to carry us forth out of Egypt? Is not this the word that we did tell thee in Egypt, saying, Let us alone, that we may serve the Egyptians? For it had been better for us to serve the Egyptians, than that we should die in the wilderness" (Exodus 14:11–12).

Of course, God opened up the Red Sea, allowing the children of Israel to cross, and closed it up on the Egyptians. The Israelites sang and danced and glorified the Lord . . .

Until three days later, when they came to a spring of bitter waters. Then "the people murmured against Moses, saying, What shall we drink?" (Exodus 15:24).

Well, God instructed Moses on how to cure the waters, but it was only a matter of days, maybe weeks, before God's people were grumbling again: "And the children of Israel said unto them, Would to God we had died by the hand of the LORD in the land of Egypt, when we sat by the flesh pots, and when we did eat bread to the full; for ye have brought us forth into this wilderness, to kill this whole assembly with hunger" (Exodus 16:3).

And so it was for forty years in the wilderness.

Eventually, God gave up on the older generation and led only the younger Israelites into the promised land. Yet the pattern continued after the death of Joshua. Israel strayed again. They began chasing after other gods—playing the harlot. Sometimes they repented and turned back, sometimes they did not, leading first to the exile of the northern kingdom of Israel, and later to the captivity of Jerusalem and Judah. And it resumed, again, seventy years later, when Judah returned through the coming of Jesus, His death, and His resurrection until, the judgment came in the first and second centuries—until most of Israel was dispersed to the four corners of the earth.

The problem was Israel's unwillingness to keep the first of God's commandments: "Thou shalt have no other gods before me" (Exodus 20:3).

It was adultery on a national scale. As God warned way back in in Exodus 34, Israel was not to go a-whoring after the false gods of the people they had succeeded in the promised land. But a-whoring they did go.

That brings us back to the main story line of Hosea, which takes place about eight hundred years before Jesus' time and presumably shortly before the fall of the Northern Kingdom to the Assyrians. The very first instruction God gave the prophet comes in the second verse of the book: "Go, take unto thee a wife of whoredoms and children of whoredoms: for the land hath committed great whoredom, departing from the Lord."

Hosea did just that—marrying a woman named Gomer, who bore him a son who would be named Jezreel. You might recall that Jezreel had been home to the wicked King Ahab and his even wickeder wife, Jezebel. Jehu overthrew Ahab. God explained to Hosea that his son was to be named after this valley "for yet a little while, and I will avenge the blood of Jezreel upon the house of Jehu, and will cause to cease the kingdom of the house of Israel. And it shall come to pass at that day, that I will break the bow of Israel, in the valley of Jezreel" (vv. 4–5). Next, Hosea had a daughter who was to be named "Loruhamah: for I will no more have mercy upon the house of Israel; but I will utterly take them away" (v. 6). Later. Hosea and Gomer had another son whose name was to be "Loammi: for ye are not my people, and I will not be your God" (v. 9).

In effect, Hosea was to be a living witness of what was shortly to befall the kingdom of Israel for its worship of other gods, for the sacrificing of its children to other gods, and for unrestrained, wanton disobedience and sinfulness.

But immediately thereafter, in the concluding verses of chapter 1, we see the promise of God to restore Israel in the future: "Yet the number of the children of Israel shall be as the sand of the sea, which cannot be measured nor numbered; and it shall come to pass, that in the place where it was said unto them, Ye are not my people, there it shall be said unto them, Ye are the sons of the living God. Then shall the children of Judah and the children of Israel be gathered together, and appoint themselves one head, and they shall come up out of the land: for great shall be the day of Jezreel" (v. 10).

There it is—the gospel of the kingdom, spoken about repeatedly by Jesus. Again, the gospel is not just about personal salvation, as we often think of it. It's also about the complete restoration of Israel and the rest of the world, with Jesus on David's throne in Israel. National salvation is much like personal salvation. It comes about through repentance when, collectively, Israel or any other nation follows the prescription God gave to Solomon at the dedication of the temple in 2 Chronicles 7:14: "If my people, which are called by my name, shall humble themselves, and pray, and seek my face, and turn from their wicked ways; then will I hear from heaven, and will forgive their sin, and will heal their land."

Notice that God only expects this from His people, those called by His name—not everyone. His people, those called by His name, thus bear a tremendous responsibility. As Jesus said in Luke 12:48: "For unto whomsoever much is given, of him shall be much required."

In the second chapter of Hosea, we see how the prophet's own family became a kind of metaphor for the nation of Israel. His wife, Gomer, had fallen into adultery like Israel. But what was her future? The Lord was going to win her back.

> Behold, I will allure her, and bring her into the wilderness, and speak comfortably unto her. And I will give her her vineyards from thence, and the valley of Achor for a door of hope: and she shall sing there, as in the days of her youth, and as in the day when she came up out of the land of Egypt. And it shall be at that day, saith the LORD, that thou shalt call me Ishi; and shalt call me no more Baali. For I will take away the names of Baalim out of her mouth, and they shall no more be remembered by their name (vv. 2:14–17).

This is a particularly tender passage. In the future, Gomer, or Israel, is going to call God "ishi," not "Baali." What does that mean? In Hebrew there are two words for husband—*Baali*, which connotes "master," and "*ishi*," which means, more colloquially, "my man." Which sounds better? *Baali* shares a root with *Ba'al*, the name of one of the pagan gods. *Ishi* sounds, well, familiar and loving, does it not? When I'm good and sweet, my wife, Elizabeth, has been known to call me "ishi." Thankfully, she has never called be Baali.

There's more redemption here—more gospel in chapter 2:

> And in that day will I make a covenant for them with the beasts of the field and with the fowls of heaven, and with the creeping things of the ground: and I will break the bow and the sword and the battle out of the earth, and will make them to lie down safely. And I will betroth thee unto me for ever; yea, I will betroth thee unto me in righteousness, and in judgment, and in loving-kindness, and in mercies. I will even betroth thee unto me in faithfulness: and thou shalt know the LORD. And it shall come to pass in that day, I will hear, saith the LORD, I will hear the heavens, and they shall hear the earth; and the earth shall hear

the corn, and the wine, and the oil; and they shall hear Jezreel. And I will sow her unto me in the earth; and I will have mercy upon her that had not obtained mercy; and I will say to them which were not my people, Thou art my people; and they shall say, Thou art my God (vv. 18–23).

The parallels between Hosea and Israel continue in like fashion in chapter 3. Hosea is instructed to buy a harlot with the purpose of restraining her from sinfulness. Why? God tells us it's symbolic of His plan for Israel: "For the children of Israel shall abide many days without a king, and without a prince, and without a sacrifice, and without an image, and without an ephod, and without teraphim: Afterward shall the children of Israel return, and seek the LORD their God, and David their king; and shall fear the LORD and his goodness in the latter days."

Once again, there's the great hope of the gospel. It's what all the prophets focused on—right through the apostles, whose last question to Jesus in Acts 1:6, before He ascended, revealed their highest hope: "Wilt thou at this time restore again the kingdom to Israel?"

Hosea 4 reveals to us that evil in people and nations can reach a point at which God no longer attempts to refrain it. In effect, the die is cast. Their fates are sealed. Take verse 14, for example: "I will not punish your daughters when they commit whoredom, nor your spouses when they commit adultery: for themselves are separated with whores, and they sacrifice with harlots: therefore the people that doth not understand shall fall." Have you ever wondered why the wicked don't seem to suffer as a result of their flaunting sinfulness? Could it be they've reached that point of no return, where correction is withdrawn? What about other evil nations? None of them seem to endure for long. Judgment eventually befalls all of them—unless, of course, they repent. Repentance is always the cure with the God of Israel. But it becomes less likely when the correction stops. Yet, it happens, as we shall see in the book of Jonah, with Nineveh being the classic example.

God, of course, knows the end from the beginning. That's why it becomes more and more difficult to seek the Lord, again, in times of total depravity, as we see in 5:3–7:

> I know Ephraim, and Israel is not hid from me: for now, O Ephraim, thou committest whoredom, and Israel is defiled. They will not frame their doings to turn unto their God: for the spirit of whoredoms is in the midst of them, and they have not known the LORD. And the pride of Israel doth testify to his face: therefore shall Israel and Ephraim fall in their iniquity: Judah also shall fall with them. They shall go with their flocks and with their herds to seek the LORD; but they shall not find him; he hath withdrawn himself from them. They have dealt treacherously against the LORD: for they have begotten strange children: now shall a month devour them with their portions.

The chapter concludes in verse 15, though, with the gospel of redemption: "I will go and return to my place, till they acknowledge their offence, and seek my face: in their affliction they will seek me early." Repentance works every time.

That message launches us into chapter 6, a familiar prophetic verse about the kingdom: "Come, and let us return unto the LORD: for he hath torn, and he will heal us; he hath smitten, and he will bind us up. After two days will he revive us: in the third day he will raise us up, and we shall live in his sight. Then shall we know, if we follow on to know the LORD: his going forth is prepared as the morning; and he shall come unto us as the rain, as the latter and former rain unto the earth" (vv. 1–3). Just as Jesus rose from the dead, so will Israel arise on the third day and live in His sight!

That's prophecy fulfilled, as Israel was resurrected after two thousand years in exile.

In Hosea 6:6, we read, "For I desired mercy, and not sacrifice; and the knowledge of God more than burnt offerings." Does it sound familiar? It should. Just read Matthew 9:13 and Matthew 12:7.

What is it that most separates people from God? We get the answer in Hosea 7:10: "And the pride of Israel testifieth to his face: and they do not return to the LORD their God, nor seek him for all this." It's pride that most separates men from God. It's the sin that leads to other sins. It's humility that leads to us back to God.

Even when judgment is near, we can still hear the loving and merciful heart of God in chapter 10: "Sow to yourselves in righteousness, reap in mercy; break up your fallow ground: for it is time to seek the Lord, till he come and rain righteousness upon you"(v. 12). That's all it takes—returning to the Creator. That's the gospel message.

It was too late in Hosea's time for a change of heart in Israel, but God offered redemption in the future. In chapter 13, it is explicit: "O Israel, thou hast destroyed thyself; but in me is thine help," we're told. "I will be thy king: where is any other that may save thee in all thy cities?" (vv. 9–10). And in verse 14 we read: "I will ransom them from the power of the grave; I will redeem them from death."

And the final chapter is pure gospel blessing:

O Israel, return unto the LORD thy God; for thou hast fallen by thine iniquity. Take with you words, and turn to the LORD: say unto him, Take away all iniquity, and receive us graciously: so will we render the calves of our lips. Asshur shall not save us; we will not ride upon horses: neither will we say any more to the work of our hands, Ye are our gods: for in thee the fatherless findeth mercy. I will heal their backsliding, I will love them freely: for mine anger is turned away from him. I will be as the dew unto Israel: he shall grow as the lily, and cast forth his roots as Lebanon. His branches shall spread, and his beauty shall be as the olive tree, and his smell as Lebanon. They that dwell under his shadow shall return; they shall revive as the corn, and grow as the vine: the scent thereof shall be as the wine of Lebanon. Ephraim shall say, What have I to do any more with idols? I have heard him, and observed him: I am like a green fir tree. From me is thy fruit found. Who is wise, and he shall understand these things? prudent, and he shall know them? for the ways of the LORD are right, and the just shall walk in them: but the transgressors shall fall therein (14:1–9).

Perfect redemption. Perfect peace. Perfect truth. Perfect justice. That is the future. That is the gospel. And it's all found in the book of Hosea.

29

THE GOSPEL IN JOEL

*And it shall come to pass, that whosoever shall call on the name of the LORD
shall be delivered: for in mount Zion and in Jerusalem shall be deliverance,
as the LORD hath said, and in the remnant whom the LORD shall call.*
—JOEL 2:32

*Multitudes, multitudes in the valley of decision: for the day of the LORD is
near in the valley of decision.* —JOEL 3:14

IT'S USUALLY HELPFUL in studying the prophets to understand to
whom the prophets were speaking, as well as when they lived and
where their ministry was based.

But that's a problem with Joel, because no one is really certain
of when and where he ministered. There are few names provided to
link him with historical events, no kings to identify the time frame,
no genealogy that places his setting. He is not mentioned or quoted

specifically or identifiably by other prophets until Peter in Acts 2:16. All we know about Joel from Scripture is that he was a prophet and the son of Pethuel, the latter name not being very helpful either because it is found only in the book of Joel.

What does this suggest? To me it suggests Joel is a prophet for all generations. And because he was focused on the events of the Day of the Lord—an event that has not yet occurred—he is most relevant to the future.

While some of Joel's descriptive language about the Day of the Lord is similar to that used by other prophets, including Isaiah, Malachi, and Zephaniah, it's also language analogous to Jesus in the Gospels and John in Revelation. Therefore, everything about which Joel wrote seems to be relevant still primarily for the future.

Let's look at a few of those cross references:

Joel 2:10 says, "The earth shall quake before them; the heavens shall tremble: the sun and the moon shall be dark, and the stars shall withdraw their shining." Compare that to Revelation 6:12–13: "And I beheld when he had opened the sixth seal, and, lo, there was a great earthquake; and the sun became black as sackcloth of hair, and the moon became as blood; And the stars of heaven fell unto the earth, even as a fig tree casteth her untimely figs, when she is shaken of a mighty wind." That hadn't happened up to the time of Jesus, nor has it happened since. So, we can conclude with assurance that it is still a future event.

In Joel 2:28–29 we read: "And it shall come to pass afterward, that I will pour out my spirit upon all flesh; and your sons and your daughters shall prophesy, your old men shall dream dreams, your young men shall see visions: and also upon the servants and upon the handmaids in those days will I pour out my spirit." Compare that to Acts 2:16–18, in which Peter quotes Joel: "But this is that which was spoken by the prophet Joel; And it shall come to pass in the last days, saith God, I will pour out of my Spirit upon all flesh: and your sons and your daughters shall prophesy, and your young men shall see visions, and your old men shall dream dreams: And on my servants and on my handmaidens I will pour out in those days of my Spirit; and they shall prophesy:" While the spirit being poured out on Peter's generation happened on Pentecost, other events noted by Joel in the subsequent verses of Joel 2 have not. Thus, we can conclude with assurance that Joel's focus was on events that remain in the future.

Next look at Joel 2:31: "The sun shall be turned into darkness, and the moon into blood, before the great and terrible day of the LORD come." Compare that to what Jesus said in Matthew 24:29: "Immediately after the tribulation of those days shall the sun be darkened, and the moon shall not give her light, and the stars shall fall from heaven, and the powers of the heavens shall be shaken:" That hadn't happened up to the time of Jesus, nor has it happened since. So, we can conclude with assurance that it is still a future event.

The book of Joel is three short chapters long, and its focus is still very much on future events—namely, the Day of the Lord, the return of Jesus to establish His kingdom on earth. Perhaps, then, it is simply unnecessary for us to know more about when he lived, where he lived, and with whom he interacted in his time. It is enough that his words were recorded for future generations.

Joel himself hinted at this immediately after scantily identifying himself as the son of Pethuel in the second and third verses of chapter 1: "Hear this, ye old men, and give ear, all ye inhabitants of the land. Hath this been in your days, or even in the days of your fathers? Tell ye your children of it, and let your children tell their children, and their children another generation."

Thus, Joel goes on to describe a time of extreme peril to what can only be the resurrected land of Israel—the one re-formed, regathered, and reborn in 1948. It sounds very much like "the time of Jacob's trouble" referenced in Jeremiah 30:7, in which the Lord comes to rescue His people and His land from attack by seemingly overwhelming forces.

"Alas for the day! for the day of the LORD is at hand, and as a destruction from the Almighty shall it come," we're told in Joel

1:15. It is further described as "a day of darkness and of gloominess, a day of clouds and of thick darkness, as the morning spread upon the mountains: a great people and a strong; there hath not been ever the like, neither shall be any more after it, even to the years of many generations" (2:2).

"And the Lord shall utter his voice before his army: for his camp is very great," Joel went on, "for he is strong that executeth his word: for the day of the Lord is great and very terrible; and who can abide it? Therefore also now, saith the Lord, turn ye even to me with all your heart, and with fasting, and with weeping, and with mourning: And rend your heart, and not your garments, and turn unto the Lord your God: for he is gracious and merciful, slow to anger, and of great kindness, and repenteth him of the evil" (vv. 11–13)

What is the message here for all times? The Day of the Lord is surely coming, when He will return to judge the living and the dead. It will be the last opportunity for people to get right with Him, to beg for His mercy, and to turn to Him with all their hearts, souls, and minds.

"And it shall come to pass, that whosoever shall call on the name of the Lord shall be delivered," we're told in Joel 2:32, "for in mount Zion and in Jerusalem shall be deliverance, as the Lord hath said, and in the remnant whom the Lord shall call."

This is the ultimate time and place of what Joel uniquely among the prophets calls "the valley of decision." It's Judgment Day. Are you for the Lord or against Him? It's a decision that cannot be forestalled. And while this judgment is a very real event in the future, all people in all times have lived similarly in a valley of decision, because Jesus will be judging the living *and the dead* at this time. You and I live here and now in the valley of decision.

Again, Joel is about repentance and grace—one facet of the gospel message. But it's also about the gospel of the kingdom, because this is the time of restoration, for Israel and the rest of the world.

"So shall ye know that I am the Lord your God dwelling in Zion, my holy mountain: then shall Jerusalem be holy, and there shall no strangers pass through her any more," God said through Joel in chapter 3. "And it shall come to pass in that day, that the mountains shall drop down new wine, and the hills shall flow with milk, and all the rivers of Judah shall flow with waters, and a fountain shall come forth out of the house of the LORD, and shall water the valley of Shittim" (vv. 17–18).

Again, take note that this is the time in which those "living waters" referenced by Jeremiah, Ezekiel, Zechariah, the Song of Solomon, Jesus in the gospel of John, and the apostle John in Revelation, will come forth from the house of the Lord in Jerusalem to help refresh and heal the land and cleanse many of their sins.

And "Judah shall dwell for ever, and Jerusalem from generation to generation," Joel concludes. "For I will cleanse their blood that I have not cleansed: for the LORD dwelleth in Zion" (3:20–21).

And we can all dwell there too.

30

THE GOSPEL IN AMOS

Seek good, and not evil, that ye may live: and so the LORD, *the God of hosts, shall be with you, as ye have spoken. Hate the evil, and love the good, and establish judgment in the gate: it may be that the* LORD *God of hosts will be gracious unto the remnant of Joseph.* —AMOS 5:14–15

In that day will I raise up the tabernacle of David that is fallen, and close up the breaches thereof; and I will raise up his ruins, and I will build it as in the days of old. —AMOS 9:11

THE BOOK OF AMOS, a prophet from Judah who preached to the northern kingdom of Israel around the time of the reign of Jeroboam II, begins by detailing the judgments that will befall the enemies of the divided kingdoms.

Then it turns the tables. Quickly and for the next eight chapters, it focuses on what God has in store for both Judah and Israel, and, at least in the short term, it's not pretty.

Both Judah and Israel had turned away from God. They were worshipping false gods. They were consumed with immorality of all kinds. They were oppressing the poor. They were full of pride. They had contempt for the Torah.

The fate of Israel seems to be set in stone, with judgment around the corner. God, speaking through Amos, was so fed up with Israel that He even, perhaps mockingly, seemed to be encouraging the people to continue in their sinful ways: "Come to Bethel, and transgress; at Gilgal multiply transgression; and bring your sacrifices every morning, and your tithes after three years: And offer a sacrifice of thanksgiving with leaven, and proclaim and publish the free offerings: for this liketh you, O ye children of Israel, saith the Lord GOD" (Amos 4:4–5).

Yet, in chapter 5, Amos reminds Israel of what the Lord requires—the simple, loving prescriptions that is resisted by most of humanity: "For thus saith the LORD unto the house of Israel, Seek ye me, and ye shall live" (v. 4).

Amos 5:14–15 advises, "Seek good, and not evil, that ye may live: and so the LORD, the God of hosts, shall be with you, as ye have spoken. Hate the evil, and love the good, and establish judgment in the gate: it may be that the LORD God of hosts will be gracious unto the remnant of Joseph." Yet, it doesn't seem as though there's much hope for the future of Israel, which, God says, He "will destroy . . . from off the face of the earth" (9:8), until the closing verses of the final chapter.

Then there's that gospel-of-the-kingdom hope once again that comes so abruptly and without segue in Amos 9:11–15:

In that day will I raise up the tabernacle of David that is fallen, and close up the breaches thereof; and I will raise up his ruins, and I will build it as in the days of old: that they may possess the remnant of Edom, and of all the heathen, which are called by my name, saith the LORD that doeth this. Behold, the days come, saith the LORD, that the plowman shall overtake the reaper, and the treader of grapes him that soweth seed; and the mountains shall drop sweet wine, and all the hills shall melt. And I will bring again the captivity of my people of Israel, and they shall build the waste cities, and inhabit them; and they shall plant vineyards, and drink the wine thereof; they shall also make gardens, and eat the fruit of them. And I will plant them upon their land, and they shall no more be pulled up out of their land which I have given them, saith the LORD thy God.

Notice this prophecy goes beyond the restoration of Israel from ruins. There's something else here. And it is so significant that this passage is quoted nearly verbatim in the New Testament. There's a promise here not just for a new Israel presided over from Jerusalem, but a place of sanctuary for all the heathen, or Gentiles, "which are called by my name."

You can find the reference to this passage in Acts 15:16–18 by James, the brother of Jesus and the head of the messianic believers in Jerusalem. It comes in the context of a debate between the leaders of the congregation about what the expectations should be for these new Gentile followers of the faith, which, until this time, was completely dominated by Jewish believers.

Here's what James said, demonstrating a clear and precise recognition of the book of Amos:

Simeon hath declared how God at the first did visit the Gentiles, to take out of them a people for his name. And to this agree the words of the prophets; as it is written, After this I will return, and will build again the tabernacle of David, which is fallen down; and I will build again the ruins thereof, and I will set it up: that the residue of men might seek after the Lord, and all the Gentiles, upon whom my name is called, saith the Lord, who doeth all these things. Known unto God are all his works from the beginning of the world.

As Paul wrote in Romans 1:16, "For I am not ashamed of the gospel of Christ: for it is the power of God unto salvation to every one that believeth; to the Jew first, and also to the Greek."

Yet recall Peter's shock in Acts 10 when Gentiles, led by Cornelius, ask him to visit them in Caesarea. Until that time, Peter was still following the customs of his generation, that Jews and Gentiles did not mix. God had to prompt him through a dream to accept the concept that the Messiah was a Savior and Redeemer to all the nations and all the people, not just the Jews.

Yet this gospel plan was there all along, throughout the Hebrew prophets: in Isaiah, in Jeremiah, in Malachi—and in Amos.

31

THE GOSPEL IN OBADIAH

But upon mount Zion shall be deliverance, and there shall be holiness; and the house of Jacob shall possess their possessions. —OBADIAH V. 17

And the house of Jacob shall be a fire, and the house of Joseph a flame. —OBADIAH V. 18

LIKE JOEL, the prophet Obadiah is a little bit of a mystery man. His was a popular name in Bible times, but there is no known connection between this prophet and the Obadiahs found in 1 and Kings, 1 Chronicles and 2 Chronicles, Ezra, and Nehemiah.

No one is exactly sure when Obadiah was preaching.

And the book of Obadiah, fewer than seven hundred words, is just one chapter in the Hebrew Scriptures—the only such book of its kind, though there are similar one-chapter writings in the Greek Scriptures, including Philemon, 2 and 3 John, and Jude.

We can thank Obadiah for perhaps the most complete explanation of the judgment of Edom, the nation founded by Jacob's brother, Esau. The brothers had a troubled relationship, to be certain, and so did their respective nations, separated by the Jordan River and the Dead Sea.

You will recall in Genesis that older twin brother Esau forsook his birthright for a bowl of soup. Jacob impersonated Esau to receive his father's deathbed blessing. They went their separate ways, and soon started their own families, which became neighboring nations. During the sojourning years of Jacob, who was renamed Israel, he feared his brother would kill him. It is thought that Esau and the sons of Ishmael, Abraham's son with Hagar, formed the mixed Semitic peoples we today call Arabs.

Edom, like many of the other lands of Israel's Middle East neighbors, will be judged by God—as, in fact, will be all nations of the world. Obadiah offers the most complete picture of that judgment on Edom.

For thy violence against thy brother Jacob shame shall cover thee, and thou shalt be cut off for ever. In the day that thou stoodest on the other side, in the day that the strangers carried away captive his forces, and foreigners entered into his gates, and cast lots upon Jerusalem, even thou wast as one of them. But thou shouldest not have looked on the day of thy brother in the day that he became a stranger; neither shouldest thou have rejoiced over the children of Judah in the day of their destruction; neither shouldest thou have spoken proudly in the day of distress. Thou shouldest not have entered into the gate of my people in the day of their calamity; yea, thou shouldest not have looked on their affliction in the day of their calamity, nor have laid hands on their substance in the day of their calamity; Neither shouldest thou have stood in the crossway, to cut off those of his that did escape; neither shouldest thou have delivered up those of his that did remain in the day of distress. For the day of the LORD is near upon all the heathen: as thou hast done, it shall be done unto thee: thy reward shall return upon thine own head.

And where is the redemptive gospel message in this book? It comes in verses 17–21, with the not-so-familiar kingdom message of restoration in an Israel-centric world ruled over by Messiah Jesus:

> But upon mount Zion shall be deliverance, and there shall be holiness; and the house of Jacob shall possess their possessions. And the house of Jacob shall be a fire, and the house of Joseph a flame, and the house of Esau for stubble, and they shall kindle in them, and devour them; and there shall not be any remaining of the house of Esau; for the LORD hath spoken it. And they of the south shall possess the mount of Esau; and they of the plain the Philistines: and they shall possess the fields of Ephraim, and the fields of Samaria: and Benjamin shall possess Gilead. And the captivity of this host of the children of Israel shall possess that of the Canaanites, even unto Zarephath; and the captivity of Jerusalem, which is in Sepharad, shall possess the cities of the south. And saviours shall come up on mount Zion to judge the mount of Esau; and the kingdom shall be the LORD's.

This does not suggest, however, that individual Edomites have no place in the kingdom. For all Gentiles who embrace the Lord God and seek forgiveness of their sins through the atoning sacrifice of Jesus can be grafted in as believers, as we saw in the previous chapter.

They will just no longer be Edomites, but Jesusites.

32

THE GOSPEL IN JONAH

But I will sacrifice unto thee with the voice of thanksgiving; I will pay that that I have vowed. Salvation is of the LORD. —JONAH 2:9

IT'S HARD TO THINK of a more familiar Bible story than Jonah's, yet, how many think of Jonah as a prophet?

Indeed, he was—a contemporary of Amos, whom you've met, another prophet to the Northern Kingdom.

Keep in mind, Israel was about to be judged, and as a prophet to the Northern Kingdom, Jonah would have been very aware of that fact, though nowhere in this book does that subject come up. But God directed Jonah to go to Nineveh to call that great city to repentance. Instead, Jonah ran away, got on a boat, and took off in the other direction, in direct disobedience to God. Everyone knows the story of how a storm broke out and threatened the boat with capsizing.

But you may have missed a few things watching the *Veggie Tales* translation of the story. So let's look more closely at the actual text.

I've never heard anyone else mention these verses as significant, but take a look at Jonah 1:5–6: "Then the mariners were afraid, and cried every man unto his god, and cast forth the wares that were in the ship into the sea, to lighten it of them. But Jonah was gone down into the sides of the ship; and he lay, and was fast asleep. So the shipmaster came to him, and said unto him, What meanest thou, O sleeper? arise, call upon thy God, if so be that God will think upon us, that we perish not."

Does that remind you of anything? How about the time Jesus was on a ship with His disciples, crossing Lake Kinneret, and a storm hit? Like Jonah, Jesus was fast asleep, when one of His followers approached, saying, "Lord, save us: we perish." (See Matthew 8:23–26.)

Coincidence?

In both circumstances, the ship's crew awakened a sleeping passenger on a perilous wind- and wave-tossed excursion that had persuaded men who had spent their lives on boats that they were goners. Both crews sought divine help from their passengers. And both took actions to calm the storm. Of course, that's where the similarity ends. It was Jonah's disobedience that caused the storm on the way to Tarshish. He could only save the ship by getting thrown overboard. In the case of the Jesus boat, the Son of God simply rebuked the wind and waves.

If this were the only analogy between Jonah and Jesus, I think you could dismiss its significance. But it's not.

Remember who Jonah was: the reluctant prophet who didn't want to offer grace through repentance to the Gentile Ninevites, for whom he had no compassion. Jesus, on the other hand, came to earth from heaven with the express purpose of giving His own life on the cross to atone for the sins of the world so that sincere repentance would offer them eternal life.

It is interesting, however, that Jonah was willing to give his life for his companions on the boat and that the incident brought his shipmates to repentance and faith. Jesus, on the other hand, before rebuking the wind and the waves, also rebuked his companions for a lack of faith.

What are the other comparisons and contrasts between Jesus and Jonah?

Jesus Himself called attention to the most striking and well-known analogy: that is, that Jonah spent three days and three nights in the belly of the fish, and only through prayer to God was, in effect, resurrected.

When the scribes and Pharisees asked Jesus for a sign, He responded, "An evil and adulterous generation seeketh after a sign; and there shall no sign be given to it, but the sign of the prophet Jonas: For as Jonas was three days and three nights in the whale's belly; so shall the Son of man be three days and three nights in the heart of the earth. The men of Nineveh shall rise in judgment with this generation, and shall condemn it: because they repented at the preaching of Jonas; and, behold, a greater than Jonas is here" (Matthew 12:39–41).

Later, after Jonah decided he'd better obey the Lord and preach to the Ninevites, Jonah asked God to allow him to die because he was so depressed about Nineveh answering his call for repentance. Jesus, on the other hand, went willingly to the cross to pay for sins that had not yet been committed nor repented of.

I'm sure I must not be the first person to have noticed this, but I have not heard or read any other similar observation. Maybe you have.

Now let's take a look at Jonah's account of the prayer he prayed while slipping in and out of consciousness in the fish's belly:

> I cried by reason of mine affliction unto the LORD, and he heard me; out of the belly of hell cried I, and thou heardest my voice. For thou hadst cast me into the deep, in the midst of the seas; and the floods compassed me about: all thy billows and thy waves passed over me. Then I said, I am cast out of thy sight; yet I will

look again toward thy holy temple. The waters compassed me about, even to the soul: the depth closed me round about, the weeds were wrapped about my head. I went down to the bottoms of the mountains; the earth with her bars was about me for ever: yet hast thou brought up my life from corruption, O LORD my God. When my soul fainted within me I remembered the LORD: and my prayer came in unto thee, into thine holy temple. They that observe lying vanities forsake their own mercy. But I will sacrifice unto thee with the voice of thanksgiving; I will pay that that I have vowed. Salvation is of the LORD (vv. 2–9).

It was a sincere petition that was answered by God. Jonah, who had been willing to die days earlier to save his boat companions, had second thoughts. He asked forgiveness of the Lord and for a second chance at life. Yet, it did not make him any more eager to fulfill his mission in Nineveh.

After being vomited out of the fish's mouth, he journeyed three days to Nineveh, and, as others have observed, did not exactly prepare a stirring call to repentance for the city. What did he say? "Yet forty days, and Nineveh shall be overthrown" (Jonah 3:4). That's all Jonah gives us. Maybe there was more. Or maybe it was just not necessary. At any rate, the entire city repented and was saved from judgment.

Was Jonah happy? No, he was "very angry" (4:1). The next verse tells us, "And he prayed unto the LORD, and said, I pray thee, O LORD, was not this my saying, when I was yet in my country? Therefore I fled before unto Tarshish: for I knew that thou art a gracious God, and merciful, slow to anger, and of great kindness, and repentest thee of the evil." Jonah had fled because he knew it was likely that Nineveh would respond even to his seemingly half-hearted call to wake up.

The story ends with Jonah sulking on one side of the city as he watches to see how Nineveh will respond. He builds a tabernacle for shade, and God causes a tall, overshadowing gourd plant to grow quickly to comfort his prophet and shield him from the sun. Jonah was pleased. But then, to make a point, God placed a worm on the gourd, and the plant withered. Next, God whipped up the wind and caused the sun to blaze on Jonah's head.

Jonah's response? "It is better for me to die than to live" (v. 8).

In the concluding verses of the book, God says to Jonah, "Doest thou well to be angry for the gourd? And [Jonah] said, I do well to be angry, even unto death. Then said the LORD, Thou hast had pity on the gourd, for the which thou hast not laboured, neither madest it grow; which came up in a night, and perished in a night: And should not I spare Nineveh, that great city, wherein are more than sixscore thousand persons that cannot discern between their right hand and their left hand; and also much cattle?" (4:9–11).

These final verses illustrate so effectively, almost comically, the differences between the ways of man and the ways of God. They also reveal the good news of God's heart of forgiveness and mercy—for Jew and Gentile alike.

33

THE GOSPEL IN MICAH

But thou, Bethlehem Ephratah, though thou be little among the thousands of Judah, yet out of thee shall he come forth unto me that is to be ruler in Israel; whose goings forth have been from of old, from everlasting. —MICAH 5:2

He hath shewed thee, O man, what is good; and what doth the LORD require of thee, but to do justly, and to love mercy, and to walk humbly with thy God? —MICAH 6:8

MICAH WAS A PROPHET in the time of Isaiah, when the northern kingdom of Israel was being judged for its sins. He introduced himself as a Morasthite, a resident of a southwest village in Judah, and he prophesied in the days of Jotham, Ahaz, and Hezekiah. He told of the coming destruction of not only Samaria, the capital of the Northern Kingdom, but also of Jerusalem.

Yet, this book is full of good news. Like so many of the prophetic books, Micah warns of terrible judgment yet also envisions the return of the children of Israel after dispersion and the glory of a revived, restored nation under the reign of Messiah—a Messiah who Micah alone among the prophets foretold would be born in Bethlehem.

Recall that in Matthew 2:1–6, Herod was troubled when wise men from the East came searching for the newborn King of the Jews. They had seen His star in the east and had come to worship Him. Herod called together his chief priests and scribes to find out where this Savior of Israel would be born. And they cited Micah 5:2: "And thou Bethlehem, in the land of Juda, art not the least among the princes of Juda: for out of thee shall come a Governor, that shall rule my people Israel."

Yet, Micah's first prophecy, in 1:2–4, is not for Israel, but for the whole earth: "Hear, all ye people; hearken, O earth, and all that therein is: and let the Lord GOD be witness against you, the LORD from his holy temple. For, behold, the LORD cometh forth out of his place, and will come down, and tread upon the high places of the earth. And the mountains shall be molten under him, and the valleys shall be cleft, as wax before the fire, and as the waters that are poured down a steep place."

This is a prediction of a future judgment of the whole world. Like other prophets, Micah often weaves the warnings of imminent judgment on the land of Israel and prophecies of the future glory of Israel almost interchangeably.

The next few verses of the first chapter focus on impending judgments on Israel and Judah, before a reference in 1:15, to an "heir" God will bring. Interestingly, He will come unto "Abdullam," which means "the hiding place." It was also an actual place in Israel's history, a cave where David hid from King Saul while he awaited his time to assume the throne. Likewise, Messiah Jesus retreated to a kind of "hiding place" following His resurrection in anticipation of the time He would assume His reign on the throne of David.

There are as many allusions in Micah to this glorious future messianic kingdom on earth as there are to the contemporary events and judgments facing his generation in Israel and Judah. Thus, in 2:12–13, we see a reference to the regathering of Israel before it has even been dispersed: "I will surely assemble, O Jacob, all of thee; I will surely gather the remnant of Israel; I will put them together as the sheep of Bozrah, as the flock in the midst of their fold: they shall make great noise by reason of the multitude of men. The breaker is come up before them: they have broken up, and have passed through the gate, and are gone out by it: and their king shall pass before them, and the LORD on the head of them."

Chapter 3 is dominated by the events of Micah's day, when "night shall be unto you, that ye shall not have a vision; and it shall be dark unto you, that ye shall not divine; and the sun shall go down over the prophets, and the day shall be dark over them. Then shall the seers be ashamed, and the diviners confounded: yea, they shall all cover their lips; for there is no answer of God" (vv. 6–7).

But the entirety of chapter 4 is replete with the gospel of the kingdom and all its glory:

> But in the last days it shall come to pass, that the mountain of the house of the LORD shall be established in the top of the mountains, and it shall be exalted above the hills; and people shall flow unto it.
>
> And many nations shall come, and say, Come, and let us go up to the mountain of the LORD, and to the house of the God of Jacob; and he will teach us of his ways, and we will walk in his paths: for the law shall go forth of Zion, and the word of the LORD from Jerusalem.
>
> And he shall judge among many people, and rebuke strong nations afar off; and they shall beat their swords into plowshares, and their spears into pruninghooks: nation shall not lift up a sword against nation, neither shall they learn war any more.
>
> But they shall sit every man under his vine and under his fig tree; and none shall make them afraid: for the mouth of the LORD of hosts hath spoken it.

For all people will walk every one in the name of his god, and we will walk in the name of the LORD our God for ever and ever.

In that day, saith the LORD, will I assemble her that halteth, and I will gather her that is driven out, and her that I have afflicted; and I will make her that halted a remnant, and her that was cast far off a strong nation: and the LORD shall reign over them in mount Zion from henceforth, even for ever.

And thou, O tower of the flock, the strong hold of the daughter of Zion, unto thee shall it come, even the first dominion; the kingdom shall come to the daughter of Jerusalem (vv. 1–8).

This is yet another picture of the return of the Messiah to Zion, where He will rule and reign forever, overseeing the complete restoration of the earth. When Jesus preached about the gospel of the kingdom, this is what He was referring to. In addition, as previously discussed, this is what all the prophets—every single one of them—pointed to with expectation, a time of peace, justice and righteousness.

In chapter 5, we get the full context of the prophecy about Messiah's birth in Bethlehem. It is not just a prophecy about Jesus' time on earth in the first century, when He came as the Lamb of God. It is also a prophecy about His return as King of kings. In verses 3–13, we see that Messiah would come to be ruler in Israel, but because the people were not spiritually ready for a Redeemer-King,

he will give them up, until the time that she which travaileth hath brought forth: then the remnant of his brethren shall return unto the children of Israel. And he shall stand and feed in the strength of the LORD, in the majesty of the name of the LORD his God; and they shall abide: for now shall he be great unto the ends of the earth. And this man shall be the peace. . . . And the remnant of Jacob shall be in the midst of many people as a dew from the LORD . . . And the remnant of Jacob shall be among the Gentiles in the midst of many people. . . . And I will cut off witchcrafts

out of thine hand; and thou shalt have no more soothsayers: Thy
graven images also will I cut off, and thy standing images out
of the midst of thee; and thou shalt no more worship the work
of thine hands.

Chapter 6 combines both prophecies of the gospel of the
kingdom with the gospel of personal salvation. In verses 3–5, we
hear God pleading with Israel to return to Him and His ways: "O
my people, what have I done unto thee? and wherein have I wearied
thee? testify against me. For I brought thee up out of the land of
Egypt, and redeemed thee out of the house of servants; and I sent
before thee Moses, Aaron, and Miriam. O my people, remember
now what Balak king of Moab consulted, and what Balaam the son
of Beor answered him from Shittim unto Gilgal; that ye may know
the righteousness of the LORD."

God asks here if we remember Balaam. It's a good time to ask
if you remember Balaam and his unusual prophecy from our study
of the book of Numbers in chapter 4. Balak was the king of the
Moabites who feared the Israelites. So he sought out Balaam, a
prophet, to curse the children of Israel on their way to the promised
land. But God told Balaam not to curse His people, "for they are
blessed" (Numbers 22:12). Balaam, thus, told the king he could
only speak the words God would allow him to speak. What words
did he speak? He spoke the words of the gospel:

How shall I curse, whom God hath not cursed? or how shall I
defy, whom the LORD hath not defied? For from th top of the
rocks I see him, and from the hills I behold him: lo, the people
shall dwell alone, and shall not be reckoned among the nations.
Who can count the dust of Jacob, and the number of the fourth
part of Israel? Let me die the death of the righteous, and let my
last end be like his!" (Numbers 23:8–10).

God is not a man, that he should lie; neither the son of man, that he should repent: hath he said, and shall he not do it? or hath he spoken, and shall he not make it good? Behold, I have received commandment to bless: and he hath blessed; and I cannot reverse it. He hath not beheld iniquity in Jacob, neither hath he seen perverseness in Israel: the LORD his God is with him, and the shout of a king is among them. God brought them out of Egypt; he hath as it were the strength of an unicorn. Surely there is no enchantment against Jacob, neither is there any divination against Israel: according to this time it shall be said of Jacob and of Israel, What hath God wrought! Behold, the people shall rise up as a great lion, and lift up himself as a young lion: he shall not lie down until he eat of the prey, and drink the blood of the slain (23:19–24).

How goodly are thy tents, O Jacob, and thy tabernacles, O Israel! As the valleys are they spread forth, as gardens by the river's side, as the trees of lign aloes which the LORD hath planted, and as cedar trees beside the waters. He shall pour the water out of his buckets, and his seed shall be in many waters, and his king shall be higher than Agag, and his kingdom shall be exalted. God brought him forth out of Egypt; he hath as it were the strength of an unicorn: he shall eat up the nations his enemies, and shall break their bones, and pierce them through with his arrows. He couched, he lay down as a lion, and as a great lion: who shall stir him up? Blessed is he that blesseth thee, and cursed is he that curseth thee (24:5–9).

I shall see him, but not now: I shall behold him, but not nigh: there shall come a Star out of Jacob, and a Sceptre shall rise out of Israel, and shall smite the corners of Moab, and destroy all the children of Sheth. And Edom shall be a possession, Seir also shall be a possession for his enemies; and Israel shall do valiantly. Out of Jacob shall come he that shall have dominion, and shall destroy him that remaineth of the city (24:17–19).

Of course, Jesus is that Star who shall come out of Jacob, and it is He who shall have dominion over the whole word when He returns.

But there's also the gospel of mercy expressed here in Micah 6:8: "He hath shewed thee, O man, what is good; and what doth the LORD require of thee, but to do justly, and to love mercy, and to walk humbly with thy God?"

And there's more in the final chapter:

- MICAH 7:7 "Therefore I will look unto the LORD; I will wait for the God of my salvation: my God will hear me."

- MICAH 7:9 "I will bear the indignation of the LORD, because I have sinned against him, until he plead my cause, and execute judgment for me: he will bring me forth to the light, and I shall behold his righteousness."

- MICAH 7:18 "Who is a God like unto thee, that pardoneth iniquity, and passeth by the transgression of the remnant of his heritage? he retaineth not his anger for ever, because he delighteth in mercy."

- MICAH 7:19 "He will turn again, he will have compassion upon us; he will subdue our iniquities; and thou wilt cast all their sins into the depths of the sea."

It's all there—repentance, forgiveness of sins, a righteous Mediator. That's the gospel of Micah.

34

THE GOSPEL IN NAHUM

Behold upon the mountains the feet of him that bringeth good tidings, that publisheth peace! O Judah, keep thy solemn feasts, perform thy vows: for the wicked shall no more pass through thee; he is utterly cut off.
—NAHUM 1:15

And it shall come to pass, that all they that look upon thee shall flee from thee, and say, Nineveh is laid waste: who will bemoan her? whence shall I seek comforters for thee? —NAHUM 3:7

ONE OF THE GREAT BENEFITS of knowing the Bible from the beginning of the book is the understanding it brings about matters less understood from the New Testament alone.

The Old Testament and the New are not different books, by authors of different character, with different standards of morality. There is one true God, and all the Scriptures are reflections of His perfect justice.

Sometimes we don't really see the similarities—the common denominators. In the past, and even in the present, there have been and are those who see Jesus as somehow "different" from the Father—less strict and unbending, more forgiving and full of grace. But that is a heresy. It's a form of Gnosticism, the kind of "dualism" taught by Marcion in the mid-second century.

Throughout this book, I have attempted to reveal the gospel messages—sometimes obscure, sometimes obvious—in every book of the Old Testament. One of those gospel principles is justice. While we see more evidence of that in the Hebrew Scriptures, you don't have to look hard for the perfectly comparative themes in the Greek Scriptures.

Before we dive into the book of Nahum, which I call "the gospel of justice," let's look at a portion of the gospel of Matthew:

> Again, the kingdom of heaven is like unto a net, that was cast into the sea, and gathered of every kind: which, when it was full, they drew to shore, and sat down, and gathered the good into vessels, but cast the bad away. So shall it be at the end of the world: the angels shall come forth, and sever the wicked from among the just, and shall cast them into the furnace of fire: there shall be wailing and gnashing of teeth. Jesus saith unto them, Have ye understood all these things? They say unto him, Yea, Lord (13:47–51).

The point? When Jesus returns, it will be a time of firm judgment and a time of the Lord's vengeance. It's difficult for many Christians to see Jesus in this light. But that is because they don't know the real Jesus. They may know the Suffering Servant, who was led to the slaughter in the first century to atone for the sins of the world. But they are unfamiliar with the personality of the conquering King who will rule the world with a *rod of iron*—yet that very phrase is found three times in the book of Revelation describing Jesus' reign (2:27; 12:5; 19:15).

No injustice, no matter how small, escapes God's attention.

For instance, have you ever noticed how many times the Bible upholds the importance of something as simple as honest weights and measures?

- Leviticus 19:36: "Just balances, just weights, a just ephah, and a just hin, shall ye have."

- Deuteronomy 25:13: "Thou shalt not have in thy bag divers weights, a great and a small."

- Proverbs 16:11: "A just weight and balance are the LORD's: all the weights of the bag are his work."

- Proverbs 20:10: "Divers weights, and divers measures, both of them are alike abomination to the LORD."

- Proverbs 20:23: "Divers weights are an abomination unto the LORD; and a false balance is not good."

- Micah 6:11: "Shall I count them pure with the wicked balances, and with the bag of deceitful weights?"

In other words, when the Lord returns to set up His throne in Jerusalem and rule the world, it will be a time of recalibrating the scales of justice. That's part of the "restoration of all things."

All that is a lead-in to the very short book of Nahum, a prophet who focused his attention on the fall of the Assyrian Empire and its capital city Nineveh. Not much is known about his personal life, but his name means "Comforter."

So how does Nahum comfort his contemporaries and readers thousands of year later? By emphasizing the Lord's righteous judgment and vengeance.

But is vengeance part of the gospel? Well, just look at Jesus' words in Matthew 13:47–51, and you decide.

Jesus tells us that the Lord's vengeance is necessary to balance the scales: "For these be the days of vengeance, that all things which are written may be fulfilled," he said in His famous prophetic look ahead at the last days in Luke 21:22.

Nahum deals primarily with the Assyrian Empire, whose judgment is near:

> God is jealous, and the LORD revengeth; the LORD revengeth, and is furious; the LORD will take vengeance on his adversaries, and he reserveth wrath for his enemies. The LORD is slow to anger, and great in power, and will not at all acquit the wicked: the LORD hath his way in the whirlwind and in the storm, and the clouds are the dust of his feet. He rebuketh the sea, and maketh it dry, and drieth up all the rivers: Bashan languisheth, and Carmel, and the flower of Lebanon languisheth. The mountains quake at him, and the hills melt, and the earth is burned at his presence, yea, the world, and all that dwell therein. Who can stand before his indignation? and who can abide in the fierceness of his anger? his fury is poured out like fire, and the rocks are thrown down by him. The LORD is good, a strong hold in the day of trouble; and he knoweth them that trust in him (Nahum 1:2–7).

In the midst of the details about what is about to overtake Assyria, Nahum offers this gospel morsel, which sounds like something right out of the New Testament, in 1:15: "Behold upon the mountains the feet of him that bringeth good tidings, that publisheth peace! O Judah, keep thy solemn feasts, perform thy vows: for the wicked shall no more pass through thee; he is utterly cut off."

Nahum is a small book, just three chapters, and most of it is devoted to the indictments against Assyria and the reasons its judgment is coming. That may not sound like it has much to do with the gospel, but maybe that's just our cultural orientation. Because vengeance precedes redemption, God tells us through another prophet: "For the day of vengeance is in mine heart, and the year of my redeemed is come" (Isaiah 63:4). Put another way, "Keep ye judgment, and do justice: for my salvation is near to come, and my righteousness to be revealed" (Isaiah 56:1).

Jeremiah 23:5 tells us it will be this way in the end when Jesus returns: "Behold, the days come, saith the LORD, that I will raise unto David a righteous Branch, and a King shall reign and prosper, and shall execute judgment and justice in the earth."

And Paul tells us in Romans 12:19 something He picked up from Isaiah 63:4: "Dearly beloved, avenge not yourselves, but rather give place unto wrath: for it is written, Vengeance is mine; I will repay, saith the Lord."

It's all the same book—the one and only Holy Bible, with consistency and congruity throughout the Old Testament and the New.

And, yes, justice and judgment are very much a part of the good news—especially the gospel according to Micah.

35

THE GOSPEL IN HABAKKUK

Behold ye among the heathen, and regard, and wonder marvelously: for I
will work a work in your days which ye will not believe, though it be told you.
—HABAKKUK 1:5

Behold, his soul which is lifted up is not upright in him: but the just shall live
by his faith. —HABAKKUK 2:4

WHAT DO WE KNOW ABOUT HABAKKUK? Very little. Most of
what we can glean is found in this small book of just three chapters.
Since this prophet focused in his writings on the rise of the Babylonians (Chaldeans), it is assumed he was active in that time period,
the early 600s BC, making him possibly an early contemporary of
Jeremiah and Zephaniah.

One of the unique aspects of Habakkuk is the way he openly
questions God. Think of it as a Q&A with the Creator of the universe.

Question 1: "O LORD, how long shall I cry, and thou wilt not hear! even cry out unto thee of violence, and thou wilt not save! Why dost thou shew me iniquity, and cause me to behold grievance? for spoiling and violence are before me: and there are that raise up strife and contention" (1:2–3). He goes on to complain that the law is not working and that judgment is never fulfilled: "For the wicked doth compass about the righteous; therefore wrong judgment proceedeth" (v. 4).

Answer 1: "Behold ye among the heathen, and regard, and wonder marvelously: for I will work a work in your days which ye will not believe, though it be told you," God says (v. 5), going on to tell His people about the Chaldeans, or Babylonians, who will take captive Judah.

Question 2: "Art thou not from everlasting, O LORD my God, mine Holy One? we shall not die. O LORD, thou hast ordained them for judgment; and, O mighty God, thou hast established them for correction. Thou art of purer eyes than to behold evil, and canst not look on iniquity: wherefore lookest thou upon them that deal treacherously, and holdest thy tongue when the wicked devoureth the man that is more righteous than he?" (vv. 12–13).

Answer 2: "Write the vision, and make it plain upon tables, that he may run that readeth it. For the vision is yet for an appointed time, but at the end it shall speak, and not lie: though it tarry, wait for it; because it will surely come, it will not tarry. Behold, his soul which is lifted up is not upright in him: but the just shall live by his faith. Yea also, because he transgresseth by wine, he is a proud man, neither keepeth at home, who enlargeth his desire as hell, and is as death, and cannot be satisfied, but gathereth unto him all nations, and heapeth unto him all people" (2:2–5).

The Babylonian king who would eventually take Judah captive for seventy years was, of course, Nebuchadnezzar. His story is an extraordinary one, given his acceptance of the God of Israel after being humbled like no other man in history. Just as Daniel prophesied, the king was driven from men, living with the beasts of the field, eating grass until he knew that the Most High ruled the kingdom of men.

Later, after recovering from this experience of utter debasement, he actually wrote part of the book of Daniel:

> And at the end of the days I Nebuchadnezzar lifted up mine eyes unto heaven, and mine understanding returned unto me, and I blessed the most High, and I praised and honoured him that liveth for ever, whose dominion is an everlasting dominion, and his kingdom is from generation to generation: And all the inhabitants of the earth are reputed as nothing: and he doeth according to his will in the army of heaven, and among the inhabitants of the earth: and none can stay his hand, or say unto him, What doest thou?
>
> At the same time my reason returned unto me; and for the glory of my kingdom, mine honour and brightness returned unto me; and my counsellors and my lords sought unto me; and I was established in my kingdom, and excellent majesty was added unto me. Now I Nebuchadnezzar praise and extol and honour the King of heaven, all whose works are truth, and his ways judgment: and those that walk in pride he is able to abase (4:34–37).

In other words, Nebuchadnezzar was used by God to execute judgment on Judah, but later was humbled and seemingly awakened to knowledge of and faith in the one true, living God of Israel.

What did Paul say in Romans 8:28? "And we know that all things work together for good to them that love God, to them who are the called according to his purpose."

Habakkuk could not possibly see how any of this judgment on his nation could be redemptive and part of God's plan. Yet, as a prophet, as he questioned God, he never rebuked him. Instead, he concluded his poetic book with a prayer.

O Lord, I have heard thy speech, and was afraid: O Lord, revive thy work in the midst of the years, in the midst of the years make known; in wrath remember mercy. . . .

Thou wentest forth for the salvation of thy people, even for salvation with thine anointed. . . .

Although the fig tree shall not blossom, neither shall fruit be in the vines; the labour of the olive shall fail, and the fields shall yield no meat; the flock shall be cut off from the fold, and there shall be no herd in the stalls: Yet I will rejoice in the Lord, I will joy in the God of my salvation. The Lord God is my strength, and he will make my feet like hinds' feet, and he will make me to walk upon mine high places (3:2, 13, 17–19).

Where's the gospel in Habakkuk? It's in his faith. It wasn't in his eyes. What he saw bewildered him, perplexed him, disappointed him. Yet he knew that one day, because of his faith, he would walk upon high places like one of those wonderful creatures in Israel, the ibex. That was not to take place during his time, he understood. It would take place at the restoration of all things during the kingdom of God on earth.

Furthermore, it was Habakkuk who first wrote these words in Scripture: "The just shall live by his faith." How important are those words to our understanding of the Lord today? They are repeated verbatim in three New Testament books:

- **ROMANS 1:17** "For therein is the righteousness of God revealed from faith to faith: as it is written, The just shall live by faith."

- **GALATIANS 3:11** "But that no man is justified by the law in the sight of God, it is evident: for, The just shall live by faith."

- **HEBREWS 10:38** "Now the just shall live by faith: but if any man draw back, my soul shall have no pleasure in him."

May you, like Habakkuk, "joy in the God of your salvation." That God is Jesus Christ, Savior of our souls—and the God of the gospel.

36

THE GOSPEL IN ZEPHANIAH

*For then will I turn to the people a pure language, that they may all call upon
the name of the LORD, to serve him with one consent.*
—ZEPHANIAH 3:9

JUST TO BE CLEAR, nowhere in the Bible are Zephaniah and the
other eleven last authors of Old Testament books ever referred to as
"minor prophets." That characterization is most often associated with
Augustine at the time of the fourth century. He's often referred to
as one of the "church fathers," but I prefer to think of the church
fathers as Peter, Paul, James, and the first-century apostles and
disciples of Jesus—those who were unquestionably empowered and
inspired by an outpouring of the Holy Spirit beginning at Pentecost, or Shavout, immediately following the ascension of Jesus, as
depicted in Acts 1.

The only reason the last twelve books of the Old Testament

are attributed to "minor" prophets is because of the length of their works. They are short, but they are not "minor." In fact, they all contribute mightily to our understanding of God's ways and, especially, our understanding of the future of our planet and its people.

Secondly, there are three biblical names that may seem confusing to Bible students not yet immersed in the "who's who" of Z-names in Scripture: Zedekiah, Zechariah, and Zephaniah.

Zedekiah was the last king of Judah and lived around the time of Zephaniah.

Zechariah was another so-called minor prophet we'll look at in chapter 38, where we'll discuss the penultimate book of the Old Testament.

And Zephaniah was the prophet and author of this three-chapter book.

Zephaniah lived in the time of Jeremiah, as well as Nahum, and bears some striking similarities to the former's prophecies. The northern kingdom of Israel had already been judged and scattered, and Judah's exile was coming.

I always like it when the prophets identify themselves, and Zephaniah offers some biographical information going back four generations to Hezekiah, presumably, but not necessarily, the king in Isaiah's day. He was prophesying in the day of King Josiah, arguably the last good king of Judah. And if he was indeed a descendant of King Hezekiah, then he was also related to Josiah and likely a part of the reforms and revival instituted under his reign between 640 and 609 BC.

It was under Josiah that the "book of the law" was rediscovered in the temple in 622 BC. Think about the spiritual depths to which Judah had fallen, that the whole Torah, the first five books of the Bible, had been lost. The law was gone. Nobody knew it or could read it. It was forgotten. This could only happen in a generation that had no interest whatsoever in God's commandments, His rulebook, His teachings, His guide to life. It was during a renovation of the temple that it was rediscovered. And this touched off the aforementioned reforms and revival that marked Josiah's reign as king as chronicled in 2 Kings 22–23.

So, with that background, let's search for the gospel in Zephaniah.

Following Zephaniah's one-verse introduction of himself, he dropped the spiritual equivalent of a

1.2-megaton thermonuclear bomb in the form of a word from the Lord: "I will utterly consume all things from off the land, saith the LORD. I will consume man and beast, I will consume the fowls of the heaven, and the fishes of the sea, and the stumbling blocks with the wicked: and I will cut off man from off the land, saith the LORD" (1:2–3).

This is obviously not good news. In fact, it sounds as though God is so angry with His people because of rampant sin that he's threatening to deconstruct creation, at least in His promised land.

In verses 4–9, we get more detail:

I will also stretch out mine hand upon Judah, and upon all the inhabitants of Jerusalem; and I will cut off the remnant of Baal from this place, and the name of the Chemarims with the priests; And them that worship the host of heaven upon the housetops; and them that worship and that swear by the LORD, and that swear by Malcham; And them that are turned back from the LORD; and those that have not sought the LORD, nor enquired for him.

Hold thy peace at the presence of the Lord GOD: for the day of the LORD is at hand: for the LORD hath prepared a sacrifice, he hath bid his guests. And it shall come to pass in the day of the LORD's sacrifice, that I will punish the princes, and the king's children, and all such as are clothed with strange apparel. In the same day also will I punish all those that leap on the threshold, which fill their masters' houses with violence and deceit.

First Israel went a-whoring after other gods, then Judah. Israel was destroyed as a result, and Judah seemingly hadn't taken notice.

The people of Judah and even God's beloved city of Jerusalem were worshipping the Canaanite and Phoenician false deity of Baal. Their priests were prostrating themselves before idols. Others were worshipping the sun, moon, and stars. Some were swearing by Malcham, another name for Molech, a pagan god to whom some Israelites even sacrificed their children. The God of Abraham, Isaac, and Jacob had had enough.

But there was something more going on here than the judgment of Judah that would send the Southern Kingdom into captivity for seventy years:

> The great day of the LORD is near, it is near, and hasteth greatly, even the voice of the day of the LORD: the mighty man shall cry there bitterly. That day is a day of wrath, a day of trouble and distress, a day of wasteness and desolation, a day of darkness and gloominess, a day of clouds and thick darkness, A day of the trumpet and alarm against the fenced cities, and against the high towers. And I will bring distress upon men, that they shall walk like blind men, because they have sinned against the LORD: and their blood shall be poured out as dust, and their flesh as the dung. Neither their silver nor their gold shall be able to deliver them in the day of the LORD's wrath; but the whole land shall be devoured by the fire of his jealousy: for he shall make even a speedy riddance of all them that dwell in the land (1:14–18).

Zephaniah was not just foreshadowing the judgment against Judah that would come in the time of a future corrupt king and people. This prophet was also describing the "great day of the LORD," which has not yet come in our time—the return of Jesus to the earth in judgment.

But lest you think God has given up on all the people, think again. This is the same God about whom Peter wrote, "The Lord .. . is longsuffering to us-ward, not willing that any should perish, but that all should come to repentance" (2 Peter 3:9). So, Zephaniah 2 opens: "Gather yourselves together, yea, gather together, O nation not desired; Before the decree bring forth, before the day pass as the chaff, before the fierce anger of the LORD come upon you, before the day of the LORD's anger come upon you. *Seek ye the LORD, all ye meek of the earth, which have wrought his judgment; seek righteousness, seek meekness: it may be ye shall be hid in the day of the LORD's anger*" (vv, 1–3, emphasis added).

This is an altar call. It is a plea for repentance. This is an example of the Lord's long-suffering character. Again, we see God holding out His outstretched arm in an offer of forgiveness. How many times have we seen it before? And here it is again. Jesus, too, talked about the danger of hellfire and damnation—to offer a choice, to hold out the hope of salvation and redemption. It's no different here. It's not too late, the Lord is saying through Zephaniah, to return to humility and righteousness like a prodigal son. Maybe then you will be hidden in the day of the Lord's anger, he says.

If that's not the essential gospel message, then perhaps I don't know what the essential gospel message is. It's the very same message Jesus preached. Jesus was no pushover. He pulled no punches. His hard sayings drove even most of His disciples away toward the close of His visitation. And that's just what we see here in Zephaniah. It's about grabbing by the throat a lost generation and shaking them out of the spiritual sleepwalk down the broad path that leads to death and destruction.

That's the choice the gospel confronts us with: life and death. This is a choice everyone faces, not just Israel, not just Judah. It is crystal clear in chapter 3 that Zephaniah's is a message to the whole planet: "I said, Surely thou wilt fear me, thou wilt receive instruction; so their dwelling should not be cut off, howsoever I punished them: but they rose early, and corrupted all their doings. Therefore wait ye upon me, saith the LORD, until the day that I rise up to the prey: for my determination is to gather the nations, that I may assemble the kingdoms, to pour upon them mine indignation, even all my fierce anger: for all the earth shall be devoured with the fire of my jealousy" (vv. 7–8)

And what's the end result? The happy ending of Zephaniah—the good news of total restoration, remaking all things as they were originally intended to be before sin entered the world:

> For then will I turn to the people a pure language, that they may all call upon the name of the LORD, to serve him with one consent.
>
> From beyond the rivers of Ethiopia my suppliants, even the daughter of my dispersed, shall bring mine offering.
>
> In that day shalt thou not be ashamed for all thy doings, wherein thou hast transgressed against me: for then I will take away out of the midst of thee them that rejoice in thy pride, and thou shalt no more be haughty because of my holy mountain.
>
> I will also leave in the midst of thee an afflicted and poor people, and they shall trust in the name of the LORD.
>
> The remnant of Israel shall not do iniquity, nor speak lies; neither shall a deceitful tongue be found in their mouth: for they shall feed and lie down, and none shall make them afraid.
>
> Sing, O daughter of Zion; shout, O Israel; be glad and rejoice with all the heart, O daughter of Jerusalem.
>
> The LORD hath taken away thy judgments, he hath cast out thine enemy: the king of Israel, even the LORD, is in the midst of thee: thou shalt not see evil any more.
>
> In that day it shall be said to Jerusalem, Fear thou not: and to Zion, Let not thine hands be slack.
>
> The LORD thy God in the midst of thee is mighty; he will save, he will rejoice over thee with joy; he will rest in his love, he will joy over thee with singing.
>
> I will gather them that are sorrowful for the solemn assembly, who are of thee, to whom the reproach of it was a burden.
>
> Behold, at that time I will undo all that afflict thee: and I will save her that halteth, and gather her that was driven out; and I will get them praise and fame in every land where they have been put to shame.

In that time will I bring you again, even in the time that I gather you: for I will make you a name and a praise among all people of the earth, when I turn back your captivity before your eyes, saith the LORD (3:9–20).

Again, this is that which all the prophets pointed to from creation onward (Acts 3:21). It all begins with repentance and ends with forgiveness: the message of the gospel.

37

THE GOSPEL IN HAGGAI

For thus saith the LORD of hosts; Yet once, it is a little while, and I will shake the heavens, and the earth, and the sea, and the dry land; And I will shake all nations, and the desire of all nations shall come: and I will fill this house with glory, saith the LORD of hosts. —HAGGAI 2:6–7

HAGGAI, the author of the second-shortest book in the Old Testament, was a contemporary of the prophet Zechariah and the governor of Zerubabel when the children of Israel returned from captivity seventy years after the Babylonian invasion to rebuild the temple and resettle the land. This was the temple that the Roman-appointed impostor "king" Herod would refurbish later in the time of Jesus.

The story told in Haggai is that the misplaced priorities of the people caused the temple rebuilding project to be stalled. It seems there were several reasons:

- Though the project was, in part, subsidized by the king of Persia, it was not as glorious as Solomon's temple, which dampened the people's enthusiasm.

- There was opposition from outside the community, foreigners who were not thrilled about the Jews coming back to their land.

- The people were more interested in rebuilding and improving their own homes than in reconstructing the temple.

For fourteen years, all efforts at rebuilding were suspended.

Haggai's prophetic warnings focused on the misguided priorities of God's people, who placed their own personal interests above the rebuilding the Lord's house.

In chapter 1, God spoke through Haggai: "Thus speaketh the LORD of hosts, saying, This people say, The time is not come, the time that the LORD's house should be built. Then came the word of the LORD by Haggai the prophet, saying, Is it time for you, O ye, to dwell in your cieled houses, and this house lie waste? Now therefore thus saith the LORD of hosts; Consider your ways" (vv. 2–5).

God commanded the people to reset their priorities. Go up to the mountain; bring wood; build the temple, He exhorted. He threatened the people with drought and famine if they did not heed His call.

"Then Zerubbabel the son of Shealtiel, and Joshua the son of Josedech, the high priest, with all the remnant of the people, obeyed the voice of the LORD their God, and the words of Haggai the prophet, as the LORD their God had sent him, and the people did fear before the LORD," we're told. "Then spake Haggai the LORD's messenger in the LORD's message unto the people, saying, I am with you, saith the LORD. And the LORD stirred up the spirit of Zerubbabel the son of Shealtiel, governor of Judah, and the spirit of Joshua the son of Josedech, the high priest, and the spirit of all the remnant of the people; and they came and did work in the house of the LORD of hosts, their God" (vv. 12–14).

Once again, the book of Haggai is a warning against complacency, self-interest, and misplaced priorities in the lives of God's people. But it's more than that. Haggai also provides a vision of the ultimate restoration that will come, not in the time of Zerubbabel, but in the future—the future that all of us who worship the God of Israel will experience in the kingdom. It is a clear, concise reminder of the gospel of the kingdom.

In Haggai 2:5–7, we're told: "According to the word that I covenanted with you when ye came out of Egypt, so my spirit remaineth among you: fear ye not. For thus saith the LORD of hosts; Yet once, it is a little while, and I will shake the heavens, and the earth, and the sea, and the dry land; And I will shake all nations, and the desire of all nations shall come: and I will fill this house with glory, saith the LORD of hosts." This is a reference to the kingdom of the Messiah, who will rule and reign physically and spiritually in Jerusalem as King of kings when Israel will live in glory at the very epicenter of the world. Of this there can be no doubt, because the concluding verses of Haggai make it clear.

> And again the word of the LORD came unto Haggai in the four and twentieth day of the month, saying, Speak to Zerubbabel, governor of Judah, saying, I will shake the heavens and the earth; and I will overthrow the throne of kingdoms, and I will destroy the strength of the kingdoms of the heathen; and I will overthrow the chariots, and those that ride in them; and the horses and their riders shall come down, every one by the sword of his brother. In that day, saith the LORD of hosts, will I take thee, O Zerubbabel, my servant, the son of Shealtiel, saith the LORD, and will make thee as a signet: for I have chosen thee, saith the LORD of hosts (2:20–23).

What we're talking about here is the very fulfillment of the gospel about which Jesus spoke, what He referred to frequently as "the gospel of the kingdom," over which He Himself will one day rule.

38

THE GOSPEL IN ZECHARIAH

And his feet shall stand in that day upon the mount of Olives, which is before
Jerusalem on the east, and the mount of Olives shall cleave in the midst thereof
toward the east and toward the west, and there shall be a very great valley;
and half of the mountain shall remove toward the north, and half of it toward
the south. —ZECHARIAH 14:4

*And the L*ORD *shall be king over all the earth: in that day shall there be one*
L*ORD, and his name one.* —ZECHARIAH 14:9

WE KNOW SO MUCH about what the return of Jesus to earth will
be like thanks to the prophet Zechariah.

For instance, we know precisely where Jesus will make His glorious return—to the Mount of Olives, a place so familiar to gospel
readers. Jesus spent time on the Mount of Olives. To this day, it is
a place pilgrims come to stand knowingly where Jesus stood and to

commune with Him in a place we know He will return in triumph. We know this because of the book of Zechariah.

How did we know that Jesus, in His first visitation, would come "lowly," making His entrance into Jerusalem riding on a donkey that had never been ridden before? We know that from Zechariah 9:9: "Rejoice greatly, O daughter of Zion; shout, O daughter of Jerusalem: behold, thy King cometh unto thee: he is just, and having salvation; lowly, and riding upon an ass, and upon a colt the foal of an ass." This was a prophecy recorded and fulfilled in Matthew 21:5: "Tell ye the daughter of Sion, Behold, thy King cometh unto thee, meek, and sitting upon an ass, and a colt the foal of an ass."

In Matthew, Jesus Himself talked about His return to earth, referencing the powerful prophecy in Zechariah 12:10–11. Compare these unmistakable and poignant parallel prophecies:

- MATTHEW 24:30 "And then shall appear the sign of the Son of man in heaven: and then shall all the tribes of the earth mourn, and they shall see the Son of man coming in the clouds of heaven with power and great glory."

- ZECHARIAH 12:10–11 "And I will pour upon the house of David, and upon the inhabitants of Jerusalem, the spirit of grace and of supplications: and they shall look upon me whom they have pierced, and they shall mourn for him, as one mourneth for his only son, and shall be in bitterness for him, as one that is in bitterness for his firstborn. In that day shall there be a great mourning in Jerusalem."

Why will there be mourning at the return of the Messiah? Because "they shall look upon me whom they have pierced." But there's another vision of this reconciliation between Jesus and His people in Zechariah 13:6: "And one shall say unto him, What are these wounds in thine hands? Then he shall answer, Those with which I was wounded in the house of my friends." I get choked up whenever I read that passage. About who else could that prophecy be but the crucified Jesus?

How do we know Jesus will be King over the entire earth when He returns? Because we're told in, among other prophecies, Zechariah 14:9: "And the LORD shall be king over all the earth: in that day shall there be one LORD, and his name one."

How did we know Jesus would be betrayed for thirty pieces of silver? Because of Zechariah 11:12: "And I said unto them, If ye think good, give me my price; and if not, forbear. So they weighed for my price thirty pieces of silver."

What prophecy was Jesus referring to in Matthew 26:31 when He said, "All ye shall be offended because of me this night: for it is written, I will smite the shepherd, and the sheep of the flock shall be scattered abroad"? It was Zechariah 13:7: "Awake, O sword, against my shepherd, and against the man that is my fellow, saith the LORD of hosts: smite the shepherd, and the sheep shall be scattered: and I will turn mine hand upon the little ones."

Jesus referenced Zechariah frequently in the Gospels and informs us in Matthew 23:35 that Zechariah was one of the prophets who, like Himself, was killed by the religious leaders of his time: "That upon you may come all the righteous blood shed upon the earth, from the blood of righteous Abel unto the blood of Zacharias son of Barachias, whom ye slew between the temple and the altar."

Need I even interject here that Zechariah is one of my favorite prophetic books—with plenty of links and insights into the gospel of the kingdom?

Of the twelve misnamed "minor prophets," just two are actually mentioned by Jesus in the Gospels—Jonah, whose "resurrection" after three days in the fish's belly foreshadows His own resurrection after three days in the tomb, and Zechariah. Like Haggai, Zechariah was a contemporary of Zerubbabel. His name means "the Lord remembers." And indeed, the Lord did in mentioning his untimely death as well as his prophecies.

It's not at all difficult to find the gospel in Zechariah. Indeed, it leaps off the page. In fact, the main theme, right from the start, is salvation.

> The Lord hath been sore displeased with your fathers. Therefore say thou unto them, Thus saith the Lord of hosts; Turn ye unto me, saith the Lord of hosts, and I will turn unto you, saith the Lord of hosts. Be ye not as your fathers, unto whom the former prophets have cried, saying, Thus saith the Lord of hosts; turn ye now from your evil ways, and from your evil doings: but they did not hear, nor hearken unto me, saith the Lord. Your fathers, where are they? and the prophets, do they live for ever? But my words and my statutes, which I commanded my servants the prophets, did they not take hold of your fathers? and they returned and said, Like as the Lord of hosts thought to do unto us, according to our ways, and according to our doings, so hath he dealt with us (1:2–6).

"Turn unto me."
"Turn ye now from your evil ways."
What did Jesus say? "The time is fulfilled, and the kingdom of God is at hand: repent ye, and believe the gospel" (Mark 1:15).

Despite what modern revisionist dictionaries may say, repentance is not just a feeling of remorse for what one has done. To repent literally means to "turn," so in this context, it means to turn back to God and to turn away from sin. Repentance is the requirement of the good news that Jesus brought in His gospel of the kingdom. It was not a new message, but it came with power because of His sacrificial atonement for our sins.

In Zechariah 1:16–17, the prophet is referring to the rebuilding of the temple by Zerubbabel in his time, yet also referencing the future kingdom and its greater glory: "Therefore thus saith the Lord; I am returned to Jerusalem with mercies: my house shall be built in it, saith the Lord of hosts, and a line shall be stretched forth upon Jerusalem. Cry yet, saying, Thus saith the Lord of hosts; My cities through prosperity shall yet be spread abroad; and the Lord shall yet comfort Zion, and shall yet choose Jerusalem."

This parallel becomes even clearer in Zechariah 2:10–12: "Sing and rejoice, O daughter of Zion: for, lo, I come, and I will dwell in the midst of thee, saith the Lord. And many nations shall be joined to the Lord in that day, and shall be my people: and I will dwell in the midst of thee, and thou shalt know that the Lord of hosts hath sent me unto thee. And the Lord shall inherit Judah his portion in the holy land, and shall choose Jerusalem again."

There's more kingdom glory foreseen in Zechariah 2:4–5: "And said unto him, Run, speak to this young man, saying, Jerusalem shall be inhabited as towns without walls for the multitude of men and cattle therein: For I, saith the Lord, will be unto her a wall of fire round about, and will be the glory in the midst of her."

There's a lot of joy expressed in this book—a great deal of anticipation about the future restoration of the kingdom and the future Israel-centric messianic world.

Zechariah 2:8–13 is one of my favorite passages:

For thus saith the Lord of hosts; After the glory hath he sent me unto the nations which spoiled you: for he that toucheth you toucheth the apple of his eye. For, behold, I will shake mine hand upon them, and they shall be a spoil to their servants: and ye shall know that the Lord of hosts hath sent me. Sing and rejoice, O daughter of Zion: for, lo, I come, and I will dwell in the midst of thee, saith the Lord. And many nations shall be joined to the Lord in that day, and shall be my people: and I will dwell in the midst of thee, and thou shalt know that the Lord of hosts hath sent me unto thee. And the Lord shall inherit Judah his portion in the holy land, and shall choose Jerusalem again. Be silent, O all flesh, before the Lord: for he is raised up out of his holy habitation.

Chapter 3 combines the personal restoration of the priest Joshua along with the ultimate restoration of the world in the future kingdom. First we see Joshua clothed in filthy garments, being demeaned by Satan, but the Lord rebukes Satan for his indictment. Rather than punish Joshua, God merely instructs an angel to provide a change of clothes, causing his "iniquity to pass"(v. 4). Joshua is then told: "If thou wilt walk in my ways, and if thou wilt keep my charge, then thou shalt also judge my house, and shalt also keep my courts, and I will give thee places to walk among these that stand by" (v. 7). Then Joshua is told about the ultimate Redeemer, called "the BRANCH," whom God would "bring forth. . . . In that day, saith the LORD of hosts, shall ye call every man his neighbour under the vine and under the fig tree" (vv. 8, 10). This is a clear reference to the future kingdom and ultimate restoration coming to all Israel and, through it, the world.

"The BRANCH" is referenced once more in 6:12–15, again, as the One who will build the temple in a glory that will surpass the one built by Solomon:

> And speak unto him, saying, Thus speaketh the LORD of hosts, saying, Behold the man whose name is The BRANCH; and he shall grow up out of his place, and he shall build the temple of the LORD: Even he shall build the temple of the LORD; and he shall bear the glory, and shall sit and rule upon his throne; and he shall be a priest upon his throne: and the counsel of peace shall be between them both. And the crowns shall be to Helem, and to Tobijah, and to Jedaiah, and to Hen the son of Zephaniah, for a memorial in the temple of the LORD. And they that are far off shall come and build in the temple of the LORD, and ye shall know that the LORD of hosts hath sent me unto you. And this shall come to pass, if ye will diligently obey the voice of the LORD your God.

Another clear ringing of the gospel is spoken by the Lord in 7:8–10: "And the word of the LORD came unto Zechariah, saying, Thus speaketh the LORD of hosts, saying, Execute true judgment, and shew mercy and compassions every man to his brother: And oppress not the widow, nor the fatherless, the stranger, nor the poor; and let none of you imagine evil against his brother in your heart."

Zechariah 8:3–9 provides another glimpse into the future kingdom:

Thus saith the LORD; I am returned unto Zion, and will dwell in the midst of Jerusalem: and Jerusalem shall be called a city of truth; and the mountain of the LORD of hosts the holy mountain.

Thus saith the LORD of hosts; There shall yet old men and old women dwell in the streets of Jerusalem, and every man with his staff in his hand for very age.

And the streets of the city shall be full of boys and girls playing in the streets thereof.

Thus saith the LORD of hosts; If it be marvellous in the eyes of the remnant of this people in these days, should it also be marvellous in mine eyes? saith the LORD of hosts.

Thus saith the LORD of hosts; Behold, I will save my people from the east country, and from the west country;

And I will bring them, and they shall dwell in the midst of Jerusalem: and they shall be my people, and I will be their God, in truth and in righteousness.

Thus saith the LORD of hosts; Let your hands be strong, ye that hear in these days these words by the mouth of the prophets, which were in the day that the foundation of the house of the LORD of hosts was laid, that the temple might be built.

There is still more good news in verses 12–17.

For the seed shall be prosperous; the vine shall give her fruit, and the ground shall give her increase, and the heavens shall give their dew; and I will cause the remnant of this people to possess all these things.

And it shall come to pass, that as ye were a curse among the heathen, O house of Judah, and house of Israel; so will I save you, and ye shall be a blessing: fear not, but let your hands be strong.

For thus saith the LORD of hosts; As I thought to punish you, when your fathers provoked me to wrath, saith the LORD of hosts, and I repented not:

So again have I thought in these days to do well unto Jerusalem and to the house of Judah: fear ye not.

These are the things that ye shall do; Speak ye every man the truth to his neighbour; execute the judgment of truth and peace in your gates:

And let none of you imagine evil in your hearts against his neighbour; and love no false oath: for all these are things that I hate, saith the Lord.

And there's more about the glorious, Israel-centric kingdom in verses 19–23:

Thus saith the LORD of hosts; The fast of the fourth month, and the fast of the fifth, and the fast of the seventh, and the fast of the tenth, shall be to the house of Judah joy and gladness, and cheerful feasts; therefore love the truth and peace.

Thus saith the LORD of hosts; It shall yet come to pass, that there shall come people, and the inhabitants of many cities:

And the inhabitants of one city shall go to another, saying, Let us go speedily to pray before the LORD, and to seek the LORD of hosts: I will go also.

Yea, many people and strong nations shall come to seek the LORD of hosts in Jerusalem, and to pray before the LORD.

Thus saith the LORD of hosts; In those days it shall come to pass, that ten men shall take hold out of all languages of the nations, even shall take hold of the skirt of him that is a Jew, saying, We will go with you: for we have heard that God is with you.

Having written a book previously on the kingdom, I found Zechariah to be a treasure trove of prophecy about it. Believers must never forget that it is this kingdom that represents the ultimate fulfillment of the gospel that Jesus preached. We're reminded in Zechariah 10:6–9 that the future kingdom will result not only in the miraculous return of the southern kingdom of Judah, but also the northern kingdom of Israel in one reunified nation:

> And I will strengthen the house of Judah, and I will save the house of Joseph, and I will bring them again to place them; for I have mercy upon them: and they shall be as though I had not cast them off: for I am the LORD their God, and will hear them: And they of Ephraim shall be like a mighty man, and their heart shall rejoice as through wine: yea, their children shall see it, and be glad; their heart shall rejoice in the LORD. I will hiss for them, and gather them; for I have redeemed them: and they shall increase as they have increased. And I will sow them among the people: and they shall remember me in far countries; and they shall live with their children, and turn again.

Likewise, as in both the prophetic books of Isaiah and Ezekiel, there's a reference in verses 9–12 to what I call "God's Middle East peace plan," the redemption of Egypt and Assyria when the kingdom of Israel is restored:

> And I will sow them among the people: and they shall remember me in far countries; and they shall live with their children, and turn again. I will bring them again also out of the land of Egypt, and gather them out of Assyria; and I will bring them into the land of Gilead and Lebanon; and place shall not be found for them. And he shall pass through the sea with affliction, and shall smite the waves in the sea, and all the deeps of the river shall dry up: and the pride of Assyria shall be brought down, and the sceptre of Egypt

shall depart away. And I will strengthen them in the LORD; and they shall walk up and down in his name, saith the LORD.

It's worth recalling the remarkable closing parallel passage in Isaiah 19:23–25: "In that day shall there be a highway out of Egypt to Assyria, and the Assyrian shall come into Egypt, and the Egyptian into Assyria, and the Egyptians shall serve with the Assyrians. In that day shall Israel be the third with Egypt and with Assyria, even a blessing in the midst of the land: Whom the LORD of hosts shall bless, saying, Blessed be Egypt my people, and Assyria the work of my hands, and Israel mine inheritance."

Zechariah closes with more vivid pictures of the future kingdom:

And it shall come to pass in that day, that the light shall not be clear, nor dark: But it shall be one day which shall be known to the LORD, not day, nor night: but it shall come to pass, that at evening time it shall be light. And it shall be in that day, that living waters shall go out from Jerusalem; half of them toward the former sea, and half of them toward the hinder sea: in summer and in winter shall it be. And the LORD shall be king over all the earth: in that day shall there be one LORD, and his name one. All the land shall be turned as a plain from Geba to Rimmon south of Jerusalem: and it shall be lifted up, and inhabited in her place, from Benjamin's gate unto the place of the first gate, unto the corner gate, and from the tower of Hananeel unto the king's winepresses. And men shall dwell in it, and there shall be no more utter destruction; but Jerusalem shall be safely inhabited (14:6–11).

No more destruction. Can you say, "Hallelujah"?

39

THE GOSPEL IN MALACHI

Even from the days of your fathers ye are gone away from mine ordinances, and have not kept them. Return unto me, and I will return unto you, saith the LORD of hosts. —MALACHI 3:7

WHAT DOES GOD EXPECT from His people?

The Lord made it clear through His prophet Malachi right from the beginning: honor and fear.

I suspect many believers are just fine with honor. But some may not be comfortable with the word "fear." I've seen many suggest that word is more appropriately interpreted as "reverence."

I can understand why, though I think it's wrong. For starters, Young's Literal Translation says "fear," not "reverence."

We typically associate fear with the following synonyms: *alarm, apprehension, angst, anxiety, despair, horror, panic, dread, terror, aversion, fright, distress,* and so on. Yet, *reverence* has always been another synonym of *fear*, though lesser so in modern English. And there's no question in my mind that we should, indeed, revere God.

I would argue, however, that both are words applicable to the way God wants us to consider our relationship with Him. After all, Proverbs 1:7 famously tell us, "The fear of the LORD is the beginning of knowledge."

But should we not fear God—an omnipotent and omniscient authority who sees all, hears all, created all, *and* who holds in His mighty hands the power of life and death? Or should we simply think of Him as our loving friend who will never think ill of what we do?

While some modern translations have substituted "reverence" for "fear," the latter is the right word. It's *yir'ah* in Hebrew. It can also mean reverence. But it unquestionably denotes *fear*.

Why should we fear God? Because He told us it's the beginning of knowledge and understanding. I suspect it's also the beginning of a relationship based on holiness, obedience, and service. The relationship with God is not one based on equality. He's our perfect heavenly Father. We're His imperfect and fallen children.

The context in Malachi 1:6 certainly states the case better than I can: "A son honoureth his father, and a servant his master: if then I be a father, where is mine honour? and if I be a master, where is my fear?"

This was written to the priests at the time of Malachi during the return of Judah to the land following the Babylonian captivity. That captivity resulted because Judah, like Israel before them, did not fear the Lord. Now, following the captivity, even the priests did not fear Him. They were not obeying His commandments about temple service and sacrifices. There are consequences to sin, or, the transgression of the law. And as our heavenly, loving Father, He wants us to know, because He wants us to be His loving and successful children. Those who have not genuinely feared their own human father are probably worse off as a result. How there could be any argument against fearing the wrath of the Lord God Almighty escapes my imagination.

The inevitable conclusion of this question comes in 1:9: "And now, I pray you, beseech God that he will be gracious unto us." That's what we all want, right? Grace. It comes with obedience and repentance when we fall short of the mark. It's key to fully understanding the good news.

In Zechariah 2:10 we see more on the practical side of this question of fear: "Have we not all one father? hath not one God created us? why do we deal treacherously every man against his brother, by profaning the covenant of our fathers?"

And this is a key to unlocking the gospel in Malachi. In 3:1–7, it becomes clear:

> Behold, I will send my messenger, and he shall prepare the way before me: and the LORD, whom ye seek, shall suddenly come to his temple, even the messenger of the covenant, whom ye delight in: behold, he shall come, saith the LORD of hosts.
>
> But who may abide the day of his coming? and who shall stand when he appeareth? for he is like a refiner's fire, and like fullers' soap:
>
> And he shall sit as a refiner and purifier of silver: and he shall purify the sons of Levi, and purge them as gold and silver, that they may offer unto the LORD an offering in righteousness.
>
> Then shall the offering of Judah and Jerusalem be pleasant unto the LORD, as in the days of old, and as in former years.
>
> And I will come near to you to judgment; and I will be a swift witness against the sorcerers, and against the adulterers, and against false swearers, and against those that oppress the hireling in his wages, the widow, and the fatherless, and that turn aside the stranger from his right, and fear not me, saith the LORD of hosts.
>
> For I am the LORD, I change not; therefore ye sons of Jacob are not consumed.
>
> Even from the days of your fathers ye are gone away from mine ordinances, and have not kept them. Return unto me, and I will return unto you, saith the LORD of hosts.

God is going to send a holy messenger to refine us, purify us, prepare us for judgment. He has called us to repentance and obedience from the beginning. Some will respond; others will not. Fear of judgment can be a great motivator. We learn in Matthew 11:7–11, Mark 1:2–4, Luke 1:13–17, and Luke 1:76 who that messenger is: John the Baptist. Notice what else is said here: "For I am the Lord, I change not." And this is in the context of a new messenger who comes to prepare the way for Jesus' appearance. Sometimes Christians have the idea that Jesus brought a new "gospel," a different spin, perhaps even an easier, less-burdensome path. What we learn with certainty from the gospel in the Old Testament is that the good news is the same as it always was—obedience, repentance, forgiveness, grace.

God tells us to test Him in Malachi 3:10–12:

> Bring ye all the tithes into the storehouse, that there may be meat in mine house, and prove me now herewith, saith the LORD of hosts, if I will not open you the windows of heaven, and pour you out a blessing, that there shall not be room enough to receive it. And I will rebuke the devourer for your sakes, and he shall not destroy the fruits of your ground; neither shall your vine cast her fruit before the time in the field, saith the LORD of hosts. And all nations shall call you blessed: for ye shall be a delightsome land, saith the LORD of hosts.

Obey, be blessed. Disobey, be cursed.

Here's that word "fear" again in Malachi 3:16–18—with a happy ending:

> Then they that feared the LORD spake often one to another: and the LORD hearkened, and heard it, and a book of remembrance was written before him for them that feared the LORD, and that thought upon his name. And they shall be mine, saith the LORD of hosts, in that day when I make up my jewels; and I will spare

them, as a man spareth his own son that serveth him. Then shall ye return, and discern between the righteous and the wicked, between him that serveth God and him that serveth him not.

And here's that word again in Malachi 4:2–3—this time in the context of the coming of Messiah:

But unto you that fear my name shall the Sun of righteousness arise with healing in his wings; and ye shall go forth, and grow up as calves of the stall. And ye shall tread down the wicked; for they shall be ashes under the soles of your feet in the day that I shall do this, saith the LORD of hosts.

The last three verses of Malachi 4 even remind us that the spirit of Elijah, who was likened to John the Baptist, will come again to prepare the way of Jesus' return: "Remember ye the law of Moses my servant, which I commanded unto him in Horeb for all Israel, with the statutes and judgments. Behold, I will send you Elijah the prophet before the coming of the great and dreadful day of the LORD: And he shall turn the heart of the fathers to the children, and the heart of the children to their fathers, lest I come and smite the earth with a curse" (vv. 4–6).

And that's the gospel of Malachi—the same gospel we heard from John the Baptist and Jesus and His apostles and disciples.

God changes not. Jesus is the same yesterday, today, and tomorrow. And He has given us His life-changing gospel from Genesis to Revelation.

CONCLUSION

WHAT'S THE BIG TAKEAWAY FROM THIS BOOK? Is the Bible really a thoroughly integrated reflection of the heart and mind of the Creator of the universe from cover to cover—Genesis through Revelation? Or, have the original Hebrew Scriptures of the Old Testament been overshadowed by the Greek New Testament, perhaps even diminished in relevance to the lives and faith of followers of Jesus?

It is my hope that this study has helped bolster the case for the first option and inspired you to recognize it's all God's Word—inextricably connected, thoroughly consistent, and, taken together, offering exponentially more insight into the Creator's purposes and the fate of the world.

While the thirty-nine books of the Old Testament represent about 75 percent of the content of the Bible's sixty-six books, from my personal experience, most believers just don't crack open those first thirty-nine books as frequently as they do the last twenty-seven. If we acknowledge, as the gospel of Luke does, that the world-shaking faith and passion of the first-century church were ignited before the Greek Scriptures were written, then today's church is missing the full story.

It is my sincere and earnest hope that this book will help stimulate renewed interest and perhaps an attractive pathway to discovering or rediscovering the beauty, majesty, and pertinency of the very foundation of God's Word from Genesis through Malachi. If we aspire to be like the Bereans of Acts 17:11, then we should acknowledge which scriptures they were searching daily, "with all readiness of mind," to measure the words and teachings of Paul and Silas.

In addition, as mentioned frequently throughout this study, it is important that believers understand the full dynamic of the gospel, or "good news," which is more than a prescription for personal salvation. It's about the complete restoration of earth, "the restitution of all things," as Peter said in Acts 3, the redemption and perfection of the world that was corrupted by sin and death in the fall of humankind in the garden of Eden.

Jesus and the gospel writers Matthew and Mark repeatedly referred to "gospel of the kingdom." Jesus said He had to be about the business of preaching the "kingdom of God" in Luke 4:43. All told, more than one hundred times the kingdom of God, this coming kingdom of heaven on earth—Jesus' kingdom—is mentioned in the New Testament. I contend that this kingdom is an essential element of the gospel, twice mentioned in Jesus' model prayer in Matthew and Luke.

Yet, there are more vivid descriptions of and allusions to this kingdom found in the Old Testament than in the New. For the first-century believers, the restoration of this kingdom was their passion—on their minds right up to the moment before the resurrected Jesus ascended after spending forty days with His disciples (Acts 1:6).

How often do today's believers give a thought to this critical component of the gospel? And do we have a complete picture of the gospel without it?

Remember what Jesus said in Matthew 13:19: "When any one heareth the word of the kingdom, and understandeth it not, then cometh the wicked one, and catcheth away that which was sown in his heart."

Lastly, while I have studied the Scriptures for more than forty years, the research for this book and my previous effort focusing on the restoration of the kingdom has intensified my zeal for the Word and quickened my faith.

I hope it has done the same for you.

NOTES

CHAPTER 1

1. Stephen Hawking, "The Beginning of Time" (lecture), Hawking.org, accessed March 16, 2018, http://www.hawking.org.uk/the-beginning-of-time.html.

2. Chuck Missler, "The Gospel in Genesis," Koinonia House, February 1, 1996, http://www.khouse.org/articles/1996/44/.

CHAPTER 3

1. Andrew Bonar, *A Commentary on the Book of Leviticus*, 3rd ed. (London: James Nisbet, 1852), 1.

CHAPTER 5

1. Dictionary.com, s.v. "coincidence," accessed March 20, 2018, http://www.dictionary.com/browse/coincidence.

CHAPTER 27

1. P. W. Goetz, ed. *The New Encyclopædia Britannica*, 15th ed. 3:937; "Dead Sea," Bibleplaces.com, accessed March 23, 2018, https://www.bibleplaces.com/deadsea/.

PATRON SUPPORT

JOSEPH FARAH WOULD LIKE TO THANK the following for their gracious support of this book through their generous tax-deductible contributions:

- Patrick J. Smith and his loving family, Song Xiao Li (宋晓丽) and Song Zi Xin (宋梓欣)

- The National Christian Foundation